"A fascinating study. Richard Burridge tackles the moral sacramental question of your COVID-19 era, namely, how do you have sacramental communion during a pandemic. He canvasses the various options, weighs the pros and cons, and sets forth his own proposal for communion in a digital and contagious age. Something all church leaders need to wrestle with!"

—**Michael F. Bird**, academic dean and lecturer in New Testament, Ridley College, Melbourne, Australia

"When the pandemic led to lockdowns and the prohibition of in-person worship services, the Ecclesiology Committee of the Episcopal Church House of Bishops which I chair took up the question of online celebrations of the eucharist. In a paper that I wrote, I was adamant that consecration of elements online is impossible. I became intrigued, however, by Richard Burridge's insistence that the question not be purely theoretical, but needed a thorough study, including a 'Zoom communion' group that I joined. Though I do not celebrate or communicate, I have come to think that, under strict guidelines and only during real emergencies, an online eucharist can be celebrated faithfully. The church's newest mission field is cyberspace, and Richard Burridge's book is a guide to its geography."

—**Pierre Whalon**, until recently bishop of the Convocation of Episcopal (formerly American) Churches in Europe

"Burridge has put together a provocative, interesting, rich, and thoughtful book, even if I am not persuaded. It is well worth the read and furthers the discussion considerably. I believe we are at our best when we do Anglican theology together and am grateful for the invitation to the table and conversation."

—**C. Andrew Doyle**, Episcopal bishop of Texas and author of *Embodied Liturgy: Virtual Reality and Liturgical Theology in Conversation* and *Citizen: Faithful Discipleship in a Partisan World*

"Sometimes it takes a crisis, sometimes a new technology, to drive the church of Christ forwards. In 2020, we had both on a global scale. The challenges of the COVID-19 pandemic and the opportunities of near-universal access to the internet created a context in which congregations and their leaders had to address afresh the question of what it means to break bread and share wine in remembrance of Christ's death. The dance between pragmatism and theology lasted eighteen months, with the lead swapping between these partners. In this book, Richard Burridge traces the developments in praxis and theory across a range of traditions, rooted in the deep question of what it means for the people of God to gather at the table of Christ. As congregations return to their buildings, and as pastors and priests resume their sacramental positions, the questions explored in this book have not disappeared, and Burridge offers some tantalizing challenges about the nature of gathering in a post-pandemic, internet-enabled age."

—**Simon Woodman**, Bloomsbury Central Baptist Church, London

"This timely book makes a sagacious contribution to the global debate over whether and how Christians might partake of the Eucharist in a pandemic. It offers a visionary eucharistic theology and ecclesiology for the future's hybrid physical and virtual expressions of church. After analyzing the eucharistic options that various parishes have chosen through the pandemic, the author makes a persuasive case for the validity of an online real-time Eucharist with participant-provided bread and wine. Burridge argues that Christ manifests himself in every human sphere, including the digital, and that therefore worship in the digital sphere is appropriate when gathering physically as a church is not possible. This book challenges Christians and churches to be theologically and liturgically imaginative in order to recognize the generative power of the Spirit at work, recreating and perpetuating the church anew in all seasons, places, and circumstances—even a global pandemic. I am part of the eucharistic community worshipping via Zoom technology that Burridge has convened. This Zoom group has become a eucharistic house church, with participants from three continents. Christ is truly present, as he promised, where two or three are gathered online."

—**Mitzi J. Budde**, deacon of the Evangelical Lutheran Church in America, head librarian and professor, Virginia Theological Seminary, Arthur Carl Lichtenberger Chair in Continuing Education and Theological Research, Alexandria, Virginia, USA

"Recognizing that the Holy Spirit of God is fruitfully active among people and communities across the world and across the churches as they face the implications for Christian worship and witness of the restrictions of the 2020–21 pandemic, Burridge offers a theological analysis that is detailed, perceptive, stretching, and highly readable. A marvelous achievement that testifies to the liberating energy of God's grace for a church which is too often hidebound in a world crying out in its suffering and need."

—**Gordon Oliver**, formerly director of ministry for Rochester Diocese, and author of *Ministry without Madness*

"This remarkable book meets the need for Christian thinking to come to terms urgently with the challenge of the digital revolution. In this carefully researched and original book of quite extraordinary scope, the author does not only show a convincing way through the problems of celebrating the eucharist online: he also brings to light the deepest meaning of the relation of God to a world that includes cyberspace."

—**Paul S. Fiddes**, FBA, professor of systematic theology, University of Oxford, principal emeritus and senior research fellow, Regent's Park College, University of Oxford

"There are few more qualified to tackle the tangled question of what communion is and does than the Reverend Canon Professor Richard Burridge. *Holy Communion in Contagious Times* brings to bear his prodigious gifts as a Bible scholar, as a priest, and as a person considering how the church balances isolation and spiritual need. This book will challenge and maybe even shift your thinking about the most sacred acts in our faith."

—**Greg Garrett**, professor of English at Baylor University and canon theologian at the American Cathedral of the Holy Trinity, Paris

Holy Communion
in Contagious Times

Holy Communion
in Contagious Times

Celebrating the Eucharist
in the Everyday and Online Worlds

RICHARD A. BURRIDGE

CASCADE *Books* · Eugene, Oregon

HOLY COMMUNION IN CONTAGIOUS TIMES
Celebrating the Eucharist in the Everyday and Online Worlds

Cascade Books
An Imprint of Wipf and Stock Publishers
199 W. 8th Ave., Suite 3
Eugene, OR 97401

www.wipfandstock.com

PAPERBACK ISBN: 978-1-7252-8577-4
HARDCOVER ISBN: 978-1-7252-8576-7
EBOOK ISBN: 978-1-7252-8578-1

Cataloging-in-Publication data:

Names: Burridge, Richard A. (1955–) [author].

Title: Holy communion in contagious times : celebrating the eucharist in the everyday and online worlds / by Richard A. Burridge.

Description: Eugene, OR : Cascade Books, 2022

Identifiers: ISBN 978-1-7252-8577-4 (paperback) | ISBN 978-1-7252-8576-7 (hardcover) | ISBN 978-1-7252-8578-1 (ebook)

Subjects: LCSH: Lord's Supper. | Sacraments. | Sacred meals. | Coronavirus. | Internet—Religious aspects—Christianity. | Cyberspace—Religious aspects—Christianity. | Religious broadcasting—Christianity.

Classification: LCC BV825 B87 2022 (print) | LCC BV825 (ebook)

VERSION NUMBER 010722

*This book is dedicated with grateful appreciation
to those who ate and drank around the Lord's table
with me these last eighteen months:*

*Peter, Don, Gordon, Ros,
Loveday, Cindy, Mags, Christopher,
Pierre, Mitzi, Liina, Alan, Richard,
Simon, Andrew, Paul, and Simon*

*And it is also offered in memory of
all those who suffered and died
in the coronavirus pandemic.*

Contents

Preface and Acknowledgements

H.G. WELLS BEGINS HIS seminal novel, *The War of the Worlds*, with these famous opening words:

> No one would have believed in the last years of the nineteenth century that this world was being watched keenly and closely by intelligences greater than man's and yet as mortal as his own; that as men busied themselves about their various concerns they were scrutinised and studied, perhaps almost as narrowly as a man with a microscope might scrutinise the transient creatures that swarm and multiply in a drop of water.

So might I begin, equally, with this pastiche: "No one would have believed in the opening years of the third decade of the twenty-first century that this world was being . . . [threatened by] . . . transient creatures that swarm and multiply in a drop of water." The end of Wells' novel, after the invading Martians have been destroyed by bacteria and a common virus, is equally portentous:

> These germs of disease have taken toll of humanity since the be-ginning of things—taken toll of our pre-human ancestors since life began here. But by virtue of this natural selection of our kind we have developed resisting-power; to no germs do we succumb without a struggle. . . . By the toll of a billion deaths, man has bought his birthright of the earth, and it is his against all comers; it would still be his were the Martians ten times as mighty as they are. For neither do men live nor die in vain.[1]

1. Quoted from the well-thumbed paperback edition from my childhood of H. G. Wells, *The War of the Worlds* (London: Penguin Science Fiction, 1964; reprint of the first 1946 Penguin edition; Wells' original was first published as a serial in *Pearson's Magazine*, April to December, 1897), 9 and 179–80. It is interesting that these are the only two direct quotations taken from the novel and narrated by Morgan Freeman at the beginning and at the end of Steven Spielberg's film of the book, starring Tom Cruise (Paramount and DreamWorks Pictures, 2005).

Similarly, I "would not have believed" in those opening weeks of 2020 when the little country church where I had just started going to a quiet mid-week celebration of holy communion shut its doors, that it would never reopen them again, nor that what began as a 'bit of fun' experiment in an online communion service at the request of a South African Roman Catholic friend on the Feast of the Annunciation, March 25, 2020, would not only still be happening on a weekly basis over eighteen months later, but would have grown into the spiritual practice sustaining a sacramental community stretching over four continents and five Christian denominations.

Equally similarly, I "would not have believed" that those few initial coughs, sneezes, headaches, and loss of senses like smell or taste, would result after only eighteen months in nearly 5 million deaths and a quarter of a billion cases infected worldwide. In the USA alone, many more people have died of COVID-19 (over 800,000) than the total deaths in combat in *all* the wars over the entire history of that country since 1775 (666,000), and no less than *sixteen* times more people have suffered illness (over 50 million) than their total casualties covering all those wounded, as well as combat and non-combat deaths, including those from bombing, massacres, disease, suicide, murder, as well as those considered 'missing' (3 million).[2]

Finally, I also "would not have believed" that the few thousand words that I wrote about this topic of holy communion during what the 1662 Book of Common Prayer calls "contagious times" over Easter 2020 would grow into a book of some hundred thousand words, nor that it would take me eighteen months, and cost me so much blood, sweat, tears, and loss—the loss of my eldest relative just short of her hundredth birthday and, later, my dearest love and closest friend and colleague. I had no idea of the toll that writing this book would take on my physical and mental health, of the weeks when I could not even get out of bed, or the months that passed with nothing written at all.

Quite frankly and simply, without the friendship, love, and support of so many people—family, friends, and colleagues—not only would this book have never been finished, but I am not sure that I personally would have survived the tribulations of these past eighteen months. To mention only a few names is so insufficient that it is almost an insult—and yet it must be done, even at the risk of the inevitable omission caused by increasing memory loss—my apologies to any not named!

First and foremost, I must pay tribute to those who have shared in our weekly online communions for most of the last year and a half, in no

2. Coronavirus numbers taken from https://www.worldometers.info/coronavirus/, while the military casualty figures are taken from the relevant Wikipedia article https://en.wikipedia.org/wiki/United_States_military_casualties_of_war.

particular order (other than our weekly email list!): Professor Peter Eccles, Don Arthurson, the Rev'd Canon Gordon Oliver, Dr Ros Oliver, the Rev'd Canon Professor Loveday Alexander, the Rev'd Cindy Kent, MBE, Dr Mags Blackie, Professor Christopher Southgate, the Rt Rev'd Dr Pierre Whalon, the Rev'd Professor Dr Mitzi Budde, Liina Sander, the Rev'd Canon Alan Amos, as well as those who joined us at various different times for part of the journey, again, in no particular order: the Rt Rev'd Dr David Walker, the Rev'd Richard Coles, FKC, Simon Jenkins, the Rev'd John MacKenzie, the Rev'd Dr Paul Roberts, the Rev'd Dr Simon Woodman, the Rev'd Professor Paul Fiddes, Dr Andrew Robinson, the Rev'd Graham Archer, the Rev'd Canon John Warner, Dr Meg Warner.

I am also grateful to the very many others, who at different times took an active interest in the development of our service, offering practical and pastoral suggestions, and sending me liturgical or theological reflections, including especially those who have read various extracts, drafts, and versions of this manuscript with appreciative thanks for all their emails, comments, and corrections, again, in no particular order: the Rt Rev'd Nicholas Holtam, the Rt Rev'd Christopher Chessun, the Rt Rev'd Michael Ipgrave, the Rt Rev'd Christopher Hill, the Rt Rev'd Graham Tomlin, the Rt Rev'd Christopher Cocksworth, the Rt Rev'd Peter Selby, the Rev'd Canon Gilly Myers, the Rev'd Martin Wroe, the Rev'd Fr Luke Miller, the Rev'd Fr Peter Anthony, Mrs Ailsa Wright, the Rev'd Professor Judith Lieu, Fr Brendan Callaghan, SJ, Dr Matthew Cheung Salisbury, Professor Mark Brett, as well as friends and colleagues from across the Atlantic Ocean, the Rt Rev'd Andy Doyle, the Rev'd Dr Chuck Robertson, the Rt Rev'd Mary Gray-Reeves, the Rt Rev'd Doug Sparks, the Rt Rev'd Bill Franklin, the Very Rev'd Professor Dr Ian S Markham, the Rev'd Professor Dr James Farwell.

Finally, I must record my thanks to my publishing colleagues at Wipf and Stock, especially to my commissioning editor, Michael Thomson, who has been a dear friend and support for over two decades, who grabbed this idea soon after Easter 2020 and encouraged me to turn into a book "in the next few weeks" (sorry!), to the Rev'd Dr Robin Parry who has been most patiently waiting over the last eighteen months, and who is the most attentive and accurate copy editor that I have ever had the privilege to read my work, and also to Ian Creeger and all involved in its production.

All that remains after compiling this extraordinary list of bishops, priests, and lay people, professors and doctors, must be to apologize again for the delay in producing this (yes, I know, we wanted—or possibly even needed—it a year ago at the height of the pandemic) and to admit that, despite the exalted readership and their scrutiny, the mistakes that still remain must be the few bits that are all my own work, sadly!

I always seem to conclude my books around major Christian festivals, and this season of Michaelmas, St Michael and all God's Angels, reminds me again that we do not struggle just against flesh and blood, viruses and infections, and also that those whom we have lost along the way are a cloud of witnesses, before whom we run this race, and with whom we will receive the unfading crown of glory from a gracious Lord who himself toiled, agonized, and died in this mortal coil, with whom we share fellowship and communion, to whom we give eucharistic thanks, and who feeds us and sends us out to serve his suffering world—*missa est*!

Richard A. Burridge,
Michaelmas, 2021

LATEST POSTSCRIPT:

As this book went finally to press, the latest variant of coronavirus, Omicron, was causing a worryingly rapid rise in infections, hospitalizations and potential deaths, and many countries were returning to lockdown and other measures. This suggests that, far from the pandemic being 'all over by Christmas', the issues and possible solutions regarding Holy Communion in Contagious Times continue to be of increasing concern and relevance. May the one who became incarnate at Bethlehem bring health and healing this Christmas and in the coming years ahead.

R. A. B.
Christmas, 2021

1

Introduction

Holy Communion and the (Inter-)national Closure of Churches in Contagious Times

AT THE END OF 2019, I moved from London to a village in north Cheshire on the edge of Greater Manchester in the hope of finding a quieter life in order to give myself more fully to my research and writing. It seemed to have all the essentials: a beautiful location on the banks of a canal, looking at the Peak District, with a welcoming 'local' pub a short walk along the tow path and a golf club about a mile further along, and it was situated halfway up a long steep hill in between two Anglican churches, one at the bottom and one at the top. Paradoxically, the parish church in the *upper* village was about as 'low' as possible in the evangelical tradition of the Church of England, while its neighbour down the hill in the *lower* village was still clearly a product of the Anglo-Catholic 'high'-church revival of the mid-late nineteenth century. Rather than their contrasting Sunday services, I began to frequent the mid-week 'said-communion with sermon' at the higher church lower down the hill on a Wednesday morning. The golf course had beautiful views all across to the north-west coast, but it was unfortunately impossible for me to cope with as I was waiting for a knee replacement operation—and buggies would not be allowed on the course until Easter. At least the pub landlord and his wife were very friendly and served excellent local ales with a wide range of gins, and I also found a music studio in the town offering tuition, music appreciation classes, and a Friday night 'open-mic' for regulars to play a party piece. Everything seemed set fair for a blissful future—if only we could deal with the persistent coughs and sniffles various people seemed to have picked up . . . .

Within a couple of months, everything had changed: the flu-like symptoms had developed into COVID-19, the pub and the golf course were closed down, my knee replacement had been cancelled by a hospital over-whelmed by victims of the pandemic, and the music studio's events were all moved online. Meanwhile, all the parish churches had been instructed by the archbishops of Canterbury and York to shut their doors. The eucha-rist or communion services offered weekly or even daily in many churches for centuries were withdrawn as a potential source of infection. This had never happened before—not even in the worst pandemics of the Plague or the Black Death. Of course, the pandemic quickly produced its rollcall of heroes, as we clapped and banged saucepans on doorsteps every Thursday night 'for the NHS', or greeted the angels of mercy, presenting as delivery drivers, leaving food orders or cardboard boxed packages at the end of the garden path—the only human beings we saw, and the cost of whose service began to emerge as many succumbed to the rising death toll. But others started to ask, where were the churches and the clergy—and how could we survive spiritually without the bread of heaven and the blood of Christ?

THE CHURCH OF ENGLAND SHUTS UP SHOP

The initial steps began with the 'first letter' from the archbishops of Can-terbury and York (March 10, 2020), which implemented the withdrawal of the chalice (resulting in communion in one kind only) and the suspension of all physical contact at the Peace (moving to so-called *namaste* greetings or bowing to each other). This was followed a fortnight later by their 'sec-ond letter' of March 24, 2020, with the announcement, that "All Church of England churches are to close with immediate effect, including for private prayer, in an effort to help limit the transmission of the coronavirus COV-ID-19," and therefore they encouraged clergy that "live streaming of services is more important than ever."[1] This was quickly confirmed by the updated 'third letter' of March 27, 2020, which however also stressed that the closure of church buildings was "to prevent them being used for streaming."[2] It is interesting that there is no mention of communion or eucharist anywhere in the press releases, announcements, or any of the archbishops' letters, and

1. https://www.churchofengland.org/more/media-centre/news/church-england-close-all-church-buildings-help-prevent-spread-coronavirus

2. https://www.churchofengland.org/news-and-media/news-and-statements/church-england-close-all-church-buildings-help-prevent-spread

it soon became the 'Elephant in the Room', which concerned everyone, but which was not being discussed openly in the national communications.

The waters were further muddied by variations from diocese to diocese, and the regular moving of the goalposts: thus on March 12, 2020 London Diocese issued a list of churches livestreaming their services, and basic instructions for doing so,[3] but then livestreaming was restricted on March 22 to the sole exception for those within 'the curtilage' that "Clergy who live adjacent to their churches may still go into the building and pray and even celebrate the Eucharist."[4]

Yet the next day, London issued clear guidance for the "huge number of London parishes who are live streaming their worship", by now too many to list individually, presumably not all within the curtilage, hence the confusion.[5] On March 31, the London College of Bishops (with particular theological input from the bishops of Kensington and Fulham from their contrasting church traditions) provided a very helpful paper on "The Eucharist in a Time of Physical Distancing" with three options—suspending celebrating the eucharist altogether; the priest celebrating it livestreamed; or the priest celebrating alone or with members of their household, but having advertised the time publicly as per instructions in the BCP so the laity could join in prayer at the same time.[6]

The wide range of interpretations across various dioceses such as Durham, Bradford, Chichester, London, Chelmsford, Leeds, prompted the Church's national adviser on medical ethics, the Rev'd Dr Brendan McCarthy, to say, "Public worship has been suspended in line with government advice in order to protect people as, together, we tackle this coronavirus epidemic."[7] On the other hand, the government issued a Statutory Instrument on March 26, allowing that "A place of worship may be used (a) for funerals, (b) to broadcast an act of worship, whether over the internet or as part of a radio or television broadcast, or (c) to provide essential voluntary services or urgent public support services" (paragraph 5.6).[8] Internet

3. https://www.london.anglican.org/articles/accessing-christian-services-and-re-sources-digitally-for-those-who-cant-get-to-church/

4. https://www.london.anglican.org/articles/closure-of-church-buildings/

5. https://www.london.anglican.org/articles/live-streaming-worship/

6. https://www.london.anglican.org/articles/the-eucharist-in-a-time-of-physical-distancing/

7. https://www.churchtimes.co.uk/articles/2020/20-march/news/uk/c-of-e-medical-adviser-gets-tough-with-differing-dioceses

8. https://www.legislation.gov.uk/uksi/2020/350/contents/made; Statutory Instrument: The Health Protection (Coronavirus, Restrictions) (England) Regulations 2020. PDF available as "uksi_20200350_en.pdf"

commentators quickly noted the contrast between the government's statutory instrument *permitting* churches "to broadcast an act of worship, whether over the internet or as part of a radio or television broadcast", while "Church of England diocesan bishops remain more restrictive . . . and broadcasting is forbidden from inside church buildings."[9]

Similar press coverage on Tuesday of Holy Week, April 7 suggesting that London Diocese was telling "Vicars to ignore guidelines banning them from their own churches" forced the London College of Bishops to issue a new statement instructing everyone, this time even including those able to access their buildings within the curtilage without going onto the public street, "to stop all live streaming from your church buildings for the time being."[10] The implication was clear, that we had been taken into a spiritual wilderness with no actual communions taking place in churches at all.

A popular meme often repeated on social media on both sides of the Atlantic depicted the police (both London's Metropolitan police, and New York's finest) called in to break up Leonardo da Vinci's Last Supper, with captions such as "I don't care who your Father is, this is an illegal gathering", or "you still need to be vaccinated", or a breach of 'social-distancing'![11]

This situation did not pass without some protest, however. Jack Lopresti, Conservative MP for Filton, Bristol, asked the government why he could go into an off-licence at Easter but not into a church.[12] More directly, the rector of St Bartholomew the Great, in London, the Rev'd Marcus Walker, writing in *The Times* on Wed April 8, 2020, said: "We're expected to say morning and evening prayer in our churches every Sunday and to celebrate communion—that's the law. Do the bishops have a right to order us not to do our legal duty? Every canon lawyer I have spoken to says 'No.'" *The Times* followed this on Good Friday, April 10, with an article entitled "Justin Welby Wrong to Close Churches at Easter, Say Clergy," noting that this was the first Easter without church services since the interdict of Pope Innocent III in 1213.[13] On that same Good Friday, *The Telegraph*'s editorial

9. https://www.thinkinganglicans.org.uk/closing-churches-now-codified-in-government-regulations/

10. https://www.london.anglican.org/articles/church-buildings-remain-closed-the-church-remains-open/

11. See, for instance,
https://imgur.com/t/police/6GDWaQf?nc=1
https://www.reddit.com/r/PunPatrol/comments/fzp3hq/those_police_are_so_impatient/
https://imgflip.com/meme/281605272/Last-supper-Covid-police-raid

12. https://www.bbc.co.uk/news/uk-england-bristol-52219164; https://www.jacklopresti.com/news?page=0 see April 8

13. https://www.thetimes.co.uk/edition/news/justin-welby-wrong-to-close-churches-at-easter-say-clergy-lbtz82ldk

opinion asked in its headline, "When Britain Needed Them Most, Why Did the Churches Lock Their Doors?"

On Easter Sunday, April 12, 2020, Andrew Marr on the BBC, after pointing out that the archbishop of Canterbury had celebrated the eucharist from his kitchen at Lambeth Palace with his toaster on view behind him, challenged Archbishop Justin to respond to the Rev'd Marcus Walker's point about canon law. After extolling the virtues of Marcus Walker as a fine priest, Archbishop Justin responded: "The answer to that is we have given guidance, not instruction."[14] Marcus Walker immediately streamed an Easter eucharist pre-recorded in his church,[15] and reverted to livestreaming from within the church the following week, Low Sunday. Other clergy also continued to resist this "guidance" or "instruction" (the confusion over its status did not help) by celebrating the eucharist in their churches, sometimes with the knowledge, or even quiet support, of their bishops.[16] If clergy are required by the Book of Common Prayer (which forms part of canon law, and thus part of the law of the land for the Established Church) to say daily morning and evening prayer as well as to celebrate regular communions in their parish churches, and if the government has not made it illegal to do so, then any episcopal instructions not to pray and celebrate in church cannot be enforced as part of a priest's sworn ordination oath to "pay true and canonical obedience to the Lord Bishop of xxxx and his successors, in all things lawful and honest: So help me God." God cannot help us, it was argued, to obey something that is not "canonical" nor "required by law", and it may not be seen as completely "honest" to assume that it is.

In a telling article entitled "Is Anglicanism Going Private?" Peter Selby, the former bishop of Worcester, suggested that there were deep ecclesiological implications for any understanding of the Church of England as the national church "by law established" being replaced by a retreat into the personal and private sphere:

> The Anglican bishops chose to go beyond government advice
> and declare church buildings closed not only for church services
> but for private prayer or even for clergy to livestream worship.
> While Mass is being livestreamed from Catholic churches, Anglican clergy have had to do so from their homes. . . .

14. https://www.churchtimes.co.uk/articles/2020/17-april/news/uk/we-have-given -guidance-not-instruction-says-welby-on-andrew-marr-show

15. https://www.churchtimes.co.uk/articles/2020/24-april/news/uk/rector-streams -eucharist-from-inside-his-church; see also, https://archbishopcranmer.com/Rev'd- marcus-walker-returns-pulpit-here-i-stand/

16. https://akma.disseminary.org/2020/04/on-streams-and-places/

Foremost among the reasons given why clergy could not enter their churches was the need to "set an example" of clergy as law-abiding citizens staying at home. The case was never made that clergy are key workers, exercising an essential public function, one rooted in the architecture and layout of their churches and the liturgical function they carry out within them, especially in Passiontide and Eastertide. . . .

The CofE bishops will surely seem to have accepted the idea that Christianity is a matter for the domestic realm, that our cathedrals and parish churches are just optional when useful and available, no longer the eloquent signs of the consecration of our public life and public spaces. The conviction that the ministry of Word and Sacrament in the places of beauty set apart is an "essential work" undertaken by "key workers" will have become a wistful "BC" [= Before Covid] memory.[17]

Like Bishop Peter writing in *The Tablet*, rather than *Church Times*, the Rev'd Ian McCormack, SSC, priest-in-charge of St. George's in the Meadows, Nottingham, had to turn to an Episcopal journal in the USA, *The Living Church*, to publish his article, "Love for Love's Sake," contrasting the response of the archbishops and the Church of England with the crucial role played by clergy and religious communities during Victorian epidemics which contributed to the rise of nineteenth-century Anglo-Catholicism.[18]

A letter published in *The Times* on Monday May 4, 2020, which attracted over 800 Anglican clergy signatories within a couple of days before the list was closed, took up Peter Selby's point, saying that "he speaks for many laity and clergy about the Church of England's current approach." Therefore, they called upon the bishops "to change their current policy" and regarded "what has happened to be a failure of the Church's responsibility to the nation, stifling our prophetic witness and defence of the poor." An editorial in the *Daily Telegraph* a couple of days later supported a group of MPs who wrote to the archbishops to permit funerals in churches, as indeed was allowed by the government's Statutory Instrument (May 6, 2020).

Meanwhile, the bishops issued a statement on May 5, 2020, claiming that "church buildings remain closed for public worship, in line with Government advice",[19] thus perpetuating the confusion from Andrew Marr's

---

17. https://www.thetablet.co.uk/features/2/17973/is-anglicanism-going-private-

18. https://livingchurch.org/2020/04/28/love-for-christs-sake/; Ian McCormack's only comment on the current pandemic was to say, "The instruction is something for which the archbishops will have to answer on the day of judgment, and it would be imprudent to comment further here."

19. https://www.churchofengland.org/more/media-centre/news/house-bishops-backs-phased-approach-revising-access-church-buildings

programme between 'instructions' and 'guidance': the 'statutory instrument' had not issued 'advice' about closing churches, but had specifically permitted them to be used for streaming services. A telling cartoon by David Walker in the *Church Times* made a number of relevant points in his own inimitable way, not least that other denominations were still using their buildings, and the vexed question of whether God is any more or less present in church than at home—and the fact that many people, such as those in wheelchairs, found access to church difficult in the first place.[20]

And so the debate about open or closed churches continued for over a year, as the pandemic waxed and waned with various 'waves' in the United Kingdom, even with different rules being issued and enforced for each of the individual nations by their devolved administrations, until the lifting of restrictions in July 2021, when the Church of England issued new guidance, complete with a letter from the Bishop of London.[21] Whether all the parish churches that had closed during the pandemic will be able to open to serve their local community in the traditional way ever again remains to be seen.

THE LOSS OF HOLY COMMUNION
WITH CLOSED CHURCHES

The whys and wherefores of the debate around the closure of Church of England churches by archepiscopal orders are, mercifully, beyond the scope of this book, which is concerned with the most important impact of such closures—the loss of the central role played by the regular weekly or even daily celebration of the eucharist in church, especially for the clergy nurtured in such a daily eucharistic tradition and lay people who would gather to join them. I described right at the start how I had just started attending the mid-week said communion in my new parish in Cheshire, when first sharing the peace was banned, then the chalice was removed so that communion was given 'in one kind' only, followed a couple of weeks later by the closure of the church in mid-late March 2020, removing all possibilities of receiving communion.

As noted above, it is as significant and it is interesting that there was no mention of communion or eucharist anywhere in the early press releases, announcements, or any of the archbishops' letters. The topic soon became the 'Elephant in the Room' which concerned everyone, and which

20. For David Walker's cartoons during the pandemic, see, for instance, https://cartoonchurch.com/content/cc/category/2020-cartoons/

21. See https://www.churchofengland.org/resources/coronavirus-covid-19-guidance#na

was beginning to feature widely on social media and discussion websites with greater urgency as Easter was approaching. I participated in several debates on Facebook about the spiritual loss we felt with the end of regular communion. An exchange of various emails with certain friends and colleagues led to my attempt at an experiment in trying to hold a communion service live online through the Zoom webinar technology on the Feast of the Annunciation, March 25, 2020. The positive response from all involved encouraged us to continue with a weekly online service—little suspecting that it would then take place every Wednesday for at least the next eighteen months up to and including the date of finally writing this section of the book last.

We also saw above that on March 31 the London College of Bishops published a very helpful paper on "The Eucharist in a Time of Physical Distancing" with three options—suspending celebrating the eucharist altogether; the priest celebrating it livestreamed; or the priest celebrating alone or with members of their household but having advertised the time publicly as per instructions in the BCP so the laity could join in prayer at the same time.[22]

A similar range of options was provided in the advice and guidance put out by the national church communications team the next day on April 1 (All Fools Day!) regarding the keeping of Holy Week and Easter 2020.[23] This noted the various broadcasts and livestreams of services during the holy season, and it was accompanied by particular instructions for Holy Week and Easter services, including a note on "Holy Communion on Maundy Thursday and Easter Day."[24] This included the following guidance:

> Particularly on Maundy Thursday evening and Easter morning, bishops and priests may wish to celebrate Holy Communion in their homes—including in chapels or oratories, in other rooms, or (on Easter morning) in their own gardens. If they do so, they should make clear that this is in intention an expression of the shared life of the Body of Christ, not the offering of an individual.
>
> Other bishops and clergy may choose to abstain from celebration of the sacrament of Holy Communion for such time as this is not physically accessible to lay people. They may choose

22. https://www.london.anglican.org/articles/the-eucharist-in-a-time-of-physical-distancing/

23. https://www.churchofengland.org/news-and-media/stories-and-features/how-church-england-adapting-plans-holy-week-and-easter-meet

24. https://www.churchofengland.org/resources/coronavirus-covid-19-guidance-churches/holy-week-and-easter-2020

to follow this course of action intentionally for the duration of the present emergency.

Recognising that they do so in real but separated company with those for whom they have spiritual care, some bishops and priests may choose to stream celebrations of Holy Communion. If so, those participating remotely should be encouraged to use the Act of Spiritual Communion on the Church of England website.

These three suggestions—the solo celebration of communion by bishops and clergy in their own homes, a eucharistic fast abstaining from communion, or replacing it with a 'spiritual communion'—were to dominate our relationship to the eucharist in the coming months, as we shall see in the next three chapters of this book. On our main concern in particular, however, this document was absolutely and explicitly clear:

> Participants in a streamed service of Holy Communion should not be encouraged to place bread and wine before their screens. Joining together to share in the one bread and the one cup as those physically present to one another is integral to the service of Holy Communion; this is not possible under the current restrictions, and it is not helpful to suggest otherwise. *Any idea of the 'remote consecration' of the bread and wine should be avoided.* (my italics for emphasis)

This meant that the online communion with which I was beginning to experiment was ruled out by the bishops in advance. Therefore, I wrote a brief reflection paper of just under 5,000 words on our experience of online communion and sent it to the bishop of Kensington, the Rt Rev'd Graham Tomlin, for his comments. His positive response led to my being invited to write an expanded version of the paper (which ended up being some 18,000 words!) which was submitted to a meeting on April 28 of the Episcopal Reference Group within the Church of England's Faith and Order Commission. After this, Michael Ipgrave, the bishop of Lichfield, who had drafted the note on "Holy Communion on Maundy Thursday and Easter Day", was asked to lead a House of Bishops Working Group on Holy Communion. I was therefore heartened to receive a very encouraging and positive emailed response from Bishop Michael after the meeting of April 28. While he had "great sympathy with what I take to be your underlying position, that an online celebration of the Eucharist is possible and appropriate in our current situation, and that people geographically separated can be drawn into this in a real participation through virtual means," Bishop Michael even more helpfully went on to debate and argue with many of the main points of my paper in some detail—which became a major stimulus in my attempt to turn those original thoughts into what has become this book, and for that I am very grateful.[25]

Nonetheless, this opposition to bringing bread and wine before a livestreamed service on a computer was repeated clearly in the first formal version of the church's "COVID-19 Advice on the Administration of Holy Communion" which included "Some Guidance on the Celebration of Holy Communion."[26] This "guidance" repeated the three main suggestions of a eucharistic fast, solo celebrations by clergy, and the practice of 'spiritual communion' for everyone else. Its concluding appendix repeated the refusal to recognize any form of "remote consecration":

> We recognise a real desire of many for some physical engagement during the online celebration of Holy Communion. In some cases, participants in online services have consumed bread and wine in their own homes during the service. Whilst we recognize that this practice may have spiritual value for some, *participants should not be encouraged to believe that any bread and wine brought before screens during online Holy Communion has been 'remotely consecrated.'* (Again, my italics for emphasis)

However, it did include one final sentence that left the door open: "However, we commend the questions raised by this practice for further theological reflection"—so I redoubled my efforts and drafted most of this book over the summer of 2020, only for this to be interrupted by an extended period of ill-health and a move back to my flat in London, which I had been unable to sell because of the pandemic and the government's regulations about fire safety in apartments following the tragedy of the Grenfell Tower fire in London.

Nonetheless, this encouragement for "further theological reflection" did lead to an online Zoom study and reflection day to which all the bishops

25. "I have just been reading through your paper, and I wanted to first of all to say how much I enjoyed it. I really appreciate the fact that you engage in some detail with the issues which are of concern to catholically minded Anglicans in relation to the Eucharist, not least the question of priestly intention. Too much of the debate around our practice in the current situation, I think, has either bypassed that and related questions, or else has taken the answer to such questions as being too obvious to require further exploration. Because you are trying to justify an unexpected position from catholic premises, you have had to explore some territory which others have missed." I am grateful to Bishop Michael for this, and all his encouragement, without which this book would not have been finished; taken from a personal email from the bishop of Lichfield, May 8, 2020, quoted with his permission.

26. Version 1.0, originally dated June 9, 2020, and updated many times subsequently; see https://www.churchofengland.org/resources/coronavirus-covid-19-guidance

of the Church of England were invited on October 26, 2020. A very helpful background note was produced by the House of Bishops Working Group on Holy Communion, chaired by the bishop of Lichfield, dated October 7, 2020. This contained substantial reflection around 'the Administration and Reception of Holy Communion' (especially with regard to communion in one kind only, the common cup, intinction, and so forth) and on 'the Eucharist in a digital medium', raising the issues covered within this book, such as the eucharistic fast, spiritual communion, livestreaming, etc. It concluded, as in the above statement, that "In some cases, participants in online services have consumed bread and wine in their own homes during the service (and in some cases this practice has been encouraged by the presiding priest)." However, the background note remains quite clear: "It is recognised that this practice may have spiritual value for some, but *to consider the possibility that such bread and wine brought before screens is 'remotely consecrated' would require a significant shift in the current understanding and practice of the Church of England*" (again my italics for emphasis). The note also posed some 'questions for discussion' that are very relevant to our concerns, including:

> c. What are the differences between live-streamed and recorded celebrations of the Eucharist, and what implications might there be for the constitution of the Eucharistic community?

> d. Where participants at a service of Holy Communion are separated geographically but present in the same digital space and at the same time, is it possible for them to receive Holy Communion by placing bread and wine before their screens? What theological issues are at stake?

The morning session was devoted to these issues around 'the Eucharist in a digital medium', with presentations from myself, the Rev'd Julie Gittoes (whose paper on the eucharistic fast we will consider in the next chapter), and Dr Colin Podmore, while the afternoon concentrated on the other aspects concerning 'the Administration and Reception of Holy Communion', also with presentations from other significant theologians, including the Rev'd Canon Professor Loveday Alexander, a member of our online eucharistic community. The presentations, papers, and notes about the day were then circulated around the bishops to encourage this "further theological reflection"—but it still has not yet led to any further publications or other theological documents.

The official statement from the House of Bishops Recovery Group on 'COVID-19 Advice on the Administration of Holy Communion' available on the Church of England website has been updated many times subsequently with regard to the practical questions about celebrating communion in church buildings, face coverings, sharing the Peace, hygiene measures, communion in one or both kinds, reserving the sacrament, etc. The latest statement on "Opening and Managing Church Buildings in Step 4 of the Roadmap out of Lockdown" deals very fully and helpfully with all these practical issues.[27]

However, it completely ignores the theological questions around 'the Eucharist in a digital medium' and online communions. All the previous statements, including the latest (version 5.3 from January 12, 2021, which is still available on the same webpage at the time of writing in September 2021, though marked as "non-current or still awaiting review"),[28] still repeated the original five-page statement of "Some Guidance on the Celebration of Holy Communion" from June 2020[29]—unchanged—with all its negative rejection of ideas about receiving bread and wine through online communion, and it still concludes with the original commendation of "the questions raised by this practice for further theological reflection"! I understand that the House of Bishops' meeting in January 2021 in fact decided not to vote upon any proposals at that point, but sent this task back to the Working Group for yet more "theological reflection" . . . .

One wonders when such "theological reflection" might be published or acted upon, especially given the recognition that no matter how much such livestreamed communions may be discouraged by bishops' pronouncements, or such 'remote consecrations' are declared not to be efficacious or sacramental, they have not only continued nonetheless but have also become the norm for thousands of people in hundreds of churches in the UK, the USA, and around the world under the pandemic for approaching nearly two years now. Speaking personally, I have to say that without participating in them, I believe that my faith and spiritual life would have withered and died—and this is despite the welcome return since July 2021 to communion services (in one kind only) being allowed in some church buildings as these words are written. It would be unfortunate if this meant that "further theological reflection" was no longer necessary. This book is therefore offered as part of that process, considering all the various options for celebrating the

27. Version 1.0, dated July 19, 2021; see https://www.churchofengland.org/resources/coronavirus-covid-19-guidance

28. Version 5.3, dated January 12, 2021, which was "Updated from version 5.2: the document has been reviewed following the announcement of a new national lockdown on the 4th January, but has not been changed," see https://www.churchofengland.org/resources/coronavirus-covid-19-guidance

29. Version 1.0, originally dated June 9, 2020, and updated many times subsequently; see https://www.churchofengland.org/resources/coronavirus-covid-19-guidance

eucharist during such "contagious times", as well as any potential problems in online services that might lead to or justify the bishops' negative assertions and prohibitive statements, and what, if anything, might be able to offset, ameliorate, or at least mitigate them. As a (not very good) ethicist is purported to have once said, "sometimes we have to give up our principles, and just do the right thing."[30]

OTHER CHURCHES IN ENGLAND

Catholics

We noted above the article "Is Anglicanism Going Private?" by Peter Selby, the former bishop of Worcester, which challenged the closure of churches in the Church of England and the move towards celebrating communions in clergy homes and kitchens. It is significant, however, that Bishop Peter's piece was published *not* in the Anglican weekly paper, *Church Times*, but in *The Tablet*, a Roman Catholic publication. It was perhaps not surprising that his pointed observations were not lost on Clifford Longley, the veteran Catholic journalist and commentator, who was first to comment below the online version on *The Tablet's* website, making the point:

> The Roman Catholic Church has become the public expression of shared faith and values, whereas the Church of England has fled to the private sphere. . . . The Catholic Church is inching, almost unwittingly, towards providing a spiritual ministry for 100 per cent of the population, not just the Catholic minority within it, while the C of E seems to be, according to Bishop Selby, vacating that space.[31]

Furthermore, various letters to the editor of *The Daily Telegraph* were published through early May from several Roman Catholic correspondents pointing out that, unlike local Anglican vicars, their priests were livestreaming mass from their churches despite the lockdown, as permitted by the government's statutory instrument. As far as I am aware, this practice of Roman Catholic priests entering their churches to celebrate mass while livestreaming it for the faithful to observe (though without any encouragement to participate with their own bread and wine, obviously) continued for

30. I must admit to having set this 'quotation' as a question for theological exploration and discussion in various ethics examinations at universities over the years!

31. https://www.thetablet.co.uk/features/2/17973/is-anglicanism-going-private-

over a year throughout the lockdown; in many places, it is still going on at the time of writing, even as in others public masses have resumed.

Methodists

The Methodist Church is governed principally by its Annual Conference, so in June 2020 the Conference discussed "responding pastorally in the light of COVID-19", particularly with regard to "deprivation", which is defined very specifically: "Deprivation is a term used in the Methodist church when there is not reasonably frequent and regular celebration of the sacrament of the Lord's Supper; but it points to the broader meaning of deprivation." To assist local churches, the Conference "directed the Faith and Order Committee, as a matter of urgency, to produce guidance on acts of Holy Communion in our current context, including reflection on ways in which appropriate on-line participation in services of Holy Communion might be encouraged."[32] This guidance, "Holy Communion: Responding Pastorally in the light of Covid-19" can be downloaded as a PDF from the main Methodist website.[33] It shares many features similar to the guidance from the Church of England bishops, including repeating this policy directive from the 2018 Conference that:

> . . . presbyters and other persons authorised to preside at the sacrament of the Lord's Supper are *not* permitted to use electronic means of communication, such as the internet or video-conferencing, in order to invite those not physically present with the presiding minister to receive the elements.[34] (my italics for emphasis)

The Rev'd Professor Judith Lieu, who had herself chaired the Faith and Order Committee until 2019, noted that there was some pressure "for approval of online communion"; however, the vote of Conference was clear, that "when people at the receiving end of an online service partake of their own bread and wine (or substitutes) it is by definition not holy communion as we understand it."[35] Instead, the guidance provides suggestions for non-sacramental participation at home, noting that "Our Roman Catholic

32. The Methodist Conference, 2020, Resolution 32/3.

33. See https://www.methodist.org.uk/our-faith/reflecting-on-faith/faith-and-order /holy-communion-responding-pastorally-in-the-light-of-covid-19/

34. The Methodist Conference, 2018, Resolution 31/2

35. I am grateful to Professor Lieu for sending me these observations and some of the following links in a private email to me of Sept 4, 2021, and for her permission to quote them here.

friends, as well as other Christians, have a tradition of 'Spiritual Communion' as a means of grace for those times when they are not able to receive sacrament of Holy Communion." This is then linked to John Wesley's sermon on the means of grace, in which "his acknowledgement that God is more than able to work in other ways is a comfort to us":

> prayer, in the letter of Scripture read, the sound thereof heard, or in the bread and wine received in the Lord's supper; but that it is God alone who is the giver of every good gift, the Author of all grace; that the whole power is of Him, whereby, through any of these, there is any blessing conveyed to our souls. We know, likewise, that He is able to give the same grace, though there were no means on the face of the earth. In this sense, we may affirm, that, with regard to God, there is no such thing as means; seeing He is equally able to work whatsoever pleaseth Him, by any, or by none at all.[36]

Sacramental participation is only possible through the Methodist practice of 'Extended Communion' in which "participants receive elements previously set apart at a service of Holy Communion", preferably "on the same day, although this is not always possible, particularly with the current restrictions and concerns for safety." Furthermore, "when someone is unable to receive visitors, consecrated elements could be delivered to them."[37] We shall revisit these suggestions in our discussions of extended communion in chapter 8 below. Finally, the Methodist tradition does also include the practice of the Love Feast, featuring the usual "prayer, praise, scripture, preaching and mutual fellowship and an offering, but in addition the Love Feast contains a time of Prepared Testimony and the sharing of the Love Feast cake and the Loving Cup."[38] Nonetheless, as with the Anglican bishops' prohibition, the Methodist guidance explicitly rules out any notion of online consecration: "Such meals, whether conducted online or in the home, are *not* a celebration of Holy Communion: there is *no question* of action towards the food/drink that is shared, other than being thankful for it and consuming it"[39] (my italics for emphasis). It is significant that the

---

36. Wesley's Sermon on *The Means of Grace*, paragraph II.3, quoted in 2020 Guidance, p. 11; in italics in the original.

37. 2020 Guidance, pp. 10–11; see also, p. 15.

38. https://www.methodist.org.uk/our-faith/worship/singing-the-faith-plus/leading-worship/additional-methodist-liturgies/a-methodist-love-feast/

39. 2020 Guidance, p. 15.

regular livestreams (and the catch-up services) from Methodist Central Hall do not include any communion services.[40]

Baptists

The ecclesiology of Baptist churches, of course, encourages each individual congregation to make their own decisions about their worship, and this, together with their 'lower' Zwinglian understanding of the eucharist more as a memorial than as a consecration (see our discussion of the theology of communion in chapter 6 below), enabled Baptists to continue to receive communion by bringing bread and wine in front of their devices as services were livestreamed, both from ministers' homes and, when allowed, from their churches.[41] During the main lockdown period, we were delighted to welcome my Baptist former colleague, the Rev'd Dr Simon Woodman, Minister of the historic Bloomsbury Central Baptist Church in central London, to celebrate communion for us in one of our weekly Zoom communions, using a liturgy and form of service that he had designed himself. Now that some members of his congregation have returned to worship in the church, Bloomsbury continues with a 'blended' approach, serving bread and wine to those present in church while encouraging those joining in online from home to have their own bread and wine as participants in the same service.[42]

ONLINE COMMUNION
AND THE EPISCOPAL CHURCH IN THE USA

It is completely natural that the debates within the Church of England were also being mirrored by our Episcopal brothers and sisters in the United

40. See https://mchw.live/ and https://mchw.live/live-stream/archive

41. As with everything else, there is a wide variety of views about the eucharist among Baptists, both historically in their tradition and today in their diversity, but in general terms there has been a shift amongst Baptists from a preference for a sacramentalist approach (the view of the Particular Baptists) towards the strong dominance of a memorialist Zwinglian position nowadays (inherited from the General Baptists). However, recent years have seen a revival of the Baptist sacramentalist tradition among Baptist theologians. These include Paul Fiddes, who bases his view "on the freedom of Christ to presence himself through all the materials of the world." I am grateful to Prof Fiddes himself for clarifying this in a private email of Oct 22, 2021, quoted by permission.

42. See for instance, the service on August 1, 2020, at https://youtu.be/BaTAuI5d-0s, see especially from 38 minutes 30 seconds for the instructions for those watching at home.

States of America. Thus, when the seminary with which I have been associated for over a decade, Virginia Theological Seminary, had to go into lockdown, it was entirely right and proper that the dean and president, the Very Rev'd Dr Ian S. Markham, should turn to his professor of liturgy, James Farwell, for advice. Farwell's immediate response was to acknowledge that "I'm not entirely opposed to the streaming of Eucharist, but . . . I have some questions." He was clear about his own position as "a great proponent of the Eucharistic recovery of the 20th century liturgical movement. No one is more supportive of the Eucharistic center of the Lord's Day than I am. No one. My own spirituality, Incarnational to the core, is eucharistically centered. I lean to the Catholic end of 'Catholic and Reformed.' That said . . . ," however, he went on to confess to a number of reservations, not least about the "fetishization of the Sacrament" in any separation from the Word: "Are we wholly deprived because the Word alone is available to us for a time? I think you know the answer." Dr. Farwell is also clear about the community basis of the communion:

> The sacrament is crucially a gathering of the social assembly, bodily, around material things. We priests do not consecrate the Eucharist alone. Nor is Eucharist consecrated or received virtually. The loss of the Eucharistic assembly for a time is a real loss to all of us. . . . But, do we serve the sacrament by gathering two or three people to fulfill the letter of the law as others watch online? . . . Or by distributing that consecrated bread and wine to be consumed privately by an individual or a family unit? . . . Might the Offices, not to mention many other devotional and meditative practices, suffice for a time? Are we suddenly not ourselves, the Body of Christ, because we cannot receive the Body of Christ in the sacrament?

Finally, he drew upon one of his mentors, the eminent Byzantine Rite Roman Catholic Archimandrite Robert Taft, SJ: "The point of the Eucharist is not the changing of bread and wine but the changing of you and me. Is God unable to change us WITHOUT the bread and wine? Might God be able to work in us through a period of sacramental deprivation? Even through it?" Farwell then concluded, "God is still at the Table that is spread among us in our hearts, in our prayers, in our service. Welcome to the Feast that does not end, the love of God from which and from whom we are never separated, even without the Sacrament."[43]

43. Personal email from James Farwell to Ian Markham, March 19, 2020, who forwarded it to me on March 25, the very day of our first Zoom communion! Used by kind permission of both colleagues; Dr Farwell also generously shared its contents with various American and Canadian bishops in the crucial months that followed. It remains

Farwell was not the only Episcopalian theologian to have reservations. The Rt Rev'd Andy Doyle, bishop of Texas, circulated some instructions, guidance, ideas, and resources around his diocese for Holy Week and Easter 2020 to which was attached a pastoral letter, containing detailed theological reflections of nearly 17,000 words. This impressive document explored "the present pastoral effects of . . . COVID-19", followed by "a survey of Christian, Anglican, and Episcopal understandings around how our praying shapes our believing", before going on to "an exploration of 'drive-by' and 'drive-in' Eucharist, when communion is not possible, virtual Eucharist, lay presidency at the Eucharist, and how the manner in which we make Eucharist challenges our secular imaginaries." Bishop Doyle was, however, quite clear: there was no permission or possibility of online eucharistic celebrations. He drew upon a reflection from Sam Wells and Abigail Kocher of St Martin in the Fields:

> This is a time when Christians can identify with and learn from Jews like never before. Since 70 AD, Jews have prayed, lit candles, and kept Sabbath without being able to be present in the Temple. They have kept the prayers, known by heart, passing down the faith generation to generation. . . . The Jews have a lot to teach Christians about knowing God's presence when the tangible signs of worship are stripped away and sacred places of gathering are not accessible for a time.[44]

Therefore, instead of the eucharist, Bishop Doyle concluded with "an invitation to lean into the creativity of Holy Week and the Easter Vigil, finding the sacrifice of the candle as an orienting theme for Easter during a Eucharistic fast."[45]

Bishop Doyle's *Pastoral Letter* quickly became an important resource for my work as I was working towards this book, while I greatly enjoyed some lively email exchanges with him, as he also directed his energies to producing his own book, completed and published months before mine![46]

© James Farwell, professor of theology and liturgy at Virginia Theological Seminary, USA.

44. The Rev'd Dr Sam Wells and the Rev'd Abigail Kocher, "Thoughts on Virtual Communion in a Lockdown Era," 27 March 2020, https://www.stmartin-in-the-fields.org/keeping-the-feast/

45. See https://www.epicenter.org/resources/covid-19-hub/virtual-liturgies/#holy-eucharist, from where it is also possible to download a pdf of Bishop Doyle's remarkable pastoral letter; it is hard to imagine any currently active bishop in the Church of England being able to produce during Lent a document of such length, let alone theological depth!

46. C. Andrew Doyle, *Embodied Liturgy: Virtual Reality and Liturgical Theology in Conversation* (London: Church Publishing, 2021).

In the late summer of 2020, I was honoured to be asked by the Rt Rev'd Pierre Whalon, recently retired bishop of the Convocation of Episcopal (formerly American) Churches in Europe, if he could summarise my work in comparison with Bishop Doyle's in a paper for consideration by the American Episcopal bishops at their "Table in the Wilderness" online conversations. However, although I understand that the American Episcopal bishops enjoyed these "Table in the Wilderness" discussions and I received some encouraging feedback from some of them afterwards, like their counterparts in the English House of Bishops, nothing concrete or further has yet emerged, as far as I am aware.

Part of the reason for this lack of further debate and action may be connected with the experience of the bishop of Western Louisiana, the Rt Rev'd Dr Jacob W. Owensby, who emailed his diocesan clergy and lay leaders over Easter 2020 with a "new standard for Sunday worship":

> I'm writing today to send you Easter greetings, but also to introduce a new standard for Sunday worship. We will now move to what many are now calling Virtual Holy Eucharist. We will continue the practice as long as the pandemic requires that we stay at home for the common good. I take this measure because there have been indications that we may be in for a longer haul than was initially anticipated. Simply put, priests who have the technical know-how, the equipment, and the inclination will live-stream the Holy Eucharist on Sunday (or other appointed times). Instead, they may refer you to my weekly Eucharist. The people will attend from their own homes, maintaining physical distance as before. The people will provide for themselves bread and wine (bread alone is also permissible) and place it on a table in front of them. The priest's consecration of elements in front of her or him extends to the bread and wine in each of family's household. The people will consume the consecrated elements.[47]

The bishop also announced that he himself planned to perform such a "virtual Holy Eucharist" over Facebook Live on Sunday, April 19, 2020. However, this was quickly met with opposition from the Rt Rev'd Dr George Sumner, bishop of the Episcopal Diocese of Dallas, who wrote on April 14 in *Covenant*, the weblog of *Living Church*:

> Since the rubrics clearly prohibit remotely consecrating bread and wine, the question of virtual communion is not one which

---

47. The Rt Rev'd Jacob W. Owensby, PhD, DD, "A Note from the Bishop on Virtual Holy Eucharist." https://myemail.constantcontact.com/Home-Based-Worship-and-Community-Resources.html?soid=1111514195724&aid=nlM3_CQpxbM

could lead to immediate action, which is for the best. We can therefore have a dispassionate discussion of it. . . . [T]he objection based on "materiality" stands. The Eucharist claims the real presence of Christ in this event of really blessing and consuming real elements by a real (bodily) congregation. . . . In our era of all-Eucharist-all-the-time, we should not absorb everything into the sacrament. . . . [T]his pestilence too shall pass, and we need to make sure in the meantime we do no harm to our more normative theology and practice.[48]

The next day, April 15, and thus two days before his planned virtual eucharist, Bishop Owensby again emailed his clergy and lay leaders, rescinding his authorization and explaining that:

After a gracious conversation with the office of the Presiding Bishop, I understand that virtual consecration of elements at a physical or geographical distance from the Altar exceeds the recognized bounds set by our rubrics and inscribed in our theology of the Eucharist. I am grateful for the collegiality of the House of Bishops and the love expressed to me, and to all of us, in the conversations I have had.[49]

The context of all of this needs to be understood. The presiding bishop, the Most Rev'd Michael B. Curry, whose extraordinary sermon in St George's Windsor at the Duke and Duchess of Sussex's wedding set the world alight, had previously formally suspended all public worship in Episcopal churches within the USA and abroad on March 17, 2020, although he wanted to "emphasise that suspension of in-person gatherings is not a suspension of worship. I very much encourage and support online worship."[50] However, on March 31, 2020, the feast of John Donne, he issued "A Word to the Church Regarding the Theology of Worship during the COVID-19 Pandemic", following conversations with a small group of theologians, which made his position clear:

Sacraments are communal actions that depend on "stuff": bread and wine, water and oil. They depend on gathering and giving thanks, on proclaiming and receiving the stories of salvation, on bathing in water, on eating and drinking together. These

48. See the Rt Rev'd Dr. George Sumner, "Against Virtual Communion." https://livingchurch.org/covenant/2020/04/14/against-virtual-communion/

49. For more details, see the report in the *Living Church*: https://livingchurch.org/2020/04/17/western-louisiana-bishop-authorizes-then-rescinds-virtual-consecration/

50. See https://www.churchtimes.co.uk/articles/2020/20-march/news/world/bishop-curry-suspends-public-worship-for-episcopalians

are physical and social realities that are not duplicatable in the virtual world. . . . From the time of Thomas Cranmer, mainstream Anglicanism has insisted that the Holy Eucharist is to be celebrated in community, with no fewer than two people. . . . Practices such as "drive-by communion" present public health concerns and further distort the essential link between a communal celebration and the culmination of that celebration in the reception of the Eucharistic Bread and Wine. . . . The Book of Common Prayer clearly expresses the conviction that even if a person is prevented from physically receiving the Sacrament for reasons of extreme illness or disability, the desire for Christ's presence alone is enough for all the benefits of the Sacrament to be received. . . . The questions being posed to Bishops around these matters are invitations to a deeper engagement with what we mean by the word "sacrament" and how much we are prepared for the Church itself—with or without our accustomed celebrations of the Eucharist—to signify about the presence of God with us.[51]

In the light of this, the "gracious conversation" of the presiding bishop with Bishop Owensby of Western Louisiana must have been very interesting! However, at the final stage of writing this book some eighteen months later, I still do not know how far the "deeper engagement", like the Anglican bishops' "further theological reflection", has reached, or where such "conversations" may lead in the future—or whether the Episcopal Church is just hoping along with Bishop Sumner that "this pestilence too shall pass", and all will return to what Americans call 'normalcy'.[52] Time alone will tell, but I suspect that we will find that the online cat, having been let out of the bag, will be more difficult to put back.

OTHER CHURCHES IN THE USA

The same debates have been taking place in all the mainstream Christian denominations in the USA.[53] Not surprisingly, Roman Catholics were

51. Published by the Episcopal Church Office of Public Affairs on April 1: https://www.episcopalnewsservice.org/pressreleases/a-word-to-the-church-on-our-theology-of-worship-from-the-presiding-bishop/

52. As one United Church of Christ minister "upping the frequency of his online Communion" put it, because "our people need normalcy": https://www.ucc.org/news_commentary_the_necessity_of_communion_at_this_time_03272020

53. For a good general survey at the time, see: https://religionnews.com/2020/03/27/as-coronavirus-keeps-parishioners-homebound-christian-clergy-debate-online-communion/

encouraged to watch livestreams of priests celebrating mass alone, while the Archdiocese of New York provided an act of "spiritual communion," explained as "an ardent desire to receive Jesus in the Most Holy Sacrament and lovingly embrace him at a time or in circumstances when one cannot receive Him in sacramental Communion."[54]

As far back as 2013, the United Methodist Church had called for a moratorium on online communion to enable further study to be done,[55] which was extended in 2014.[56] Furthermore, in 2015, it was made clear that not only was online communion prohibited, but so also was 'pre-consecration' of "elements ahead of time for the convenience of the pastor not having to go to small or remote congregations" and similarly "Self-Serve or Drop-In Communion".[57] However, with the advent of the pandemic, some Methodist bishops started issuing guidance to permit the practice, thereby breaking the moratorium, including Bishop Kenneth Carter of the UMC's Florida Conference, who had chaired the original taskforce on online communion and the moratorium. He explained to the Religion News Service that "we have given that permission with the guidance that this is an extreme situation to meet pastoral and missional needs", pointing out that "churches were doing it anyway. . . . This was not driven by denominational officials handing down an edict. It came from congregations."[58] It is not surprising, therefore that Justus Hunter described the situation as "chaos in the UMC" in his plea in *Covenant* for restraint.[59]

The Evangelical Lutheran Church in America (ELCA) also issued a statement encouraging livestreaming on online services during the pandemic, including some helpful short and clear practical suggestions "to honor the body of Christ in your virtual community", such as allowing people to see each other, using "chat features to communicate prayer requests", singing "short, repetitive songs", lighting candles, etc. On the other hand, while the statement welcomed recent encouragement towards "weekly communion", it argued that Lutherans should employ a eucharistic "fast" during the pandemic:

54. https://archny.org/mass/acts-of-spiritual-communion/

55. https://www.umnews.org/en/news/moratorium-study-urged-on-online-communion

56. https://web.archive.org/web/20150825032155/http:/www.gbhem.org/about-gbhem/publications/online-communion

57. https://www.umcdiscipleship.org/blog/three-communion-practices-to-quit-doing

58. https://religionnews.com/2020/03/27/as-coronavirus-keeps-parishioners-homebound-christian-clergy-debate-online-communion/

59. https://livingchurch.org/covenant/2020/03/27/communion-in-chaos-in-the-umc/

Fasting from Holy Communion for a time might be a good discipline. This absence makes God's presence more profound. During this limited fast we might become more aware of God's presence around us and in creation in ways that we have never noticed before. . . . We recommend that we do not urge people to employ virtual Communion, that deacons, pastors, and bishops use this time as a teaching moment about the Lutheran understanding of the Word of God, and that we make use of the Service of the Word and Morning Prayer, Evening Prayer, Night Prayer and Responsive Prayer.[60]

Finally, other churches have changed their stance as the effects of the global COVID-19 outbreak dragged on. Leaders of the Presbyterian Church of the USA initially suggested in early March 2020 that pastors should avoid celebrating communion online. But on March 27, the PCUSA's Office of the General Assembly performed an about-face. It published an "Advisory Opinion from the Stated Clerk of the General Assembly" with a simple one-word answer in reply to two basic questions:[61]

- May a congregation celebrate the Lord's Supper within an electronic worship service during an emergency or pandemic? **Yes**
- Is this advice different from the advice given in early March, 2020? **Yes**

The PCUSA webpage does point out that "Advisory Opinions are just that, opinions, and they are neither authoritative nor binding upon the Presbyterian Church (U.S.A.)." Nonetheless, the advisory opinion provides various references and long quotations from the PCUSA Book of Order about how "the Session or other council" may "authorize the Lord's Supper" in both "an emergency situation or during a pandemic" or at other times: "In emergency circumstances there may be situations in which the pastoral needs of that moment require that the church take actions that run contrary to normal practice. . . . The council should be clear that their decision is one of emphasizing the unity of the body in an extraordinary time when we are not able to worship or be together in person." To undergird the importance of maintaining the communion during the pandemic, it also quotes extensively from PCUSA's Directory of Worship, identifying "several theological reasons for this [opinion] including embodiment, . . . community, . . . [and]

---

60. "Worship in Times of Public Health Concerns: COVID-19/Coronavirus." Issued 20th March 2020; downloadable as a PDF from https://www.elca.org/publichealth

61. The advisory opinion can be downloaded as a PDF from https://www.pcusa.org/resource/advisory-opinion-communion-emergencypandemic/

meaning. . . . The Sacrament of the Lord's Supper offers an abundant feast of theological meaning, including: thanksgiving to God the Father; remembrance of Jesus Christ; invocation of the Holy Spirit; communion in the body of Christ; and a meal of the realm of God."

CONCLUSION

This introductory chapter has outlined how the coronavirus pandemic has led all mainstream Christian churches on both sides of the Atlantic and around the rest of the world into previously uncharted territory, where the initial instructions, guidance, or advice from governments and church authorities led to the closure of churches in line with the general lockdowns that came into force in most countries as the virus spread apparently unabated. As what was assumed or intended to be only a temporary measure dragged on for weeks, months, and then over a year, it was inevitable that this would also affect the central act of Christian worship, the eucharist, mass, holy communion, or Lord's supper.[62] After more than a century of liturgical renewal across many denominations, which had restored holy communion to a central place in the life of most churches, this was bound to come as a great shock, and cause severe heart-searching and theological dilemmas about the best and proper way to proceed. We have charted in a little detail how the Anglican tradition as well as other mainstream churches reacted in the USA and United Kingdom—and similar debates and reactions went on in many countries, as the eucharist stopped being the quintessential corporate rite around the Christian world. Some countries, which relied more on a strict and immediate shutting down of borders, such as Australia and New Zealand, where infection rates were so much smaller, were able to maintain public eucharistic services longer than the northern hemisphere; however, as such places currently attempt to negotiate rejoining the wider international community and are facing new waves of coronavirus and lockdowns at the time of writing, the same issues are again raising their heads there also.

What this survey has shown is that several solutions quickly rose to the fore, such as masses being said by individual priests alone, but watched by the (spiritually hungry?) faithful online, or—at the other extreme—embarking

62. Of course, it also had a profound impact on another major Christian rite also referred to in the government's Statutory Instrument, that of funerals, especially as thousands were dying as a result of the virus and infection. This important area is beyond the scope of this book—but it would be wrong not least to acknowledge this fact, and all the hard work and effort put in by clergy to minister to the bereaved within such difficult circumstances.

upon the previously hardly known discipline of an extended eucharistic fast. Many church authorities quickly took refuge in the generally little-known and less-used practice of 'spiritual communion', found mostly in the Catholic tradition, but which came to be adopted across Protestant denominations with amazing rapidity. While such solutions may have seemed acceptable, at least initially, to many church leaders and authorities, as the weeks and months went by, and a year's anniversary passed, the lay people faced the parody of the old pastoral description of ministry in which "the hungry sheep look up and are fed," into the increasingly difficult situation where the Lord's sheep look hungry and fed-up, but actually they are *not* being fed with his body and blood. Despite the general opposition of most church hierarchies and leaderships to online celebrations of communion, together with their 'directives', 'instructions', and 'guidance', the anecdotal evidence was growing on both sides of the Atlantic that hundreds, if not thousands, of churches, with thousands, if not tens of thousands of Christians, were quietly (or not so quietly in some cases) ignoring the official line and participating in online celebrations of communion.

Therefore this book, begun in great haste at the arrival of coronavirus, and subsequently written in fits and starts as the pandemic wore on, not least because of the author's own health issues, is offered as a resource at the current stage of the pandemic, where increasing use of vaccination is beginning to permit regular gathering of eucharistic communities to celebrate communion once again in churches and other places of worship, although in many places still only 'in one kind', with the common chalice or communion cup being withheld. However, even on such occasions, there are still many rules and guidelines in force, and large numbers of the faithful do not yet feel comfortable or ready to return, or to join in physically, preferring to stay at home and watch online, even if they cannot receive communion as a result.

The structure of the book follows the author's own personal search for possible answers and a solution to the challenge of sharing holy communion in what the 1662 Book of Common Prayer calls "contagious times". The first half explores all the possible ways of celebrating the eucharist in the everyday physical universe, often mistakenly called 'the real world'—before going on to consider all the extraordinary opportunities now offered by new technologies in the equally 'real' world of digital, online, and cyber-space. Through coronavirus, a biblical *kairos* moment—the possibility of opportunity or judgement—has come upon us, and Jesus Christ, the Lord of the sacrament who commanded us to break bread and drink wine to remember him, calls us to follow, like Aslan in Narnia, "further up and further in". Who are we to refuse his gracious invitation?

PART I

Holy Communion in "Contagious Times" in the Everyday World

2

Proposal 1

The Eucharistic Fast

IN A PROFOUNDLY MOVING article in the Church of England's *Church Times* at the start of the COVID-19 pandemic, the Rev'd Dr Julie Gittoes, Vicar of St Mary's and Christ Church, Hendon, in London, wrote about "Why I am fasting from the feast."[1] This is obviously the most extreme reaction to the place of holy communion in "contagious times"—that is, to *abstain from it altogether*. There are several possible reasons for such abstention:

- by clergy and laity out of fear of possible infection;

- by lay people who cannot consecrate the sacrament of bread and wine;

- by clergy who follow the Anglican tradition and rubrics of the Book of Common Prayer, which forbid it without a certain minimum number of participants, usually four or three at least;[2]

- by clergy acting out of a sense of solidarity with those who cannot receive it, especially the lay people in their pastoral care.

Dr Gittoes makes it abundantly clear in her article that the eucharist has been "at the heart of my spiritual life" since childhood; it is "the lens through which I see everything; it is the pulse and plumb line of life; it is a point of encounter with Christ, feeding and forming us in the midst of joy and grief, the mundane and the complex." She rightly notes that it is

1. https://www.churchtimes.co.uk/articles/2020/17-april/comment/opinion/why-i-am-fasting-from-the-feast

2. See further, chapter 3 on solitary communion on one's own.

"intimate" in its "physicality of touch, taste, and sight," but at the same time, it is also "cosmic, enfolding us into the story of creation and redemption, restoring our vision of God's Kingdom." As part of our lives, it is "endlessly repeated, but never the same."

And yet, because churches were closed by (arch-)episcopal order at that time, holy communion was simply not possible in any recognizably 'normal' way. In such a "contagious time" of crisis, "I find myself mourning the loss of celebrating the eucharist with my congregation, but also embracing a chosen fast from this feast—not only because I live alone, but out of a sense of being with God's people in this unchosen wilderness." Thus, she picks up two of the reasons cited above—that because she lives alone, she has no one else with whom to celebrate it in accordance with the BCP's instructions, but also in order to be in solidarity in the wilderness with her people. This must be a very difficult and deeply painful place to be for someone who has valued the eucharist since childhood—and yet she does not merely endure it, but actually *embraces* and *chooses* it, as a "fast from the feast."

In undertaking this fast, Dr Gittoes is following the first option suggested by the London College of Bishops in their paper of March 31, 2020, "The Eucharist in a Time of Physical Distancing": "Some parish churches may wish temporarily to suspend the celebration of Holy Communion until they are able to meet together in person again. We are already having to cease the practice of public Baptism for the duration due to the restrictions placed upon us, and so a church may choose to do the same with the other dominical sacrament. As one incumbent put it recently: 'We will take this opportunity to fast from the Sacrament while we feast on the Word.'"[3]

Writing in a similar vein in the Roman Catholic weekly journal *The Tablet*, Thomas O'Loughlin, professor of historical theology at the University of Nottingham and a former president of the Catholic Theological Association of Great Britain, seizes this "time of loss" as an opportunity to reflect on the commodification of the eucharist, which is revealed when worshippers talk of 'getting mass' or 'taking communion', as though "the Eucharist is something 'out there', which we watch or somehow obtain and make our own, as if we were theatregoers or consumers."[4] His response is that the eucharist is not an object, which we 'get', but a verb, which we *do*; the very word 'eucharist', in its meaning in Greek, indicates "the *activity* of

3. https://www.london.anglican.org/articles/the-eucharist-in-a-time-of-physical-distancing/. This paper was written with particular theological input from the bishops of Kensington and Fulham from their contrasting church traditions.

4. Thomas O'Loughlin, "Open New Doors to Prayer," *The Tablet*, March 28, 2020, 4–6; https://www.thetablet.co.uk/features/2/17770/reimagining-the-eucharist

thanking God." Therefore, he 'reimagines' the eucharistic thanksgiving in several ways: that the Lord is always with us everywhere, not just in churches; that one's room is "a basic place of prayer" (Matt 6:5–6); and lastly that "every table is a sacred place." He anticipates our next chapter by concluding with the observation that "Some have been tempted to reach for the idea of 'spiritual communion' as a sort of 'fix' in this emergency." But he considers that it is "better to simply acknowledge that this is a weird time" and "Until we can get back to normal, let's just note its loss, concentrate on what we can do while we are living in isolation from one another," namely to "rediscover that *we* are the church," not a building, and "we must be *eucharistic* every day (it is an act of attitude of thankfulness for all the good things of creation)."

At the other end of the ecclesiological candle and on the far side of the globe, we should note an important contribution from the renowned Australian Baptist Old Testament scholar from Whitley College, Professor Mark Brett, together with his Anglican colleague at Trinity College, Dr Rachelle Gilmour, both colleges being part of the University of Divinity, Melbourne.[5] In seeking a parallel for the current crisis, Brett and Gilmour turn to the exile in Babylon after the capture of Jerusalem and destruction of the temple in 586 BC. Out of the experience of being physically separated from their place of worship, which lay far away in ruins, "came significant portions of what we now call the Hebrew Bible, *Tanakh* or Old Testament." They compare the "signs of intense grief, like weeping, mourning and groaning: 'She weeps bitterly in the night with tears on her cheeks' (Lam 1:2), . . . guilt and a sense of confusion" in the book of Lamentations (probably written at the start of the exile) with our current "deep grief arising from the cessation of public worship."

Yet by the end of the exile, this has become the opening cry of second Isaiah (Isaiah 40–55), forever immortalized in the haunting tenor aria that opens Handel's *Messiah*, "Comfort ye, my people": "A voice cries out: In the wilderness prepare the way of the LORD, make straight in the desert a highway for our God" (Isa 40:1–3). "This transformation of *Lamentations* in *Isaiah* 40 is not a negation of Judah's grief and trauma, or even a replacement of it. Rather, it reflects a practice of hope that grows from experiences of trauma." Brett and Gilmour argue that it came about in part through a "renewal of sabbath theology," "a community observance of sacred time, rest from work on the seventh day . . . when people could not travel to a distant shrine." Learning from this experience of God's ancient people, they exhort

5. https://www.abc.net.au/religion/hebrew-bible-worship-in-exile-as-essential-service/12102306

us, "let us revitalise our communities on the sabbath. In sacred time, we can lament together, and we can wait for the good news: . . . whether or not we lift the bread and wine together, [we should] continue to pray in the one sacred moment, 'Blessed are you, Lord God of all creation.'"

Much of the current debate is, of course, being conducted through social media. In a long post on his Facebook page on March 25, 2020, the Rev'd Dr David Hilborn—who came from a Free Church background, became an Anglican, and is now principal of a Free Church College[6]—outlined four possible options for holy communion during COVID-19. He dismissed option 2 (a form of 'spiritual communion', as discussed in the next chapter) as "docetic and hyper-clerical" and option 3 (a form of 'extended communion', as discussed in chapter 8) as "potentially contaminative." As an evangelical theologian, it is not surprising that he ended up with option 4 as "scripturally and theologically the least worst option," namely streaming a president's celebration online and allowing everyone watching to partake of their own bread and wine (although, not surprisingly, he got some considerable pushback from respondents of a more traditional or catholic churchmanship!).

However, his consideration of option 1 ("Suspend it completely, reject all attempts at online celebration on the grounds that they're inauthentic, and see the privation as something that will help us appreciate it all the more when it resumes") is not that far from the position suggested by Dr Gittoes, Professor O'Loughlin, Professor Brett, and Dr Gilmour. It did commend itself to at least one respondent from a 'higher tradition', the Rev'd Ian Mobsby, the assistant dean for fresh expressions & pioneer ministry for the Diocese of Southwark, who posted: "As a Priest where the sacraments are important, we need to remember that other forms of sacramental presence are possible and called for. I don't think we need to compromise the Eucharist or Holy Communion, but instead emphasis[e] the presence of God through contemplative forms of prayer and sacred reading . . . promoting prayer practices, drawing on Ignatian, Franciscan, and Benedictine Spirituality [and] some of the wisdom of the new monasticism movement."

Despite this, I find myself drawn towards Hilborn's rejection of such a eucharistic fast, in which holy communion is replaced by prayer, worship, and spiritual practices, agreeing with his grounds that it is "a misapplication of a more general principle of self-denial." Normally fasting is a spiritual discipline in its own right, freely chosen by a believer, to go without particular

---

6. David Hilborn was formerly a minister of the United Reformed Church and the theological adviser to the Evangelical Alliance, who then became an Anglican priest, and principal first of the North Thames Ministry Training Course, and then St John's Nottingham, but who is now principal of the non-denominational evangelical Moorlands College.

foodstuffs or drink, or certain habits or pleasures (even sexual intimacy in 1 Cor 7:5, and probably Dan 6:18)[7] for a particular period, such as Lent (or Ramadhan for Muslims), in order to promote self-control over the needs and passions of our human nature and to allow us to give more time to prayer, study, and seeking God. For those for whom the eucharist is at the heart of their spiritual life and personal discipline and who believe that regular, even daily, reception of it is necessary for growth in prayer and holiness, it is hard to see how a compulsory withdrawal of the eucharist because of unfortunate circumstances, including terrible suffering, economic disaster, and millions of deaths around the world, can be considered as comparable to a 'fast' voluntarily chosen by a disciple. The bishop of Lichfield, Michael Ipgrave, made a similar point concerning "a Eucharistic fast, for which I can think of little precedent (at least, when entered into voluntarily rather than of necessity)."[8]

The internet abounds with brief video lectures from clergy, especially priests from a more (Anglo-)Catholic tradition reflecting on this situation. In a wide-ranging exposition of eucharistic theology, the Rev'd Dr Thomas Plant, chaplain of Lichfield Cathedral School,[9] rightly points out the importance of the *whole* people of God in a sacramental, eucharistic theology, with lay people making bread and wine to serve both the church and all those in need for the glory of God. His part in the eucharistic offering (to go into the oratory in his garage to celebrate communion) is "only my part, as a priest in the eucharistic offering, and it's only *one* part" (his emphasis in the video); "if I were to neglect that, if I were to fast from it, I would have nothing to offer anyone at all, because I offer nothing. Christ offers, through me."[10] He goes on to argue that "the laity who serve and volunteer, who pre-

---

7. After being tricked by his wicked advisers into condemning Daniel to be sealed into the lions' den, Darius the king retreated "to his palace and spent the night fasting" (NRSV), although the Greek Septuagint says he was "lying in the open courtyard fasting"; then in the original (which is in Aramaic, unusually, rather than Hebrew here) "no *dahavan* was brought to him", an unclear word which NRSV translates as "no food", whereas since, whatever its meaning, the word is feminine plural in form, other translations hint at something more explicit: "no entertainment" (NIV; NASB; CEV; GNT; ISV), or no "diversions" (RSV; ESV; NET; JPS Tanakh); the Darby Bible (1890) is clearest, with its "neither were concubines brought before him", which, if he was "lying in the open courtyard" is not surprising! However, that would not have stopped the "instruments of musick" preferred by the KJV/AV and its descendants (RV; ASV; NKJV). The point is clear that King Darius' fasting and going without anything is a particular mark of his concern and prayer for Daniel, shown by how he rushes to the lions' den the next morning (Dan 6:19).

8. Personal email to me on April 26, 2020; quoted with his permission.

9. See https://mistergog.blogspot.com/

10. See his video at https://www.youtube.com/watch?v=zlwbo6ouSzw

pare and deliver food, who provide jobs for people, and who pray the divine office of the hours . . . participate in exactly the same eucharistic action as me"; therefore, even if not receiving communion is "not ideal . . . people can participate through their loving service and their gift of self to Christ."

In a similar vein, Father Peter Anthony, then vicar of St Benet's, Kentish Town, but later elevated to become priest of All Saints Margaret Street, another Anglo-Catholic video blogger, examines Paul's account of the institution of the Last Supper, concluding with his explanation "for as often as you eat this bread and drink the cup, you proclaim the Lord's death until he comes" (1 Cor 11:23–26). He argues that Paul's use of *katangellō* ("proclaim") for an *action* as well as for *speech* suggests that "the eucharist is not just about those gathered receiving the body and blood of Christ; it is about bringing the power of the cross into this world of ours. . . . The eucharist is a necessary thing, and an important thing, which changes the world. . . . The eucharist is of consequence, and worth, and power, for those outside that particular celebration as much as it is for those who receive holy communion."[11]

According to this kind of sacramental approach to the world as well as to the eucharist, the practice of clergy fasting from communion is not an act of solidarity with their people—quite the reverse: it is actually a neglect of their God-given role to celebrate the Lord's supper itself, so that all God's people can participate in the continuing eucharistic offering of the church through each of their individual actions in turn. Far from being a fast or identifying with other people's situation, it is an abdication of priestly responsibility to be one channel (and only one) through which Christ is made present in the world.

Furthermore, initial discussions about a fast from the eucharist took place in Lent, the one period of the church's year when it might be argued that abstinence could make some liturgical sense. However, fasting from the eucharist at Easter sends out very confused liturgical messages. Here is the feast by which we participate in the benefits of the redemptive work of Christ and spiritually commune with the Risen Lord and the body of the *ekklēsia*. And here is the season in which we celebrate that very redemptive work and the new creation it inaugurates. Fasting from the eucharist in Eastertide makes only for liturgical doublespeak.[12]

Therefore, while I applaud the concept of a 'eucharistic fast' as an attempt to find something positive in such a negative situation, I do not think such an approach is *helpful*, even or especially for lay people who also cannot

11. https://www.youtube.com/watch?v=T_XrWsFd88Y

12. I'm grateful to the Rev'd Dr Robin Parry for the argument of this paragraph.

receive communion, let alone *sustainable*, certainly in the longer term. We must, therefore, explore other avenues that might provide some criteria or framework for finding valid and effective ways of celebrating the eucharist and sharing in communion during what the 1662 Book of Common Prayer terms "contagious times".

3

Proposal 2

Spiritual Communion

THE FIRST POSSIBLE SOLUTION has been to turn to the concept of 'spiritual communion' as noted in the rubric instruction in Thomas Cranmer's 1549 Prayer Book at the end of the service for "The Order for Visitation of the Sick and the Communion of the Same":

> but if any man, either by reason of extremity of sickness, or for want of warning in due time to the Curate, or for lack of company to receive with him, or by any other just impediment, do not receive the Sacrament of Christ's Body and Blood: then the Curate shall instruct him . . . that if he truly repents and believes, he can nonetheless receive the benefits of communion "*although he do not receive the Sacrament with his mouth.*"[1]

No less a theologian than Thomas Aquinas himself defined spiritual communion as "an ardent desire to receive Jesus in the Holy Sacrament and a loving embrace as though we had already received Him."[2] From the

---

1. Taken from the Book of Common Prayer, with our italics for emphasis. For the original 1549 version in the ancient spelling, see Grant Bayliss' blog, quoted below; see note 16 later in this chapter.

2. This is a summary by Alphonsus Liguori of Aquinas' teaching about spiritual communion, "*Whether there are two ways to be distinguished of eating Christ's Body, namely, spiritually and sacramentally?*" in Aquinas' *Summa Theologiae* III, q. 80, a. 1; in *The Complete Works of Saint Alphonsus de Liguori, The Ascetical Works, Vol VI, The Holy Eucharist* (translated by Eugene Grimm. New York: Benziger, 1887), 121. My thanks to Fr Stephen Brock at the University of Chicago for chasing down the source of the quotation.

sublime (the angelic doctor) to the rather more ridiculous, Wikipedia (fortunately?) agrees with him: "Spiritual Communion is a Christian practice of desiring union with Jesus Christ in the Holy Eucharist. It is used as a preparation for Holy Mass and by individuals who cannot receive Holy Communion." It goes on to note that "the practice of Spiritual Communion has been especially used by Christians in times of persecution, such as during the era of state atheism in the Eastern Bloc, as well as in times of plagues, such as during the 2019–20 coronavirus pandemic, when Christians were unable together to celebrate the Eucharist on the Lord's Day."[3]

THE ROMAN CATHOLIC VIEW

Following our reference to St Thomas Aquinas, Pope John Paul II opened his 2003 encyclical about the relationship of the church and the eucharist, *Ecclesia de Eucharistia*, with the simple, yet all embracing, statement: "The Church draws her life from the Eucharist." Later on, he explains that, because of this fact,

> it is good to cultivate in our hearts a constant desire for the sacrament of the Eucharist. This was the origin of the practice of 'spiritual communion', which has happily been established in the Church for centuries and recommended by saints who were masters of the spiritual life. St. Teresa of Jesus wrote: "When you do not receive communion and you do not attend Mass, you can make a spiritual communion, which is a most beneficial practice; by it the love of God will be greatly impressed on you" (*The Way of Perfection*, 35).[4]

In the coronavirus situation, Pope Francis also commended spiritual communion, according to *The Tablet* on March 15, 2020: "With so many Catholics unable to attend Mass, because of the restrictions on public celebration of the liturgy, Pope Francis on Sunday recalled the Church's spiritual communion as the Body of Christ, united in prayer."[5] The Catholic News Service similarly noted that "Pope Francis, after reciting a livestreamed Angelus prayer March 15, told people, 'United to Christ we are never alone, but instead form one body, of which he is the head. It is a union that is

---

3. See https://en.wikipedia.org/wiki/Spiritual_Communion

4. Ecclesia de Eucharistia, section 34, 17 April, 2003; available at http://www.vatican.va/content/john-paul-ii/en/encyclicals/documents/hf_jp-ii_enc_20030417_eccl-de-euch.html

5. https://www.thetablet.co.uk/news/12597/pope-francis-urges-catholics-to-unite-in-spiritual-communion

nourished with prayer and also with spiritual communion in the Eucharist, a practice that is recommended when it isn't possible to receive the sacrament." CNS went on to reassure the faithful by explaining that

> Obviously, receiving Communion is the way to participate most fully in the Mass, but it is not always possible for everyone to receive at every Mass, nor do many Catholics in the world even have regular access to Mass. The idea of 'spiritual Communion'—inviting Jesus into one's heart and soul when receiving the actual sacrament isn't possible—is part of Catholic tradition. In the 1700s, St. Alphonsus Liguori wrote a special prayer for spiritual communion: "My Jesus, I believe you are really here in the Blessed Sacrament. I love you more than anything in the world, and I hunger to receive you. But since I cannot receive Communion at this moment, feed my soul at least spiritually. I unite myself to you now as I do when I actually receive you."[6]

THE METHODIST CHURCH

According to the Methodist Church's official website in the UK, "In these days of social distancing and self-isolation, many Methodists feel the lack of being able to share communion as normal." According to their founder, "In his sermon on the means of grace, John Wesley taught that God can give us grace with or without physical means: God can work through anything or indeed nothing," and so they produced a short "Act of Spiritual Communion." This contains suggestions for readings and prayers, but at its heart is a prayer, which draws upon the Catholic tradition, thus:

> Jesus my brother, who brought divine Life out of human death, you are meeting me here and now in this place, in this moment. I pause to remember that the one thing I desire above all others is for you to be with me. Though I cannot receive you in bread and wine today, come into my heart and show me you were already there within me, by your love lighting my darkness from within. Open my eyes to your sacred presence in each thing you have created and in every moment you give. As each of your followers does their part where they are, may we all grow together in love and in richer, fuller communion. Make us one with you and with all who love you in every time and place. Help us to feel and to know that we are united as members of your body.

6. https://cruxnow.com/church-in-europe/2020/03/public-mass-ban-in-italy-leads-to-new-focus-on-spiritual-communion/

With all your people, may I share your risen life, which renews all creation. I offer myself to you in service, as an act of spiritual worship. Amen.[7]

Similarly in the United States of America, Mitchell Lewis, an ordained United Methodist elder of thirty-nine years in the North Georgia Conference who also served as an Army chaplain for twenty-seven years, wrote this prayer of spiritual communion for use in the Methodist tradition: "My Jesus, I love you above all things. How I long to receive you with my brothers and sisters at the table you have prepared. Since I cannot at this moment receive you in bread and wine according to your promise in the sacrament of Holy Communion, I ask you to feed me with the manna of your Holy Spirit and nourish me with your Holy presence. I unite myself wholly to you. Never permit me to be separated from your love. Amen"[8]

EPISCOPALIANS AND ANGLICANS IN THE USA

At Philadelphia in October 1789, "the Bishops, the Clergy, and the Laity of the Protestant Episcopal Church in the United States of America" formally ratified their version of the Church of England's 1662 Book of Common Prayer, which was subsequently modernized and revised in 1882, 1928, and 1979. It does not appear to have provision for any formal "act of spiritual communion," except that the order for the *Ministration to the Sick* (p. 457) includes their version of the relevant 1549/1662 BCP rubric noted above: "*If a person desires to receive the Sacrament, but, by reason of extreme sickness or physical disability, is unable to eat and drink the Bread and Wine, the Celebrant is to assure that person that all the benefits of Communion are received, even though the Sacrament is not received with the mouth.*"[9]

Following the break away by various conservative Episcopal churches to form the Anglican Church of North America (ACNA), they produced their own version of the Book of Common Prayer in 2019, which *does* include Occasional Prayer No 106 "For Spiritual Communion" (p. 677):

---

7. See https://www.methodist.org.uk/our-faith/worship/singing-the-faith-plus/seasons-and-themes/worship-during-the-coronavirus-pandemic/ which contains a downloadable PDF.

8. https://milewis.wordpress.com/2020/03/20/an-act-of-spiritual-communion/

9. A downloadable edition of the Episcopal Book of Common Prayer can be found here: https://episcopalchurch.org/files/book_of_common_prayer.pdf; see also, https://episcopalchurch.org/book-common-prayer, and http://justus.anglican.org/resources/bcp/bcp.htm

Dear Jesus, I believe that you are truly present in the Holy Sacrament. I love you above all things, and I desire to possess you within my soul. And since I cannot now receive you sacramentally, I beseech you to come spiritually into my heart. I unite myself to you, together with all your faithful people [gathered around every altar of your Church], and I embrace you with all the affections of my soul. Never permit me to be separated from you. Amen.[10]

The Anglican bishop of Pittsburgh, Jim Hobby, issued a 'Suspension of Services' on March 16, 2020, in which he also provided an outline form of service or prayer around this Collect:

If you or your family would like to participate in 'spiritual communion', you might consider this format:

1. Say, "In the name of the Father, and of the Son, and of the Holy Spirit."
2. Read the Collect, the Epistle, and the Gospel of the Day.
3. Recite the Nicene Creed (BCP 2019, p. 127).
4. Pray for your needs and the needs of others (BCP 2019, p. 128).
5. Confess your sins, read the Comfortable Words and exchange the Peace. (BCP 2019, p. 130).
6. Pray the Collect for Spiritual Communion (BCP 2019, p. 677).
7. Recite the Lord's Prayer (BCP 2019, p. 134).
8. Recite the Grace (BCP 2019, p. 26).

You may want to do this in the context of a meal, as was the custom in the early church.[11]

It is significant that from this brief study of the Roman Catholic, Methodist, and American Episcopalian and ACNA churches quite a unified picture emerges of 'spiritual communion' being suddenly embraced as a possible solution to the current difficulties arising from not being able to celebrate holy communion in our churches and congregations in the usual way. It is therefore time to consider how this idea has played out in the Church of England.

---

10. A downloadable edition of the ACNA's Book of Common Prayer can be found here bcp2019.anglicanchurch.net/wp-content/uploads/2019/08/BCP2019.pdf

11. https://www.pitanglican.org/blog/bishop-hobby-issues-suspension-services

THE SITUATION IN THE CHURCH OF ENGLAND

In his treatment of *"Extended Communion,"* written ten years before any of us had heard of coronavirus (2009) and to which we shall return in chapter 8 below, the Rev'd Dr Phillip Tovey, warden of licensed lay ministry in the Diocese of Oxford, notes that "Spiritual Communion is another part of the Anglican tradition. The 1549 Prayer Book said that if the person is so sick as to be unable to receive the elements but is repentant, then they eat and drink spiritually. This statement is incorporated into many prayer books of the Communion. Anglican devotional material developed this into a set of prayers."[12]

Just over ten years later, on March 7, 2020, the archdeacon of London, Fr Luke Miller, thought that it was "still possible that Coronavirus will not spread into the population, but it does look as if it might," even though at that point, it was "highly unlikely that there will be any ban on gatherings which would force churches to shut"! A well-known and widely respected leading Anglo-Catholic traditionalist who is committed to maintaining and holding together the diversity found in the Church of England, Fr Luke presciently posted a blog noting that "concerns about receiving at least the Precious Blood even among those who are able to get to church suggests a need to renew Spiritual Communion. This is a devotion by which a communicant who is in church but not receiving, or one who is not able to be in church unites themselves spiritually with the act of Holy Communion being made in a particular church at a particular time."[13] To provide an example of what he was talking about, Fr Luke kindly posted photographs of an old order of service and provided a link to *A Form of Spiritual Communion* compiled by the Bishop of Melanesia, Cecil John Wood, and published at Easter 1916.[14]

After various rubrics and instructions, the good bishop provided his "missionaries and others . . . far removed from the ministrations of a Priest" with a "form of service to be used by communicants when no Priest is present, and when therefore a celebration of the Holy Communion is impossible," consisting of a proper preparation and confession, before coming to the "Act of Communion" with this prayer:

---

12. Phillip Tovey, *The Theory and Practice of Extended Communion* (Farnham: Ashgate, 2009), 62.

13. http://frlukemiller.blogspot.com/2020/03/spiritual-communion-and-coronavirus.html

14. It was transcribed eighty years later by the Rt Rev'd Dr Terry Brown, Bishop of Malaita, in Melanesia (2006) and is available at: http://anglicanhistory.org/oceania/wood_communion1916.html

In union, O Dear Lord, with the faithful at every Altar of Thy Church, where Thy blessed Body and Blood are being offered to the Father, I desire to offer Thee praise and thanksgiving. I present to Thee my soul and body, with the earnest wish that I may ever be united to Thee. And since I cannot now receive Thee sacramentally, I beseech Thee to come spiritually into my heart. I unite myself to Thee, and embrace Thee with all the affections of my soul. O let nothing ever separate me from Thee. Let me live and die in Thy love. Amen."[15]

It also included a lovely prayer echoing the story of the haemorrhaging woman in Mark 5:25–34: "Grant, O Lord Jesus Christ, that as the hem of Thy garment, touched in faith, healed the woman who could not touch Thy Body, so the soul of Thy servant may be healed by like faith in Thee, Whom I cannot now sacramentally receive; through Thy tender mercy, Who livest and reignest with the Father in the unity of the Holy Ghost ever one God. Amen."

Less than two weeks later, on March 19, 2020, and thus still early in the outbreak of the coronavirus, a former student from my days as the chaplain to the University of Exeter, the Rev'd Canon Grant Bayliss, who is now the diocesan canon precentor at Christ Church Cathedral, Oxford, wrote a moving and honest reflection entitled, "Thoughts from a Cloistered House":

I don't know about you but I'm shut in—cloistered in the Cloisters since Tuesday. . . . All my life I've found hope in the darkness by going to church. . . . At the heart of that has been the eucharist—a reliable moment of grace, a tangible encounter that I can touch, taste, smell, as God's presence is made known through the very matter of creation. . . . So what do I do when the matter has been taken away? When I can't touch the blessed bread or taste the wine? Well, this Sunday, I'll be making a 'spiritual communion.' It's an old idea that was important in the medieval Church and has often got a little lost or confused. But even when the Reformers rewrote our service books to bring back all the tasting and the touching, restoring the breaking of real bread and the sharing of a common cup to the people, it found a home in the new Anglican theology of Cranmer's 1549 Prayer Book. At the end of his service for "The Order for Visitation of the Sick and the Communion of the Same," he wrote:

15. The echo of the Ignatian prayer, *Anima Christi*, ("do not allow me to be separated from you," *ne permittas me separari a te*) is clearly deliberate—and in the photos of the old order for Spiritual Communion in Fr Luke's blog post, the actual prayer of spiritual communion is followed by the Our Father, the Hail Mary, and then *Anima Christi* is printed out in full, in English!

But yf any man eyther by reason of extremitie of sickenesse, or for lacke of warnyng geven in due tyme, to the curate, or by any other just impedimente, doe not receyne the sacramente of Christes bodye and bloud then the curate shall instruct hym, that yf he doe truely repent hym of his sinnes and stedfastly beleve that Jesus Christ hath suffered death upon the crosse for hym, and shed his bloud for his redempcion, earnestly remembring the benefites he hath therby, and geving hym hertie thankes therfore; he doeth eate and drynke spiritually the bodye and bloud of our savioure Christe, profitably to his soules helth, although he doe not receyve the sacrament with his mouth . . .

And there it has stayed through all the editions ever since. A little disclaimer—or small print, if you like—that, even as the main Communion service put a renewed and powerful emphasis on eating and drinking, on God coming close through the chosen things of his creation, he was never limited. God chooses sacraments like the eucharist to meet us but he never said he would *only* meet us there, *only* love us *if* we physically ate, *only* bless us *if* we literally drank. And as Bishop Steven [bishop of Oxford] lifts up the bread and holds the cup, I will cross myself and pray like St Thomas, "My Lord and my God!" And be reassured by the Prayer Book and the testimony of Christians throughout the ages that I am eating and drinking spiritually the body and blood of our Saviour Christ, profitably to my soul's health, although I do not receive the sacrament with my mouth.[16]

Around the same time, Stephen Cottrell, then bishop of Chelmsford (who was appointed as archbishop of York several months later), recorded a short video and issued a statement saying that, "Throughout Christian history some Christian people have found themselves isolated from the sacramental life of the Church for all sorts of reasons, and particularly in times of plague, famine and warfare. At such times the Church has encouraged people to make what is called *a spiritual communion.*" He referred to this as a *"little Order of Service"* and so issued one entitled "Spiritual Communion When Unable to Attend a Celebration of Holy Communion," which included a version of Melanesia's prayer about the haemorrhaging woman being healed by touching the hem of Jesus' garment, rather than his actual body.[17]

16. See https://www.chch.ox.ac.uk/blog/thoughts-cloistered-house? for his full discussion.

17. https://www.chelmsford.anglican.org/spiritual-communion; with the Order downloadable as a pdf, Spiritual_Communion_Order_Chelmsford.pdf

The Church of England soon similarly included in its "Guidance for Churches" a downloadable pdf for "Guidance on Spiritual Communion and Coronavirus", which comprised relevant prayers, if not an "order of service", little or not. This begins: "The term 'Spiritual Communion' has been used historically to describe the means of grace by which a person, prevented for some serious reason from sharing in a celebration of the Eucharist, nonetheless shares in the communion of Jesus Christ."[18]

REFLECTIONS

From these early beginnings, this approach was frequently reproduced around the Church of England's dioceses (and also by other denominations and across the globe, as we have seen) as the apparently preferred option to deal with the coronavirus crisis, and so one must be cautious in criticizing it, but some comment at least is needed. While it is true that there is ample evidence in the tradition (at least of Catholic Church) of the practice of 'spiritual communion', it has not been easy to find evidence, within the Anglican tradition at least, of any so-called 'order of service'—little or not— other than Fr Luke's 1916 "*form* of service" from Melanesia. Far from being a service in its own right, 'spiritual communion' is a shorthand for a rubric in the Book of Common Prayer Order of Service for the Communion of the Sick, which does conclude, "*but if a man, either by reason of extremity of sickness, or for want of warning in due time to the Curate, or for lack of company to receive with him, or by any other just impediment, do not receive the Sacrament of Christ's Body and Blood*" then the Curate shall instruct him that he can nonetheless receive the benefits of communion "*although he do not receive the Sacrament with his mouth.*"

The bishop of Melanesia was very careful to draw attention to the 'certain circumstances' outlined in this BCP rubric at the start of his 1916 "*form* of service"—note that even this is not called an "*order* of service." Therefore, he compiles his own, rather daunting, list of 'conditions' that need to be met, beginning with the "need for repentance, as in the case of Sacramental Communion" and "the need of a real faith that Christ died to save mankind"; further, he makes it clear that "the act of Spiritual Communion is not a substitute for Sacramental Communion, nor is it a make-believe"; and furthermore that "it would not be right to use this devotion of Spiritual Communion when the Sacramental Communion could be readily obtained"; he

18. https://www.churchofengland.org/more/media-centre/coronavirus-covid-19 -guidance-churches with download, Guidance on Spiritual Communion and Coronavirus.pdf

especially warns against things like "unwillingness to rise in the morning nor slackness in preparing for Communion," before concluding "That God in His love provides many special means of Grace can never be sufficient warrant for neglecting the normal means."

It is not immediately clear, therefore, how this rubric from the BCP Visitation and Communion of the Sick (much less the bishop of Melanesia's strict conditions) applies to a perfectly healthy person capable of receiving communion, who gives due notice to the curate (or the vicar or rector!), especially perhaps with other members of their household so that they are not receiving alone. As for the latter point about "*lack of company to receive with him*," which does sound like lockdown, the rubric concludes that "*in the time of the plague, sweat, or such other like contagious times of sickness or diseases, when none of the Parish or neighbours can be gotten to communicate with the sick in their houses, for fear of the infection, upon special request of the diseased, the Minister may only communicate with him.*"

Before anyone objects in the manner of St Paul's imagined interlocutor, pointing to the "*may* only communicate," this does not mean in sixteenth- and seventeenth-century English, that the priest "may" choose to do so or not, in the modern sense of "may"; instead, it is giving not only permission for "the Minister only" (= 'alone') to receive with the infectious person, but actually the canonical *requirement* to do so, thus dispensing with the usual rubric at the end of BCP Communion requiring that even in a small parish "*if there be not above twenty persons in the Parish of discretion to receive the Communion: yet there shall be no communion, except four (or three at the least) communicate with the priest.*" Thus, far from the clergy telling parishioners to be satisfied with 'spiritual communion' while receiving the body and blood of our Lord Jesus themselves safely on their own in their own houses, this BCP rubric actually requires ordained ministers to visit the infectious person at their request and to communicate with them alone if the sick person so requires them to do!

However, over the centuries the consequences of this last clause of course led to the deaths of many 'heroic' clergy (often Anglo-Catholics, who were celibate, ministering in poorer slums while others, including Evangelicals, who were more likely to be married, preferred to live in safer areas for their families). This is reflected in the contemporary concerns of one clergy wife's letter to the *Church Times* on April 9, 2020,

> I, for one, would like my husband and the rest of my family to be alive and well at the end of this. This is not about clergy putting themselves out there as some sort of superheroes; they are also husbands, wives, fathers, and mothers. My husband is

a dedicated priest and wants nothing more than to help his parishioners; he also has the intellectual understanding to realise how serious the current situation is. At the beginning of this crisis, I saw him being put under intolerable pressure by a few church members who could not accept that the church was having to be closed or that their regular activities were having to be postponed. I saw him really struggling with that pressure to 'have faith' and put himself and us in danger. So, please, think before you advise against following the safety rules.[19]

Of course, other frontline essential workers, especially in the NHS, care-homes, and delivery drivers, are battling with exactly such pressures on a daily basis—and the list of those who have given their lives through serving others in this way continues to grow, sadly, even as I write these words.[20] However, as Angela Tilby wrote in the *Church Times*, "So much for clergy as key workers. When the postman, the bus driver, not to mention health workers, put themselves at risk for Christian values and the common good, the Church's position [the archbishops' instructions] looks uncomfortably like moral cowardice."[21] Of course, I do not want to add lots of the names of numerous clergy to this roll-call of those who have given the ultimate sacrifice—but the BCP rubric and the bishop of Melanesia's 'conditions' ought make us think carefully at least, before rushing to embrace 'spiritual communion' as the panacea for the difficulty of celebrating holy communion in "contagious times".

19. https://www.churchtimes.co.uk/articles/2020/9-april/comment/letters-to-the-editor/letters-to-the-editor

20. The Office for National Statistics published an analysis of deaths up to April 20, 2020 by occupations (as well as by gender and ethnicity) in which "men working in the lowest skilled occupations had the highest rate of death involving COVID-19, with security guards at 45.7 deaths per 100,000" followed by taxi drivers and chauffeurs, 36.4; chefs, 35.9; bus and coach drivers, 26.4; social care workers, 23.4; sales and retail assistants, 19.8." Interestingly, "healthcare workers, doctors and nurses, were not found to have higher rates of death involving COVID-19 when compared with the rate among those whose death involved COVID-19 of the same age and sex in the general population." Perhaps relevant to our point here, there is no mention of clergy, priests, or ministers at any point in this document. While this is to be welcomed, of course, not least by those like the clergy wife I quoted above, it is an interesting contrast to the previous pandemics, such as the cholera outbreak in the nineteenth century. https://www.ons.gov.uk/peoplepopulationandcommunity/healthandsocialcare/causesofdeath/bulletins/coronaviruscovid19relateddeathsbyoccupationenglandandwales/deathsregistereduptoandincluding20april2020

21. https://www.churchtimes.co.uk/articles/2020/8-may/comment/columnists/angela-tilby-the-c-of-e-has-become-member-only

We have given this topic of spiritual communion detailed treatment since it has suddenly become the universal 'go-to' solution for the situation under coronavirus. However, Grant Bayliss' description of the BCP mention of spiritual communion as "a little disclaimer—or small print, if you like," and the fact that Fr Luke has to resort to particular provision made in 1916 for missionaries in Melanesia to find any "form of service" (much less an order of service) both suggest that in fact 'spiritual communion' has a limited place in the Anglican tradition. Such a personal act of devotion is permitted in the 1662 Book of Common Prayer in the exceptional circumstances of a person so sick that they physically cannot receive the eucharist being offered to them by a priest, and it was also proposed by the bishop of Melanesia in 1916 specifically for "missionaries and others . . . far removed from the ministrations of a Priest" and under strict conditions. Like many others, I suspect, I have found such an act of personal devotion to be helpful when facing the pain of being excluded from receiving communion at certain times and places, such as being present in a Roman Catholic mass.

On the other hand, no matter how beneficial this personal practice may be on such particular circumstances, the point of these rubrics suggests that 'spiritual communion' does not solve the problem of holy communion in "contagious times", nor is it sufficient to satisfy the canonical instructions and rubrics of the 1662 Book of Common Prayer, requiring the clergy to conduct daily offices and regular communions in their parish churches and chapels. Furthermore, it is also not clear that such 'spiritual communions' were required in order to meet UK Government regulations in force at the time. In addition, it is hard to see how a provision so particular and circumscribed with such strict conditions can bear the weight currently being imposed upon it. Finally, given it is clearly meant to be a 'last resort' by both Cranmer and the bishop of Melanesia, it is surprising how quickly it was adopted, even among less sacramentally minded Protestants, as the universal 'go-to' way of dealing with times like coronavirus, rather than other possibilities. Our search for a solution must move on to the next option, which is often combined with spiritual communion in an even more painful manner.

4

Proposal 3

Solitary or 'Solo' Communion on One's Own

MOVING ON FROM SPIRITUAL communion, the next possibility is to allow for a priest to celebrate the eucharist on their own. Such a 'solitary communion' has a long tradition within the Roman Catholic Church, where it is linked into the idea of the 'offering of the mass' in eucharistic sacrifice, especially in the mediaeval practices of paying for masses to be offered for one's soul in chantry chapels. Even in larger churches or abbeys, especially in monastic communities, it is not uncommon to see lots of individual niche chapels where each of the priests could celebrate each day.

However, for Anglicans, such solitary communions on one's own are *explicitly forbidden* by the 1662 Book of Common Prayer rubric at the end of the Communion service, as we have just seen with regard to 'spiritual communion': "*there shall be no Celebration of the Lord's Supper except there be a convenient number to communicate with the Priest, according to his discretion*"; and even for small parishes of up to twenty people, "*yet there shall be no Communion, except four (or three at the least) communicate with the Priest.*" For many clergy, the "*four (or three at the least)*" have been decreased in our tradition to at least one other person, but that is the minimum. I can recall various occasions when I was ready to do a small midweek lunchtime or early morning communion in the chapels at the University of Exeter, or King's College London, but had to abandon that plan when no one else turned up, and instead settle for prayer on my own (perhaps in front of the reserved sacrament, when available, as an act of 'spiritual communion').

Cranmer's shift in emphasis from just the eucharistic words of the narrative being said by the priest on their own to including also the role of worthy reception by some people present may be seen in the Book of Common Prayer's first Exhortation: ". . . our spiritual food and sustenance in that holy Sacrament. Which being so divine and comfortable a thing to them who receive it worthily, and so dangerous to them that will presume to receive it unworthily; my duty is to warn you . . . ." The same point is made in the second Exhortation: "For as the benefit is great, if with a true penitent heart and lively faith we receive that holy Sacrament; . . . so is the danger great, if we receive the same unworthily." Clearly, in both cases, even if the communion elements have been consecrated by the one priest saying the right words with the right manual actions, their salvific effect depends upon the attitude of the person receiving them. Similarly, the important line in the Prayer of Consecration which says, "grant that we receiving these thy creatures of bread and wine, according to thy Son our Saviour Jesus Christ's holy institution, in remembrance of his death and passion, may be partakers of his most blessed Body and Blood" comes immediately *before* the words of institution with the manual acts. Thus, it could be argued that this means that the object of the eucharistic prayer is not so much a change to the elements in themselves effected by the priest alone, but to a corporate reception *"we receiving these thy creatures."*[1] Thus, for Cranmer himself and Anglicans ever since, communal participation is *part of the meaning of the sacramental act itself* (we are one body because we all share in the one bread). Celebrating eucharist without anyone else present is perhaps akin to celebrating it without the bread or wine—depriving it of a fundamental aspect of the ritual. It is at best ritually problematic and perhaps even theologically unintelligible.[2]

The significance of this prohibition of solitary communion on one's own can best be illustrated by the spiritual discipline and practice instilled in Archbishop Desmond Tutu through his early experiences with Trevor Huddleston and many other Mirfield fathers of the Community of Resurrection who were his mentors. My first experience of meeting the archbishop with his wife, Leah, and two accompanying staff members off an overnight plane from Cape Town in May 1990 was his immediate need to be able to celebrate the eucharist at the start of his day as usual. Therefore, as soon as he was brought into the special immigration room at Heathrow provided by the then archbishop of Canterbury, he asked if it would be possible to

1. I am grateful to +Graham Tomlin, bishop of Kensington, for the point made in this paragraph.

2. I am grateful to the Rev'd Dr Robin Parry for making this point.

celebrate communion there and then, but, because of the pressures of time and security concerns, we were rushed into armour-plated police vehicles to be taken to Reading station, where we were due to catch the train to Exeter, where I was then university chaplain. In fact, after various delays, we eventually ended up celebrating it much later (but still without breakfast!) according to the rites of the Church of the Province of Southern Africa (CPSA) in the first-class railway dining car, speeding across Salisbury Plain at 125 mph, with me worrying about the Church of England rules about all the diocesan bishops I should have sought permission from, let alone the number of parishes traversed![3] Over the subsequent three decades, I have been privileged to make sure that on all of the archbishop's visits to England, and especially to King's College London as his *alma mater*, there have been people ready and willing to join him in celebrating his daily eucharist, a task made easier as advancing years have also brought the originally very early start forward into the day![4] However, the significant point relevant here is that even someone with such a daily invariable spiritual discipline would not have allowed himself to celebrate or receive communion on his own.

THE CHURCH OF ENGLAND BACKTRACKS

Despite this long-standing tradition, as exemplified by Bishop Tutu's spiritual discipline and the clear BCP rubrics, many English dioceses have now given permission for clergy to celebrate communion on their own during the time of coronavirus. Thus, the first Bulletin of Southwark's Coronavirus Task Group included this paragraph: "We have been asked if a priest can celebrate alone. As you will be aware it is standard Anglican practice to have at least one respondent for a Eucharistic celebration. However, in these exceptional circumstances Bishop Christopher is prepared to permit priests to say the Eucharist alone. If you are able to have someone with you, please make sure that you observe all the prescribed precautions and consider

3. Particularly memorable was the dining steward's deadpan reaction to my pre-breakfast order of a small bottle of wine and a slice of bread; first he enquired whether he should provide bread for everyone, and then when I explained that one slice would be sufficient for the archbishop to break up, he kindly offered to "cut it up for him"; his last desperate attempt to be helpful was to ask "if the archbishop would like it buttered"! Fortunately, there was plenty of toast and butter afterwards with the rest of a traditional cooked breakfast—even if we had had to wait several hours since touchdown. See my chapter, "Praying at 125mph" in *Tutu as I Know Him*, edited by Lavinia Crawford-Browne (Cape Town: Umuzi/New York: Random House, 2006), 89–93.

4. Again, see my contribution to *Tutu: The Authorized Portrait*, edited by Allister Sparks and Mpho Tutu (London: Arcadia, 2011), 238–39.

leaving the host on the altar for the person to come and consume rather than distributing it."[5] The point about "these exceptional circumstances" is reinforced as being "in the context of the lockdown and needing to operate within the restrictions at home."

Similarly, the circular letter of March 31, 2020 from the College of Bishops in the Diocese of London on "The Eucharist in a Time of Physical Distancing" is clear that the BCP rubric "reflects a 'rule', which is both desirable and to be enjoined in all normal circumstances, that there should be communicants other than the minister at every celebration of Holy Communion. In teaching and holding this position, the Church of England does so in common with Christian tradition reaching back to apostolic times. The Eucharist is intended, normatively, to be a corporate, not a private act, because it is given to offer the people spiritual nourishment." Therefore, the London bishops suggest three possible options: first, a eucharistic fast, or secondly, "to ensure congregational involvement, where a parish church wishes to continue to celebrate the eucharist within the current advice issued by the London College of Bishops, and only the priest can be present, it should, whenever possible, be livestreamed." Thirdly, where such livestreaming "is not feasible, at the very least, it should be clearly advertised in the parish and among the congregation when the Holy Communion is to be celebrated in the home of the priest. . . . This way, others can be invited to pray and perhaps read the scriptures at that time, so that the service takes place within some kind of extended communal act of worship in that parish, even if dispersed, and does not become merely a private act of devotion. Some prayers that would enable people to take part in such a celebration might be prepared." Finally, the London bishops emphasize that "in granting permission, exceptionally, for the clergy to celebrate Holy Communion in this way, our prayer must be that this time will be short."[6]

However, a number of commentators, including those from a more (Anglo-)Catholic tradition, are less comfortable with this permission or encouragement of solitary communions. Thus, the Rev'd Dr Paul Roberts, who teaches liturgy at Trinity College Bristol, sent me this reflection:

> It is worth saying . . . that I also have considerable discomfort
> about the practice of a priest celebrating the eucharist on his
> or her own, even to the point of its validity. In terms of tradi-
> tion, this only emerged (or makes sense) once various medieval

5. Southwark Coronavirus Task Group Bulletin 1, April 23, 2020; https://southwark.anglican.org/news/press-releases/2020/bulletin-no-1-monday-23-march

6. https://www.london.anglican.org/articles/the-eucharist-in-a-time-of-physical-distancing/

theologies of priesthood (with implications for the theology of the mass) had developed, focussing more on the two aspects of the sacramental category of *character indelibilis* and the role of eucharistic consecration being dependent upon a priest's *potestas* rather than other matters. In the late-medieval period these two aspects became determinative of the understanding of the mass, and the response of reformers, Luther in particular, marked a welcome return to a more scriptural and patristic foundation which had become distinctly shaky in the previous few centuries. It is worth noting that the Liturgical Movement, and Vatican II itself, also marked a move back toward corporate celebrations and a distinct cooling towards single celebration, with the introduction of *concelebration*, allowing religious communities of priests to celebrate together, rather than each separately at an altar of their own. At All Saints, Clifton, we have followed a policy of not having a celebration of Communion by a priest on his or her own: in our daily mass, the liturgy will only proceed to the Liturgy of the Word unless at least one other person is present. This is not uncommon in many other parishes of a Catholic tradition—so the tendency of some places now routinely having a priest 'offering the mass' solo, is something of a step backward to older practice, which does not attune with more recent reforms in both Anglican and Roman Catholic contexts.[7]

Even Fr Peter Anthony, the Anglo-Catholic regular video lecturer, appeared very reluctant about such solitary celebrations on one's own: "they should only happen with permission and in very particular times of crisis or emergency or when a priest for very definite reasons cannot celebrate with a congregation. It is an imperfect celebration, in the sense that it is not the fullness that it should be."

However, he does argue that, "it is certainly a valid celebration of the eucharist" because you have the priest present as "the bishop's delegate"; furthermore, even if the priest is on their own at this solitary communion and although "the body of Christ is not physically present in the body of the laity," he argues that the priest is still celebrating "in the presence and company of the whole body of Christ, living and departed, for no celebration of the eucharist is ever completely alone." Therefore, Fr Peter is "convinced that a solitary celebration by a priest is a legitimate response to the present crisis," but because it is "less than perfect," such a practice should cease as

7. Personal email of April 25, 2020; quoted with his permission.

soon as the crisis is over and we can return to celebrations with the people of God.[8]

**Fr Peter Anthony presiding on his own with his back to the camera
at St Benet's, Kentish Town, Easter Day, 2020,
https://www.youtube.com/watch?v=6dePvFYKH5E&t=1649s at 27 mins 20 sec**

REFLECTIONS

As a priest holding permission to officiate (PTO in CofE speak) in South-wark Diocese, I duly attended the 'livestreamed' Chrism Mass on Maundy Thursday, 8 April 2020.[9]

While it was good to feel still part of the diocese by reaffirming my ordination vows at the same time as the bishop and my other 220 fellow

8. See his video lecture, "How should we celebrate the Eucharist at a time of lock down and social isolation?" https://www.youtube.com/watch?v=T_XrWsFd88Y, at around 21–23 minutes. I note that Fr Peter subsequently returned to celebrating solitary consecrations in St Benet's on his own, facing east, with his back to the cam-era, and therefore also to any people watching. https://www.youtube.com/watch?v= -HHMrX7JMYE

9. Still available to watch on https://www.youtube.com/watch?v=q3BqNJTobKY&t =39s

clergy, any such sense of being an ecclesial and eucharistic community was quickly dashed after the consecration. As the bishop broke the consecrated bread, we were encouraged to join in saying "though we are many, we are all one body because we all share in one bread." However, of course, all we could do then was to watch Bishop Christopher communicate himself, after which he said "we receive Christ's most precious gift to us, his Body, his Blood, as we make our spiritual communion."

The Bishop of Southwark breaks the consecrated bread with the words "though we are many", despite being on his own at his Chrism mass, Maundy Thursday, 2020, https://www.youtube.com/watch?v=Tq78tYvEThc at 35'30"

As canon theologian for Salisbury, I also subsequently watched the similarly livestreamed chrism mass from the bishop of Salisbury on Maundy Thursday, which is still available on YouTube at the time of writing.[10] Bishop Nick began by noting that his little chapel in South Canonry, his home, felt a bit like Dr Who's Tardis, with everyone else crowding in by

10. https://www.youtube.com/watch?v=ZBnMls43jec&t=2s; see also the order of service at https://bit.ly/dosalchrism-oos and the Bishop's sermon, https://bit.ly/dosal-chrism-ser

watching through the technology. Nonetheless, he was alone throughout (except for possibly someone operating the camera, although since it never moved, it could have just been fixed on a stand) with no one else visible, other than a pre-recorded reading of the Gospel by the precentor. He explained at the start that "in receiving communion, I will do so for us all. It is a strange eucharistic theology for these strange separated times in which we are united in Christ." The service then proceeded as usual, including the bishop's sermon, the blessing of the oils and the eucharistic prayer, followed by the Lord's Prayer and the breaking of the bread with the words, "though we are many, we are all one body because we all share in one bread," after which the bishop communicated himself, and then moved straight to the final blessing. There was no mention of spiritual communion, and little time in which such an act of devotion could have been undertaken. It felt "strange" indeed, to use Bishop Nick's word, especially when watched on a later recording!

This rapidly became the pattern for most, if not all, other such livestreamed or broadcast eucharists, such as the archbishop of Canterbury's Easter Day celebration from his kitchen table.[11] Once again, as the archbishop broke the consecrated bread, we were encouraged to join in as the TV subtitles indicated "[All:] though we are many, we are all one body because we all share in one bread." Similarly, after Archbishop Justin proclaimed "Alleluia, Christ our Passover is sacrificed for us," the TV subtitles instructed "[All:] Let us keep the feast, Alleluia." However, instead of having to watch the archbishop give bread and wine to himself alone, at least the camera cut to the Church of England version of spiritual communion, based on the prayer of St Richard of Chichester:

> Thanks be to you, Lord Jesus Christ,
> For all the benefits you have given me,
> For all the pains and insults you have borne for me.
> Since I cannot now receive you sacramentally,
> I ask you to come spiritually into my heart.
> O most merciful redeemer, friend, and brother,
> May I know you more clearly,
> Love you more dearly
> And follow you more nearly, day by day.

11. Still available at https://www.youtube.com/watch?v=6bmhRCJ3YAI; at 48'00"

[All] Though we are many, we are one body, because we all share in one bread.

The Archbishop of Canterbury breaks the consecrated bread with the words "though we are many", on Easter Day in his kitchen on his own, https://www.youtube.com/watch?v=6bmhRCJ3YAI at 48'00"

However, I am not alone in feeling uneasy about this practice of watching a bishop or a priest celebrate on their own, give themselves the bread and wine, and then encourage the rest of us simply to receive God's grace spiritually. I was grateful while writing this to receive a detailed response from the bishop of Lichfield, Michael Ipgrave, not least because he is a member of both the Church of England's Faith and Order Commission and the Liturgical Commission, as well as chairing the House of Bishops Working Group on Holy Communion as they discuss these issues:

> I was interested in your comments on the Southwark Chrism Mass. In fact, in this diocese we held an online Renewal of Ordination Vows and Ministerial Commitment, in a non-eucharistic context (and without the blessing or consecration of oils). However, I did celebrate and livestream a daybreak Eucharist on Easter Day (in my garden), with an invitation to those participating to make a spiritual communion at the normal point of the people's communion. I have not received any comments of people feeling excluded at that point; quite the contrary. We were careful to omit both the words of the fraction you mention and also the post-communion prayer of thanksgiving; at the moment of spiritual communion, we kept the camera focused on the host and chalice, with suitably meditative music playing, and included at that point in the downloadable order of service the prayer of St Richard of Chichester suggested on the CofE

website. I mention that, not especially to commend those arrangements, but because I think that the way in which people
experience occasions like this, and particularly whether they
have a sense of exclusion or not, is not just a function of theological principle, but is shaped in large measure by the actual
choreographic and rubrical arrangements.[12]

Bishop Michael's practical comments are very helpful and we shall
return to them when we discuss livestreaming in chapter 14 and elsewhere
below. However, unlike his worshippers on Easter Day, my experience of
those three video services from Southwark, Salisbury, and Lambeth Palace
was primarily a sense of being excluded at the climax at the end of the service. Although all three services included the expected congregational response, in bold typeface in the printed orders of service for Southwark and
Salisbury, and even more pointedly in the TV subtitles for the archbishop,
"[All:] though we are many, we are all one body because we all share in one
bread," the simple fact is that we did *not* "all share in one bread"; we watched
the leader help himself to it, and to make matters worse, in one case we were
told he was doing it "on our behalf"! We could not even "gather the crumbs
from under his table," to echo the words of the feisty Syro-Phoenician woman to Jesus (see Mark 7:28; Matt 15:27), which are reflected in our Prayer of
Humble Access.

It was perhaps significant that none of the services concluded with the
usual post-communion prayer, "thank you for feeding us with the body and
blood of your Son Jesus Christ. Through him we offer you our souls and
bodies to be a living sacrifice." On the other hand, if what the bishops and
archbishop said about spiritual communion was really believed to be true,
those words could—and maybe should?—have been used. The bishop of
Melanesia is quite clear about it in the introduction to his 'form' of spiritual
communion:

> In recollection of these benefits and in thanksgiving for them
> the *Communicant will receive the Body and Blood of Christ*, to
> his soul's good *as surely as if he were partaking of the consecrated
> elements* in the service of the Church. Thus the act of Spiritual
> Communion is not a substitute for Sacramental Communion,
> nor is it a make-believe. At the close of the devotion the Com-
> municant gives thanks to God for *something definitely received*,
> and during the day he can look back to his morning devotion

12. Personal email to me on April 26, 2020; quoted with his permission.

and say, This morning *I received the Body and Blood of my Lord.*"[13]

Was the omission of the post-communion prayer actually a tacit admission that far from receiving "something definite," namely "the body and blood" of our Lord, what we were engaged in was actually what Bishop Wood dared to term "make-believe"? Certainly, I am sorry to admit that I felt far from spiritually nourished, and equally far from being in any position, lockdown or no lockdown, to ask God and/or the bishop that I might be "sent out in the power of your Spirit to live and work to your praise and glory." I presume that the bulk of the large number of solitary communions being livestreamed on Facebook or YouTube, or even pre-recorded for those channels, will also have featured the president enjoying a solo communion, feeding themselves, while the 'audience'—not a congregation—can only watch, feeling spiritually hungry and deprived.

But I don't know, since I have not watched, still less participated, in any such broadcasts, nor will I in future, as it is all just too painful. Such solitary communions, flights of fancy taking off to fly 'solo', just leave the rest of us still on the ground—as well as being completely un-Anglican and uncanonical, against not only the rubrics of the 1662 Book of Common Prayer but also contrary to all the liturgical and eucharistic reforms of the last century or so. Those who persist in streaming, 'live' or otherwise, such communions must in future surely take care to ensure that there is always another person present and visible—even if 'socially distanced.' And while the habit of the eucharistic president receiving the sacrament themselves first may be hallowed by tradition, and something you can get away with at the high altar off in the distance, especially if the celebrant, facing east, has their back to the congregation, the image of someone feeding themselves first in close up across all the computer's screen just looks greedy—and even rude, stuffing your face while being watched by hungry people! It is a basic rule of television that it does not matter what words you say if what people see is screaming the opposite.

As with spiritual communions, so here we should be very cautious in our search to find a solution for 'holy communion in contagious times' about rushing to something so counter to Anglican tradition, belief, and practice as this "imperfect celebration" to use Fr Peter Anthony's phrase. We must surely explore every other option first and so, therefore, it is time to move on from solitary communions to consider other possibilities that might satisfy this first criterion or requirement for a valid and effective

13. http://anglicanhistory.org/oceania/wood_communion1916.html; my italics for emphasis.

communion, which has emerged from this chapter, namely that solitary communions make no sense and run counter to the development of the eucharistic tradition that there shall always be at least one other person present, and preferably more.

5

Proposal 4

Simultaneous/(Con)celebration
and the Role of the People

"IT IS WORTH NOTING that the Liturgical Movement, and Vatican II itself, also marked a move back toward corporate celebrations and a distinct cooling towards single celebration, with the introduction of *concelebration*, allowing religious communities of priests to celebrate together, rather than each separately at an altar of their own."[1] We noted this comment from the liturgist Paul Roberts in the previous chapter—but it also gives us the bridge into our next option, simultaneous celebration (concelebration) of the eucharist by two or more priests together. I can best illustrate this point by taking my personal story on from that Maundy Thursday online service in which I had felt excluded and, like the rich in Mary's Magnificat, "sent empty away."

Such is the bishop of Southwark's pastoral care and kind self-effacement, that he permitted—indeed encouraged—me to explain frankly all my disappointment with his Maundy Thursday Chrism Mass (discussed in the previous chapter) in a helpful—and long—personal videocall two days later on Holy Saturday, perhaps a good day to reflect on grief and being alone with Jesus in the tomb. During our conversation, I made the suggestion that since the intended audience (congregation?) for such a service of the renewal of ordination vows was the 220 clergy of Southwark Diocese,

---

1. Personal email from the Rev'd Dr Paul Roberts of April 25, 2020; quoted with his permission.

there could have been the opportunity for us all to have our own bread and wine, preferably in suitable containers, such as a small chalice and paten or perhaps in a sick home communion set if we are fortunate enough to have one. Since the bishop had given permission for his clergy to celebrate the eucharist on their own, it would have been a valid and efficacious sacrament if we had all celebrated or presided over our own bread and wine at the same time as he did over his in Bishop's House. Then, he could have invited us to be one body by receiving our bread and wine all together at the same time as he received his. Such a 'simultaneous celebration', I felt and humbly suggested, would have resulted in a much stronger sense of inclusion and identification with both our bishop and our diocese, rather than my disappointing feeling of exclusion and rejection.

I was grateful for Bishop Christopher's positive response to this idea. Indeed, he went further in responding that, of course, those clergy from a more Catholic tradition would also have interpreted this as a chance to 'concelebrate' with their bishop, and would have rejoiced therein. This would also be in line with more recent Catholic liturgical reforms and the tendency in religious communities or groups of priests living together to move away from each one saying a solitary mass towards concelebration all together, as noted at the start of this chapter.

Of course, such a suggestion would only have worked for those watching or participating who were priests; it would still have excluded all the deacons present, and any readers, pastoral assistants (Southwark pastoral assistants are known as SPAs!), or other lay people present and observing—unless they were fortunate enough to be part of a priest's family or household in the same lockdown. The bishop of Lichfield, Michael Ipgrave, responded to an earlier draft of this chapter as follows: "I am quite taken by the suggestion you made to +Christopher of a remotely concelebrated Chrism Mass. However, as you say that would in itself have the effect of excluding similar participation by deacons and laypeople; and it is in any case a fairly unusual situation."[2]

I found it interesting that on Easter Day when the good bishop (of Southwark) livestreamed the eucharist again from his chapel in Bishop's House, now decked with the paschal candle and other signs of new life, his only non-liturgical comment came immediately after the words, "Though we are many, we are one body because we all share in one bread" when he looked directly into the camera and invited the online participants "to join me in making your communion spiritually on this Easter Day" before he himself received communion. This may be only a small development, yet

2. Personal email to me on April 26, 2020; quoted with his permission.

it marks a significant change from only suggesting 'spiritual communion' after he had received first and alone, as had happened on Maundy Thursday, towards us all receiving communion in one, possibly spiritual, concelebration[3]—and one that went this time some way towards making me feel included on the special Day of Resurrection.

Furthermore, since then, in fact, the bishop of Southwark adopted a new default invitation in his subsequent communions livestreamed from his chapel at Bishop's House that any priests watching should actually participate by concelebrating with their own bread and wine along with him.[4] However, this raises at least two other problems: first, while this suggestion might work for a clergy gathering of priests, like the renewal of ordination vows, or more widely for those priests fortunate not to be living alone, since this also provides an opportunity for them to give communion to members of their family or household, it still remains the case as we saw above that for deacons and all lay people watching, they would presumably still feel—or actually be—excluded. We shall return to this point in the next chapter on lay presidency and our understanding of the eucharist.

ONE BODY, ONE BREAD, ONE CUP?

The second issue follows from the fact that at least with concelebration with multiple priests in one community or church, there is still the issue of the

possible impact on the important symbolism of the "one body" because we are all sharing in the "one bread" and the one cup. Using one bread and one cup symbolizes the unity of the church. This is, of course, the reason behind a long-standing objection by some Anglicans, especially those of a more Catholic churchmanship, to

---

3. By inviting the online participants to join in making spiritual communion I wondered whether he was implicitly inviting them to concelebrate (if they were priests) or to engage in spiritual communion (if they were not) while he celebrates.

4. Bishop Christopher has graciously expressed his thanks that an early draft of this chapter "spurred me on to much deeper reflection on participation and how merely talking about people making their spiritual communion can add to the sense of exclusion—so my position is gratitude to being stimulated to think this through"; he now makes this invitation to his clergy via social media, and he has told me that he knows that "this offer has been taken up by a number of priests" (personal email of May 16, 2020).

the practice in many free churches of passing around trays of little individual cups, a practice that originated out of a fear of infection in previous times of contagious infection.[5]

It is clear that originally the free churches followed the Catholic and Anglican tradition of the one, common cup. For example, in 1725, the Baptist church in Exeter commissioned two silver wine cups "of exquisite workmanship, two handled, 3¾ inches in height, 3½ in diameter" and a further pair to match in 1764.[6] However, during the late nineteenth century after various outbreaks of diphtheria and tuberculosis, pressure grew to adopt little individual cups. John G. Thomas, a physician and pastor of the Vaughnsville Congregational Church in Ohio, designed a communion outfit after noticing "a communicant with a diseased mouth condition" and applied for a patent on August 2, 1893, which was granted on March 6, 1894. Early advertising for his individual cups includes the claim to be the "originator of the individual communion service", although the Rev. H. Webb, pastor of Scovill Avenue Methodist Church of Cleveland, Ohio, believed his church's first use of individual cups on December 6, 1891 was "absolutely the first time or case where it has been thus served".[7]

Within the (Presbyterian) Church of Scotland, in 1906 the Presbytery of Glasgow asked the General Assembly to consider a move to individual cups, which resulted in significant debate and controversy before a majority decision was eventually made in 1909; however, even in 1978, A. K. Robertson could note in his presidential address to the Liturgical Service Society that, "the individual cup remains an innovation—it is not part of the living body of the Christian Church."[8] Significantly, the move to unfermented wine had been made in 1878—and, of course, alcohol was well known as a

---

5. https://www.dreamstime.com/royalty-free-stock-photos-communion-tray-image4390378

6. F. M. Sleeman, Kenneth Palmes, and A. de M. Chesterman, "Notes," *Baptist Quarterly* 14.8 (1952) 366–67; https://www.tandfonline.com/doi/abs/10.1080/0005576X.1952.11750857; I am grateful to the Rev'd Dr Simon Woodman from Bloomsbury Central Baptist Church, London for this information.

7. For a fascinating description of the debate about who was first, complete with a timeline, see https://sharperiron.org/article/who-first-adopted-individual-cups-as-regular-communion-practice; I am grateful to Dr Meg Warner, tutor in Old Testament and co-ordinator of the United Reformed Church Research Network, Northern College, Luther King House, Manchester for this information, and for that which follows concerning the Church of Scotland.

8. A. K. Robertson, "The Individual Cup: Its Use at Holy Communion," *The Liturgical Review* 8.2 (1978) 2–12; see http://www.churchservicesociety.org/journals/volume-08-number-02-nov-1978/individual-cup-its-use-holy-communion or download the pdf as https://www.churchservicesociety.org/sites/default/files/journals/1978-Nov-2–12.pdf

disinfectant. Similarly, letters to the *Baptist Times* and *Freeman* in the early 1900s argued that the common cup was unhygienic, especially since by 1904 most Baptist churches used unfermented wine. Significantly for our purposes here, in order to preserve some sense of unity in a common drink, if not a single cup, the Baptist church in London Road, Lowestoft, developed the habit of everyone drinking *at the same time,* hence the custom of receiving the individual cups passed around but waiting for the invitation to drink together at the same time still common today.[9]

Of course, the irony of the Anglo-Catholic objection to the use of many individual cups is that while the wine (or unfermented grape juice) may be served in individual cups, there is usually the impressive symbolism of one large, real loaf in free church practice. The paradox is that the high-church traditionalists who object to these little glasses are those who are most keen on having one special or large priest's wafer, or 'host' as they would prefer to call it, with all the people receiving *individual little wafers,* often stamped with the image of the crucifixion upon them. It seems most odd to break up one big wafer solely for the celebrant as we say "Though we are many, we are one body because we all share in one bread," and then follow a practice that proclaims exactly the opposite, namely distributing individual wafers.

During my twenty-five years as dean of King's College, our normal practice was to use large wafers that were pre-scored with lines to enable them to be broken easily into eight equal slices, each would then be broken again into three, giving twenty-four pieces for distribution.

For larger services, one could use several large wafers or hosts—and if a quick headcount revealed a few more people than a multiple of twenty-four, but not enough for another whole host, we could break one into half, or quarters or even eighths at the laying of the table or altar before it gets consecrated in the eucharistic prayer, and return it to wafer box on the side credence table for use another time.[10]

9. See Ian M. Randall, *The English Baptists of the Twentieth Century* (A History of the English Baptists, 4; Didcot, UK: The Baptist Historical Society, 2005), 57–58; I am grateful to the late Rev'd Dr Anthony R. Cross from the International Baptist Theological Seminary in Amsterdam for this information.

10. See for example,
https://www.celebratecommunion.com/large-whole-wheat-communion-wafers;
https://fmchurchsupplies.com/products/concelebration-hosts;
https://vanpoulles.co.uk/products/concelebration-wafers;
https://www.church-supplies.co.uk/shop/25-concelebration-wafers-24-section/

The other obvious alternative is to use a real loaf of bread, which is precisely what Cranmer envisaged in the rubrics of the Book of Common Prayer:

> And to take away all occasion of dissension, and superstition, which any person hath or might have concerning the Bread and Wine, it shall suffice that the Bread be such as is usual to be eaten; but the best and purest Wheat Bread that conveniently may be gotten. And if any of the Bread and Wine remain unconsecrated, the Curate shall have it to his own use: but if any remain of that which was consecrated, it shall not be carried out of the Church, but the Priest, and such other of the Communicants as he shall then call unto him, shall, immediately after the Blessing, reverently eat and drink the same. The Bread and Wine for the Communion shall be provided by the Curate and the Church-wardens at the charges of the Parish.

Here we also see clearly the expectation that a sufficient amount of the bread or loaf is broken off before the service (or at least the prayer of consecration) begins, and similarly the wine is opened and enough poured into the chalice or suitable cup, with the rest of the bread and wine being put to one side to "*remain unconsecrated*" so that "*the Curate shall have it to his own use.*" After quite some period of time, when people got used to wafers being used, traditionalist objectors would object to the use of real bread, lest 'fragments of our Lord' should fall all over the church carpet. To this, Bishop Mark Santer, the former bishop of Birmingham, and a good liberal Anglo-Catholic theologian himself, was apparently wont to say to, "If Jesus can get himself *into* the bread and wine, he can presumably get himself *out* again!"

However, to return to the idea of using concelebration for services like a bishop livestreaming over the internet with clergy all celebrating with their own bread and wine before them, as in the bishop of Southwark's practice, this actually suggests that we are not really all celebrating in *one* eucharist together, sharing in the one bread. Rather, there are multiple eucharists all going on at once, with various priests repeating the eucharistic words, in synch with the bishop perhaps, but actually consecrating their own bread and wine. That would, indeed, seem ritually detrimental to the idea that we are sharing in one meal together with one bread and one cup.[11] That said, both the high-church tradition of individual wafers and the free church practice of individual communion cups are very common without everyone arguing that these are not valid eucharistic expressions of one bread and one cup. Nonetheless, it is a real open debate about whether all the clergy

11. I am grateful to the Rev'd Dr Robin Parry for this reflection.

watching the bishop online are really 'concelebrating' with him or her in the same one eucharist, or actually just celebrating their own inidividual communions for themselves, and, if they have others present, their households.

"WHO IS PRAYING THE EUCHARIST?"[12]
THE PEOPLE (CON)CELEBRATING WITH THE PRIEST

In his fascinating pastoral letter to his Episcopal Diocese of Texas, "A Reflection on the Eucharist during the time of COVID-19," Bishop Andy Doyle answers his above question thus:

> The people and the priest are praying the Eucharistic prayer. It is the very nature of the liturgy of the Anglican and Episcopal tradition received through the ages that it is necessary to have our people gathered. This gathering is the *synaxis* nature of our Eucharistic prayer. In the early language of church theologians like Ignatius, it was the *union* of the church. It was the *collecta*, in other writings. But most of all, it was the notion of pulling forward into our Eucharistic theology the prayer of the synagogue, which was understood as *reunion*. The Eucharistic prayer is *reunion* theologically—a coming together of people who have been apart. The Eucharistic prayer, prayed by priest and people, is a reunion from being apart [to now being] gathered to pray, hear the word of God, and to say the words over the bread and wine. The priest may say the prayer aloud, but it is the solemn assembly reunited and praying in one voice the liturgy of Eucharist—the Great Thanksgiving.

We saw in our discussion in chapter 2 above that both Fr Thomas Plant and Fr Peter Anthony argued against the 'eucharistic fast', in part, on the grounds that the eucharist belongs to the whole people of God, and therefore the priest should not neglect to play his part in celebrating communion. However, Bishop Andy's argument, like that of Cranmer and the Anglican mainstream tradition, is that if the people need the priest to celebrate the eucharist for them, then equally the priest needs the people in order to be able to do so, which is why solitary communion is essentially 'un-Anglican'.

---

12. I am very grateful to the Rt Rev'd C. Andrew Doyle, Bishop of Texas, for sharing with me his pastoral letter "A Reflection on the Eucharist during the time of COVID -19." Both this question and much of what follows in this section is taken from this letter, which can be downloaded from this page: https://www.epicenter.org/resources/covid-19-hub/virtual-liturgies/#holy-eucharist; see pp. 4–7.

Doyle further notes that Marion Josiah Hatchett (1927–2009)—a liturgist and pastoral theologian who helped to form the Episcopal 1979 revision of their Book of Common Prayer—wrote that everyone stands at the beginning of the eucharistic prayer as a way to "[foster] and [signify] the participation of the congregation in the action." Hatchett emphasizes the idea of *reunion* in the liturgy and upholds the early church's stress that the whole gathered community actively shares in the eucharistic prayer. "We stand to give thanks; we stand because we have been raised in baptism; we stand because all of us are part of the action. And when the celebrant says, 'Let us give thanks to the Lord our God,' the celebrant is asking for 'permission to offer thanks in the name of those present.'"[13] Similarly, Louis Weil, who was also integral to the development of the 1979 Episcopal Book of Common Prayer, notes that "all the members of the assembly are celebrants."[14] Rick Fabian, from St. Gregory's Church in San Francisco, agrees and goes further: "Following rabbinical custom, the Presider secures the congregation's assent ('Let us give thanks . . . . It is right . . .')." Therefore "all present 'concelebrate' at the eucharistic table, while the Presider prays aloud."[15] Therefore, at the end of the great thanksgiving prayer, all the people join in with the '*Great Amen*' or the '*People's Amen*' which goes back at least to the second century, according to the rite of Justin Martyr.[16]

Nor is the eucharist something that the priest and people do together just for their own sake. The great liturgist Dom Gregory Dix argued that the eucharist is a social work, the work of the people in bringing the church back together and presenting their labour together to God with word and action in the eucharistic feast at the table.[17] Similarly, Massey Shepherd's historical work on the 1928 American Prayer Book points to the Anglican tradition that it is *the church* that is making the sacrifice of its labour both liturgically and missiologically.[18] Ruth Myers explains that, "It is in the eucharist that the assembly is drawn into God's mission." The eucharistic

13. Marion J. Hatchett, *Commentary on the American Prayer Book* (New York: Seabury, 1980), 361 and 373. This was a commentary on the 1979 BCP.

14. Louis Weil, *A Theology of Worship* (Boston: Cowley, 2002), 46–48.

15. Rick Fabian, "The Worship of St. Gregory's." St. Gregory's Episcopal Church, 2001, www.saintgregorys.org/uploads/2/4/2/6/24265184/worship_at_st._gregorys_1_.pdf, 12.

16. See Justin Martyr's early description of the communion in his *First Apology*, written c 153–155 A.D; https://www.catholicculture.org/culture/library/fathers/view.cfm?recnum=1610

17. Dom Gregory Dix, *The Shape of the Liturgy* (London: Dacre, 1945), 733.

18. Massey H. Shepherd Jr., *The Oxford American Prayer Book Commentary* (New York: Oxford University Press, 1955), 83.

prayer "is the prayer of the community, the assembly's worship," and when we go out and gather away from the existing church building, we repeat in ever-new settings the same action of making *ecclesia* in ever-new settings.[19]

Therefore, Bishop Doyle concludes, "What our Anglican heritage reveals, and Episcopal tradition reveals, is that the very reunion and participation of all those gathered at every point of the service is what constitutes the liturgical act. This is not an act the priest makes, and the people then receive. We are singing, praying, administering, and acting as one—physically together. Our agreed-upon Eucharistic Theology found in our tradition and exemplified in the 1979 Book of Common Prayer is that the Eucharistic act is not about the priest doing something for others."[20]

CONCLUSION

This consideration of concelebration has taken us into several other areas, which need careful consideration. First, it is true that by encouraging those priests watching him or her celebrate communion on their own to join in by also presiding over their own bread and wine, such an invitation draws upon the contemporary practice of concelebration, which is, as we saw in chapter 4, to be preferred to solitary masses. Obviously, we will have to return to the questions about whether such communion services can be livestreamed, particularly when actually the service is pre-recorded (as many of those apparently being 'live'-streamed have been in fact), in our later consideration of so-called 'virtual' (or 'digital') communions online in subsequent chapters in Part II. But before we leave this discussion of concelebration, we need to note two other crucial issues that have surfaced: first, that there is a risk in everyone concelebrating over their own bread and wine (especially if they are actually watching or participating in a different place physically) that the important symbolism for being *one body* through sharing the *one bread* and the *one cup* is lost. On the other hand, we have noted that both the Anglican tradition of using individual wafers and the free church use of separate little glasses of wine could both similarly compromise that symbolism—and yet people and churches continue to use such individualistic elements without the loss of being one body in Christ.

Secondly, while the practice of priests joining in concelebrating with the president, especially if it happens to be their bishop, marks a welcome

19. Ruth Myers, *Missional Worship/Worshipful Mission: Gathering as God's People, Going Out in God's Name* (Grand Rapids: Eerdmans, 2014), 52; 188–90.

20. Doyle,   https://www.epicenter.org/resources/covid-19-hub/virtual-liturgies/ #holy-eucharist, p. 7.

step forward from the unsatisfactory regression in the "contagious times" of coronavirus to solitary communions, further consideration of the emphasis—especially in the Anglican tradition, but actually found much wider—on the role of the *people* in enabling their priest to celebrate the eucharist, and even the need for their permission or participation, means that this option of concelebration has still not resolved our difficulties, but has in fact given us a second criterion or requirement for a valid and effective eucharist, namely *the full participation of all the people of God, including the laity.* Therefore, our search must move on yet more widely to examine the role of lay people in more detail.

6

Proposal 5

Lay Presidency, the Eucharist, and the Priesthood

IN RECENT CHAPTERS, WE have noted that one way to avoid the twin problems of fasting from holy communion entirely or only participating in it 'spiritually', was for priests and bishops to celebrate a solitary communion on their own. However, ever since Cranmer and the Reformation, the Anglican tradition has been firmly against this practice because of the important corporate role of the people in the sacrament, and therefore we have argued that it is better for a bishop or priest to have someone else present with them at least, and to livestream their celebration if at all possible. To avoid the unfortunate exclusive impression of the celebrant merely feeding themselves, while the rest go hungry, it was also suggested that any priests watching could concelebrate over some bread and wine, which they themselves could then receive, together with any of their household who are present with them. There are (at least) two ways of interpreting this: either in terms of the bishop and priests all concelebrating together in one glorious eucharist across space and time, or rather to see what is happening as a collection of lots of mini-eucharists sharing the same *time* simultaneously, but happening separately with different presidents and different breads and wine cups in various different *places*.

Whichever understanding you opt for, it still leaves those who are *not* priests facing the unhappy prospect of being excluded from communion while having to watch others sharing in it. So what might happen if such lay people placed bread and wine in front of their laptop, tablet, phone, or whatever device they happen to be watching upon? We will return to the question of whether the priest's consecration on screen can reach to wherever they are watching and consecrate their bread and wine later in Part II below. In this chapter, however, we will begin with the question of whether, in these extreme circumstances, those who are not ordained can somehow 'preside' or 'celebrate' over their own bread and wine and it be in any way valid, sacramental, or effective: in other words, does it *work*?

IS LAY PRESIDENCY POSSIBLE?

The understanding of most of the Christian tradition, regardless of denomination, over the centuries is that holy communion must be celebrated by a priest or some other form of ordained or officially recognized person for it to be sacramentally valid and effective. This tradition of reserving eucharistic presidency to authorized ministers goes right back to antiquity. Of course, our knowledge of practice in the earliest congregations is very sparse, but the practice of the bishop (a word that comes direct from the Greek New Testament, *episkopos*, which means literally, 'overseer') being the one who presides (or a presbyter—which means 'elder', but gives us the word 'priest'—as his representative *in absentia*) is certainly very ancient and, as far as we can tell, universal.[1]

From time to time, there has been debate over whether lay people (possibly with some form of training or authorization) can celebrate communion—so-called lay presidency. This has been a desire in the conservative Anglican Diocese of Sydney, Australia, for many years, following a vote in their own synod to allow it, which was vetoed by their archbishop in 1999.[2] A number of subsequent attempts have been made over the years since.[3] These have been resisted by the rest of Australia, and indeed by most of the Anglican Communion. Thus Bosco Peters, a renowned and ebullient New Zealand liturgist, characteristically does not mince his words: "The context of Sydney diocese's advocating of lay presidency is the pressing of an anti-catholic theology and practice. There is nothing more sacred than the Eucharist as the heart of catholicism. Sydney Anglicans are forbidden such 'popish' practices as wearing a chasuble, adding water to the wine, . . . [and] if they could get rid of the connection between priesthood and Eucharist

1. I am grateful to Rev'd Dr Robin Parry for this point.

2. See the various news articles posted on the Anglican Communion News Service on Nov 10, 1999, https://www.anglicannews.org/tag/lay%20presidency.aspx

3. https://web.archive.org/web/20071212160507/http://your.sydneyanglicans.net /sydneystories/1655a;   https://web.archive.org/web/20070902112452/http://www.sds. asn.au/Site/103704.asp?a=a&ph=sy

they would have removed a central piece of the catholic hardware on which Anglicanism runs."[4]

Part of the reason for this desire flows from the passage we have already noted in chapter 2 above (p. 34) from St Paul, "for as often as you eat this bread and drink the cup, you *proclaim* the Lord's death until he comes" (1 Cor 11:23–26). Paul's use of *katangellō*, which is normally used for preaching or proclaiming the gospel, here in an unusual connection with holy communion, suggests for Sydney Anglicans that "the sacrament is a 'symbolic preaching of the gospel'. Those who are not bishops or priests are allowed to preach the gospel (but not preside at the sacrament). The perception is that this elevates the importance of the sacrament over the preaching of the gospel—in other words, the symbolic preaching of the gospel is more important than the literal preaching of the gospel."[5] Reserving eucharistic presidency to ordained clergy only is thus perceived to suggest that bishops and priests are more important than lay people, and that the sacrament of holy communion is more important than preaching. Thus the revisionist stance is a consequence of the more evangelical theology and churchmanship in Sydney Diocese, which owes more to puritan and Calvinist ecclesiology than to traditional Anglican (and catholic, both 'big-C' and 'little-c') understandings of the church and sacraments. It is not surprising that this debate is promoted from time to time all over the world, especially in certain parts of the UK and (the southern states of) the USA when those from such a puritan/Calvinist tendency manage to get control of Anglican churches or dioceses.[6]

Indeed, if I may admit to another personal story to illustrate this point, I held a similar view myself during my ordination training. With hindsight, it is clear that I had been running away from the call to ordination for most of a decade in my twenties, although I had trained and been licensed as a lay reader (a form of Licensed Lay Ministry in the Church of England) and I had exercised that lay ministry for some eight years before I was ordained. To be honest, it seemed to the younger me somewhat 'daft' that, according to my LLM/reader's licence, I could preach and teach (thus risking taking

4. See the Rev'd Peter Bosco's essay on his very helpful liturgical website, following the publication by Sydney Diocese of its proposal "The Lord's Supper in Human Hands—Epilogue" in April 2011; https://liturgy.co.nz/lay-presidency-again. This page also provides helpful links to some of his previous posts about lay presidency—and his website is well worth visiting for all sorts of liturgical matters.

5. Bosco, https://liturgy.co.nz/lay-presidency-again.

6. See Muriel Porter's careful analysis in *The New Puritans: The Rise of Fundamentalism in the Anglican Church* (Melbourne University Press, 2006); available at https://www.amazon.co.uk/dp/0522851843.

the church into error?), administer communion elements that had been previously consecrated by a priest (allowing me access to the homes of the elderly and vulnerable?), lead any Service of the Word, such as Morning and Evening Prayer by myself (disrupting the regular worship of the church?), receive the offerings of the people (financial embezzlement?), catechize the young (child abuse?), and even take funerals, and if necessary, baptisms (with the possibility of messing up people's entry and exit into not only the church, but into and out of this life and world?!)—but in order to be able to say a few 'magic words' over bread and wine, I had to go to train at theological college for three years and then spend an extra year as a deacon, before I could preside at the eucharist. It made little sense to me at the time, so I even wrote my main paper about it for the module at theological college on liturgy.

My views on the matter changed. In fact, the Rt Rev'd David Say—an imposing figure some 'eight feet by four feet in cope and mitre', capable of putting the 'fear of God' into anyone after over twenty-five years of being bishop of Rochester[7]—cross-examined me carefully about it on my second ordination retreat to check that I was now 'sound of doctrine', before he was prepared actually to ordain me a priest in 1986! And I remember with great joy, my subsequent 'first mass', nervously presiding over holy communion for the very first time, in a church packed not only with the usual congregation but also all my family and friends, with a special guest star preacher who had played a very significant role in helping me get to finally being ordained a priest, followed by a party and much celebration—and this is typical for newly ordained Catholic and Anglican priests. Yes, it is that important, dear reader . . . !

In July 1994, less than a decade later, the General Synod of the Church of England embarked on the first in a long and tortuous sequence of debates about 'extended communion', as we shall discover later in chapter 8. However, that debate included a number of significant points that are relevant here.[8] Thus, Michael Till argued that "where pastoral presidency becomes detached from eucharistic presidency, priesthood is diminished" (*Proceedings*, 280). Stephen Sykes, the bishop of Ely and a renowned theologian at Cambridge in his own right, was quite clear and forthright: "in my view the literature in favour of lay presidency is not very impressive" and he pointed out that Canon B12 rejects it (*Proceedings*, 282). Even the then archbishop of Canterbury, George Carey, who was well-known as an evangelical himself,

7. The assessment of the chairman of the House of Laity at Bishop David's Silver Jubilee!

8. See General Synod of the Church of England, *Report of Proceedings* (London: General Synod, 1994) for a full report of the debate.

argued, "lay presidency is a contradiction in terms if we are to keep faith with the received doctrine of ministry of our Church" (*Proceedings*, 287).

Celebrating holy communion is considered to be *so special* as an expression of the action of the whole church together in making real the presence of our Lord Jesus Christ in the bread and wine, that in the Catholic, Orthodox, and Anglican traditions eucharistic presidency is reserved only for ordained priests, and in most Protestant denominations—such as Lutherans, Methodists, Reformed, Presbyterian, and Congregationalist churches—it is reserved for ordained and authorized ministers, although some of the latter and other free churches, such as some Baptists, do permit certain lay people to preside. However, even these people do have to have some form of training and authorization by the wider church before they are allowed to celebrate communion. Some go so far as to argue that this is tantamount to ordination training, and that the very act of presiding at the eucharist itself 'ordains' someone a priest as much as any bishop's hands.

Therefore, even if one was to permit lay presidency in the extreme circumstances of "contagious times", it is not going to help us in this situation where a priest or a bishop presides over communion online, perhaps assisted by a number of priests, all (con)celebrating with their own bread and wine as they participate in their own homes but everyone else 'watching' is excluded—unless one is willing to countenance *indiscriminate presidency* and *wholesale ordination*. Nonetheless, it is suggested often enough in these extreme difficulties that it is worth still spending a little more time examining whether it could be a solution, and if it is not, determining why not?

First, we note a widespread agreement across Christian denominations, that the priest or the minister is the properly authorized and accredited leader and representative, not just of the church, but even of God in Christ himself. Bishop Doyle quotes the Orthodox priest and theologian Alexander Schmemann putting it like this: "If the 'Assembly as the Church' is the image of the body of Christ, then the image of the head of the body is the priest. He [or she] presides over, he [or she] heads the gathering, and his [or her] standing at their head is precisely what makes a group of Christians the gathering of the church in the fullness of her gifts."[9] Like Christ, the priest or minister is at one and the same time leader and servant, given all power and authority and yet this is to be exercised in serving all the people of God.

Such 'service' is what the very word 'minister' or 'ministry' means. The mediaeval Catholic stress on the mediatory role of the priest as a

9. Alexander Schmemann, *The Eucharist* (New York: St. Vladimir's University Press, 1988), 24–25.

'go-between', standing in the middle between God and the people, representing God to the people and the people to God, may be emphasized less today and makes some clergy uneasy, as well as certain lay people. Yet in times of sorrow, sickness, and confusion, such as during the coronavirus pandemic,[10] many people, especially in the media, turned to clergy in general, and the hierarchy of (arch)bishops to ask them, as representatives of God and the church, both what they thought God was doing or saying through it all and also what the church's response and activity should be. On the other hand, it is also at times of great joy and celebration, like the arrival of a new baby or a wedding, that it seems a human compulsion to turn to the church and its clergy and ministers for a celebration like baptism or marriage, 'holy matrimony' as it used to be called.[11]

These 'liminal' experiences of joy and sorrow at the threshold of our very existence, at the beginning and end of life itself, or certain key stages along its way, seem to drive us beyond ourselves, to seek answers about 'what it all means', or bring the need for Someone or Something Bigger than ourselves to help us make sense of it all, to celebrate or to mourn, to rejoice or to grieve. Such 'hatching, matching, and despatching', births and baptisms, weddings and marriages, funerals and memorial services, make up a large part of the time of many clergy and ministers, not only in actually presiding over the occasion itself and making sure it all goes well, but also in preparation, advising, and counselling the family beforehand, and in follow up, providing whatever is needed by way of pastoral care. It is also very significant that the most important liturgical service that the church can offer at these liminal moments of transition is to celebrate them in the context of holy communion—which, surprisingly enough, seems to be appropriate and fitting for all these very contrasting occasions.

This is probably the primary reason why all, or nearly all, of the mainline Christian churches and denominations insist that communion should, or even can, only be presided over by a duly and properly *trained and*

10. See especially Megan Warner, Carla Grosch-Miller, Hilary Ison, and Christopher Southgate (eds.), *Tragedy and Congregations: A Practical Theology of Trauma* (London: Routledge, 2019); see the Tragedy and Congregations project at the University of Exeter, funded by the Sir John Templeton Foundation, https://tragedyandcongregations.org.uk/; on this turning to the church in times of tragedy and crisis, see Warner's blog of May 2018, https://megwarner.wixsite.com/bible/single-post/2018/05/16/Churches-in-Crises---a-National-Necessity; for the coronavirus situation, see also May 2020: https://megwarner.wixsite.com/bible/single-post/2020/05/05/Re-visiting-Aberfan-The-Church-of-England-and-COVID-19

11. See further, Richard A. Burridge, *Four Ministries, One Jesus: Exploring Your Vocation with the Four Gospels* (London: SPCK, 2017), 83–87; international edition (Grand Rapids: Eerdmans, 2018), 76–79.

authorized priest, minister, leader, or representative. Because the eucharist is in some form or other—whatever particular theology or understanding of it is held—seen as the both the pinnacle and the staple diet of the church, equally suitable for birth or death, joy or sorrow, it is felt that it is somehow important that the properly accredited person should lead it.

ORDINATION SERVICES AND LITURGIES

This is confirmed by even a quick look at the manuals and guidance, and also the orders or forms of services, for ordination or the licensing or commissioning of clergy and ministers across the various different churches and denominations in our world today, most of which connect together the two ministries of preaching the word and presiding over the sacrament. Thus, the Evangelical Lutheran Church of America ordains "rostered ministers of Word and Sacrament" to "1. Preach the Word; 2. Administer the sacraments" (ELCA Manual 26); "A Word and Sacrament rostered leader demonstrates the ability to plan worship, preach, and administer the Sacraments; to adapt the Lutheran liturgical tradition, and to invoke in worship a sense of the holy and a welcoming spirit" (ELCA Summary 6). Interestingly, for a more congregational and reformed tradition, the Disciples of Christ ordination service makes it clear in its introduction (p. 5) that

> The 'priesthood of all believers' refers to the persons who have entered into a covenanted relationship through confession and baptism. It ought not be confused with the role of congregational elders in the administration of the Lord's Supper. Although in some circumstances anyone can administer the Sacraments/Ordinances of the Church, in Disciples practice it has usually been the duly appointed congregational leaders who administer baptism and the Lord's Supper. This practice derives not from the 'priesthood of all believers' but from early distinctions between the roles of elder and evangelist/preacher. The evangelist, called from outside the congregation, was restricted to ministries of preaching/teaching. The elder(s), called from within the congregation, bore responsibility for congregational governance, including the administration of baptism and the Lord's Supper. The right and responsibility to preside at the Table is increasingly a role shared by elders and ministers.[12]

---

12. http://disciples.org/wp-content/uploads/2015/04/Ordination_Service_Guidelines.pdf

Most liturgies or orders of services for ordination begin with the bishop or senior church leader reading out a 'declaration' or description of the minister's role, almost like a kind of job specification: the Church of England's service starts with a 'declaration' by the bishop of the ministry of priests: "They are to preside at the Lord's table and lead his people in worship, offering with them a spiritual sacrifice of praise and thanksgiving."[13] Similarly, the *Anglican Prayer Book for New Zealand* states, "above all they are to proclaim God's word and take their part in Christ's prophetic work, ... to preside at the Eucharist, to administer Christ's holy sacraments."[14] The Ordinal of the Episcopal Church in America describes "the presbyters, or ordained elders, in subsequent times generally known as priests. Together with the bishops, they take part in the governance of the Church, in the carrying out of its missionary and pastoral work, and in the preaching of the Word of God and administering his holy Sacraments" (p. 510).[15]

The Roman Catholic liturgy is even more explicit: "For by your ministry the spiritual sacrifice of the faithful will be made perfect, being united to the sacrifice of Christ, which will be offered through your hands in an unbloody way on the altar, in union with the faithful, in the celebration of the sacraments."[16] The Presbyterian Church of the USA service book notes,

> within the community of the church, some are called to particular service as ministers of Word and Sacrament, as elders, and as deacons. Recognizing the importance of each office, the church ordains in order to assure fulfillment of the primary responsibilities of preaching the Word and administering the sacraments, ordering the governance of the church, and providing for ministries of care and compassion in the world. Representing the one, holy, catholic, and apostolic church, the Presbytery of N., by means of this commission, now ordains N. to the ministry of Word and Sacrament. (p. 53)

The United Church of Christ wishes to ordain a candidate "to the ministry of the church, committing to him/her the authority to preach your word, administer the sacraments" (p. 410), while the African Methodist Episcopal church tells the candidate, "you are to be a faithful dispenser of

---

13. https://www.churchofengland.org/prayer-and-worship/worship-texts-and-resources/common-worship/ministry/common-worship-ordination-services

14. https://anglicanprayerbook.nz/898.html, p. 901

15. https://www.episcopalchurch.org/files/book_of_common_prayer.pdf

16. *The Roman Pontifical, as renewed by decree of the Second Vatican Ecumenical Council; published by authority of Pope Paul VI, and further revised at the direction of Pope John Paul II*, section 123

the Word of God and of God's Holy Sacraments in the name of the Father, and of the Son, and of the Holy Ghost."

This is usually followed by questions to the ordinand, who makes solemn vows and promises in response, especially regarding presiding over the sacraments. Thus, for example, a Roman Catholic bishop will ask, "Do you resolve to celebrate faithfully and reverently, accord with Church's tradition, the mysteries of Christ, especially the sacrifice of the Eucharist and the sacrament of Reconciliation, for the glory of God and the sanctification of the Christian people?" For the Church of England, ministering the sacrament is also connected with teaching the doctrine: "Will you faithfully minister the doctrine and sacraments of Christ as the Church of England has received them, so that the people committed to your charge may be defended against error and flourish in the faith?" To this the person waiting to be ordained priest must reply "By the help of God, I will." A similar connection of word and sacrament is found in rest of the Anglican Communion, such as New Zealand, Australia, and the USA,[17] as well as in the main Protestant churches, including the African American Episcopal Church and the Presbyterian Church of the USA.[18] Similarly, some churches include the sacrament in the words of ordination with the laying on of hands, and in the case of the United Methodist Church the elevation of the appropriate vessels: "faithfully administer the sacraments of Holy Baptism and Holy Communion" with the rubric, "*Here a paten and chalice may be lifted.*"[19]

There may be other additional symbolic acts later as the candidate is given a copy of the Bible to remind them to preach and teach it, or a chalice and paten to use at communion services, or they may be robed with a stole or some other vestment denoting their office. Thus, the PCUSA service suggests that "symbols appropriate to the ministry of the Word and Sacrament may be presented", while the Methodist rubric has "*As instruments of office they may receive a Bible, a chalice and paten*"; the Disciples of Christ Guidelines explain why: "Since Communion is integral to weekly worship in the Christian Church, the presentation of a chalice and paten is also appropriate as a sign of office."[20]

17. https://anglicanprayerbook.nz/898.html page 906; the Ordinal of the Episcopal Church, p. 532.

18. PCUSA Ordinal, pp. 57, 64–65, 93–94.

19. UMC Ordinal, 26.

20. PCUSA, 68; NZ, 909; TEC, 534; UCC, 411; UMC, 28; DoC Guidelines, 17; all these liturgies and ordination services are discussed and quoted more fully throughout Richard A. Burridge, *Four Ministries, One Jesus: Exploring Your Vocation with the Four Gospels* (London: SPCK, 2017); international edition (Grand Rapids: Eerdmans, 2018).

THE 'SPECIAL CHARACTER' OF THE PRIEST/PRESBYTER
AND THE UNDERSTANDING OF THE SACRAMENT

While this survey of ordination services has made it abundantly clear that for nearly all the mainline churches (some Baptist or independent churches may differ) the celebration of the eucharist and presiding over communion is inextricably linked to the ordination of the priest or minister, this is mainly for reasons of *authority*, with the priest being a trained and duly accredited representative of the church, who is able to lead the church through word and sacrament.

However, within the catholic tradition (again with both a large-C and small-c), there is another, even deeper reason. The traditional definition of a 'sacrament' is "the outward and visible sign of an inward and spiritual grace." In catholic understanding there is a direct connection between the 'inward and spiritual grace' conveyed through the outward sign of the laying on of the bishop's hands at the ordination of a priest, itself also seen as a sacrament in this tradition, and that effected by the priest's words over bread and wine at communion. We noted in chapter 4 on solitary communion above a point made by one liturgist, the Rev'd Dr Paul Roberts: "this [i.e., solo eucharists] only emerged (or makes sense) once various medieval theologies of priesthood (with implications for the theology of the mass) had developed, focussing more on the two aspects of the sacramental category of *character indelibilis* and the role of eucharistic consecration being dependent upon a priest's *potestas* rather than other matters."[21] This is made explicit in the introduction to the Roman Catholic liturgy for ordination: "By sacred Ordination a sacrament is conferred on priests through which, 'by the anointing of the Holy Spirit, they are signed with a special character and are so configured to Christ the Priest that they have the power to act in the person of Christ the Head,'" quoting from the Second Vatican Council's *Decree on the Ministry and Life of Priests*.[22] This 'special character' is permanent, *character indelibilis*, making a real—or even ontological—change in the character of the priest, which is what enables him also to make a real and ontological change of bread and wine into the body and blood of Jesus Christ, which is sacrificed for us: "For by your ministry the spiritual sacrifice of the faithful will be made perfect, being united to the sacrifice of

---

21. Personal email to me of April 25, 2020; quoted with his permission.

22. *The Roman Pontifical, as renewed by decree of the Second Vatican Ecumenical Council; published by authority of Pope Paul VI, and further revised at the direction of Pope John Paul II*, section 101, quoting the Second Vatican Council, Decree on the Ministry and Life of Priests, *Presbyterorum Ordinis*, no. 2.

Christ, which will be offered through your hands in an unbloody way on the altar, in union with the faithful, in the celebration of the sacraments."[23]

Of course, in mediaeval times, this connection relied upon the doctrine of *transubstantiation*, which was itself based on Platonic concepts of an 'ideal form' and Aristotle's distinction between something's 'properties' or 'accidents' and its actual 'substance' or 'essence'. Thus, we all know and recognize a table, even though it can have three, four, or many legs, be made out of wood, plastic, metal, or whatever, and be round, square, oblong, or any shape you like. No matter how much we may change these 'properties' or 'accidents' of its manufacture, there is an essential 'tableness' that we recognize as its substance, literally 'standing-under' in Latin, *sub-stans*. In the celebration of holy communion by a priest—who may look like any other human being in their *accidental properties* (tall or short, black, white, brown or yellow, young or old, male or female, etc., though of course whether someone who is female can actually be ordained a priest remains an issue in the catholic tradition), but whose underlying *essential substance* has this special, indelible priestly character—the reverse happens: the bread and wine retain their *accidental properties*, still looking like and tasting like bread (whether it is brown, white, sliced, or wafers) and wine (regardless of whether it is red or white, sweet or bitter) but whose underlying *essential substance* is transformed, or 'transubstantiated', from 'breadness' or 'wineness' into the body and blood of our Lord Jesus Christ. That is why Catholics will reverence the sacrament, elevate it, or bow their head, or genuflect before it, because it now conveys the 'real presence' of Jesus Christ, "before whom every knee shall bow . . . and every tongue confess that he is Lord" (Phil 2:11).

It was this doctrine of transubstantiation that was challenged in various ways through the Reformation. In its most explicit form, Luther thought that it meant that Jesus, as really physically present in the substantial essence of the bread and wine, was actually being sacrificed again, dying repeatedly at every eucharist—so he preferred the idea of *con*-substantiation, where the substance or essence of Christ's body and blood *co*-existed alongside the substantial essence of the bread and wine, rather than completely replacing it. Other reformers argued that while there is a 'real presence' of Christ in the consecrated elements, it is more 'spiritual' than the mechanistic, woodenly literal understanding of Aristotelian metaphysics—while for Anglicans, it is a 'holy mystery' about which a wide variety of views are acceptable. At the other extreme, particularly in those churches that tend to

23. *The Roman Pontifical, as renewed by decree of the Second Vatican Ecumenical Council; published by authority of Pope Paul VI, and further revised at the direction of Pope John Paul II*, section 123.

follow Zwingli's teaching, it is believed that nothing happens to the bread and wine at consecration. Instead of the first clause of the eucharist words—"*This* is my body/blood"—such 'memorialist' understandings stress instead the second half of Jesus' command: "Do this in *remembrance* of me." John Dyer (dean of enrolment and distance education and adjunct professor of media arts and worship at Dallas Theological Seminary as well as a computer coder and blogger) depicts the possible range of understandings in a diagram like this:[24]

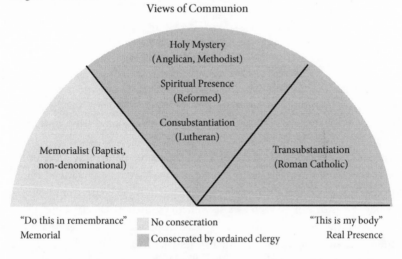

Views of Communion

Holy Mystery
(Anglican, Methodist)

Spiritual Presence
(Reformed)

Consubstantiation
(Lutheran)

Memorialist (Baptist,
non-denominational)

Transubstantiation
(Roman Catholic)

"Do this in remembrance"   No consecration   "This is my body"
Memorial   Consecrated by ordained clergy   Real Presence

Of course, today, most people no longer see things in such Greek philosophical or mediaeval metaphysical terms. The development of the modern sciences—especially physics, chemistry, and biology—took place in large part by setting aside questions regarding an underlying 'substance' or 'essence' somehow underpinning particular objects. Consequently, views like transubstantiation feel very alien to contemporary ways of thinking about reality and so they struggle for plausibility in the modern world. On the other hand, Catholics, Anglicans, Lutherans, Methodists, and various other church traditions continue to believe strongly that the consecration of bread and wine by a duly ordained and properly accredited priest or

24. Taken from John Dyer's very interesting article, "The Digital Church in the Age of Corona," available at https://j.hn/digital-communion-summary-of-theology-practices/. One caveat to the diagram is that there is a growing movement among Baptists away from memorialist understandings of the eucharist towards a doctrine of real presence. Such Baptists often argue that more sacramental understandings of baptism and eucharist were common among seventeenth-century Baptists and ought to be restored today. See, for instance, Philip Thompson and Anthony Cross (eds.), *Baptist Sacramentalism* (Carlisle, UK: Paternoster, 2003); *Baptist Sacramentalism 2* (Eugene, OR: Wipf and Stock, 2009); *Baptist Sacramentalism 3* (Eugene, OR: Wipf & Stock, 2020).

minister does actually bring about the 'real presence' of Christ in the communion elements, even if understandings of the mechanics or the theology of this vary, and many are content to believe as a holy mystery which we can never understand. For me personally, I find the words of the saintly Bishop Thomas Ken (1637–1711) still express this mystery for me, especially since they were written at a particularly contentious time: "I believe Thy Body and Blood to be as really present in the Holy Sacrament as Thy divine power can make it, although the manner of Thy mysterious presence I cannot comprehend."[25]

CONCLUSION

It is time to draw this discussion to an end, and answer our opening question of whether, in these extreme circumstances, those who are not ordained can somehow 'preside' or 'celebrate' over their own bread and wine, and can it be in any way valid, sacramental, or effective. In other words, does it *work*? There are several possible answers to this question, depending on one's beliefs, theology, and ecclesiology. First of all, we have noted that the catholic tradition stresses that the sacrament of ordination (since this tradition also believes it is or can be seen as a sacrament) somehow effects some sort of change in the person of a priest, a special or indelible character. It follows, therefore, that this change in the priest's character enables him or her to effect a similar sort of change of bread and wine into the body and blood of our Lord Jesus Christ, however defined or understood, such that the real presence of Jesus is present in the communion elements to feed and nurture the believer. From this position, it is clear that any kind of lay presidency is a complete non-starter, regardless of how extreme the circumstances may be. If a lay person tries to preside then the bread and wine remain simply bread and wine—nothing happens. In fact, as we noted above, some have tried to argue that the logic and power flow the other way—that it is the real presence of Jesus Christ in the consecrated bread and wine that nurtures and sustains the special character of the priest; therefore, if a lay person did somehow manage to consecrate the eucharistic elements, that would be tantamount to them becoming an ordained priest.

Secondly, all the ordination services and liturgies that we examined were very clear that the ministry, privilege, prerogative, or right (choose your understanding) to preside at the eucharist belongs solely to the order

25. I am extremely grateful to Canon Gordon Oliver for this quotation, taken from Georgina Bettiscombe *John Keble: A Study in Limitations* (London, Constable 1963), 320.

of priests or ordained ministers, because of their office as duly authorized and accredited representatives of God and the church, regardless of what one may or may not believe about any special character. Once again, on such an understanding, lay presidency at the eucharist is not possible, either generally or in such extreme times of contagious disease.

Thirdly, even people who argue for lay presidency, like those in the Anglican Diocese of Sydney, do so because they want to emphasize the parallel ministries of word and sacrament. The argument runs that if a lay person can be carefully trained over several years, and then duly licensed and properly accredited to be able to preach the word, why do they have to be ordained in order to be able to "say a few words over bread and wine"? This seems to them to imply a tacit understanding that the ministry of the sacrament in its "proclaiming the Lord's death until he comes" is more important than the verbal proclaiming of the gospel in preaching and teaching. For evangelicals centred on the importance of the Bible and its exegesis and exposition, such is unacceptable—hence their desire for lay presidency. And this is also why it is possible—if not common—in certain Baptist or independent church traditions for a properly trained lay person to be licensed or given official permission to preside at communion in the absence of an ordained minister.

However, even if one accepts the logic of this third position generally, this is still not going to solve our problem in the particular and extreme circumstances of "contagious times", i.e., that allowing priests to concelebrate along with a bishop or priest on a broadcast or livestreamed communion means that lay people are left out of the eucharistic feast, and so go hungry and unfed spiritually. The argument of those like Sydney Diocese or these independents would lead simply to another category of Licensed Lay Ministers, like readers, who have been trained and are permitted and accredited to celebrate communion alongside other ministries such as preaching and teaching. If one happened to live in the household of such a licensed lay person, then here it might be possible to receive communion, but all that has happened is that the boundary of the lucky few who receive has been extended a little. Only wholesale and indiscriminate allowing of *any and all* lay people to preside or celebrate communion, regardless of their theological understanding, pastoral training, and without any kind of formal recognition or accreditation, will enable everyone to receive—and not even Sydney Diocese argues for that.

*****

Over these chapters so far, therefore, we have seen a gradual progression, like ripples on a pond, towards more people being able to have 'holy communion in contagious times', beginning with a *eucharistic fast*, which provides nothing (except greater spiritual discipline perhaps?), through *spiritual communion*, which has its place in certain limited situations such as extreme sickness or being present in the eucharist of a denomination that does not permit you to receive, and *solitary communion*, where only the bishop or priest receives, to *concelebration*, where the bishop and priests can receive, to this consideration finally of *lay presidency*, where the circle is expanded one more step to include certain trained and authorized lay people. Sadly, none of these options are going to solve our problem, since in addition to the criteria and requirements for at least *one other, and preferably several people, to be present and receiving* in addition to the celebrating president, and secondly that *the laity must be present* to exercise their role in participating with, or even inviting, the celebrant to preside, we now have a third necessity, namely that the *presiding celebrant must be an ordained priest or minister authorized* so to preside at holy communion. Therefore, we must press on with our search for a solution to explore whether, if the churches are all closed, celebrating holy communion outdoors might be the answer.

7

Proposal 6

Drive-in Churches and Drive-thru Communions

THIS CHAPTER, UNLIKE THE others, will not contain any personal stories, for this topic is not something I have experienced personally, and indeed, it is not something I ever thought I would be taking seriously enough to include in a book of mine. Certainly, it did not feature in the original paper that I wrote for the English bishops out of which this book has grown, nor in any of our subsequent conversations. But, and it is a big 'but', I admit that I was somewhat surprised when I found it in Bishop Andy Doyle's paper and that, as bishop of Texas, he thought he had to devote a couple of pages to it.[1] A few moments searching online for 'drive-in/drive-thru communion' reveals that it has been happening all around America, and across different churches and denominations. After all, it makes complete sense, especially in American culture, where you have lots of space and lots of cars to fill it up with! Therefore, as Bishop Doyle demonstrated, it needs some serious consideration, especially in case it proves of some assistance in our search for ways to celebrate holy communion in "contagious times".

DRIVE-IN CHURCHES AND COMMUNIONS

To my surprise, I discovered that 'drive-in church services' are not at all new in the United States. In fact, the Reverend Robert Schuller is credited with

1. Doyle, https://www.epicenter.org/resources/covid-19-hub/virtual-liturgies/ #holy-eucharist, pp. 7–9.

having popularized this form of church in the 1950s in Garden Grove, California, together with his extraordinary Crystal Cathedral.[2] Whatever one's initial reaction, the fact remains that many churches all around the USA offer this ministry, as can be demonstrated in a short online search—and this was happening long before the coronavirus pandemic. Back in March 2014, Amy Kiley from National Public Radio broadcast a programme about the benefits of such a drive-in church.[3] The Daytona Beach Drive-in Christian Church in Florida uses an old drive-in theatre, where cars park in rows on the grass facing an altar erected on its balcony; to hear the service, worshippers merely have to switch on their car radios.[4] Bob Kemp-Baird has been the pastor there since 2012, and, as well as his preaching, the church offers communion. As NPR's Kiley reported in 2014, "Liturgical purists might balk at a worship style in which even Communion isn't very communal. Parishioners in their cars drink wine from plastic ramekins with tiny rectangles of bread under the lids. As they do so, the radio pipes out instructions over organ music: 'Remove this inner lid and, holding this cup, join me in prayer.'"

With the arrival of the coronavirus pandemic, *Time* magazine investigated a new phenomenon: "Come As You Are—in the Family Car," as "an increasing number of pastors have turned instead to a seemingly old-fashioned option to gather their flock: the drive-in. Churchgoers are driving into church parking lots, pulling up a respectable distance away from the next car, and tuning into their radio to hear their pastor speak from the church steps."[5] They reported on Genoa Church in Westerville, Ohio, where "300 cars carrying roughly 600 parishioners arrived in the Genoa church parking lot, amounting to about 40% of its typical weekly population. [Pastor Frank] Carl preached from a scissor lift and was broadcast over a low frequency FM station, which the congregation tuned into in their cars." *Time* also visited a number of other churches that were using their own parking lots, including places as far apart as Liquid Church in New Jersey, Bethel Church in Evansville, Indiana, and Double Springs Baptist Church in Taylors, South Carolina.

The article goes on to note that when Nathan McDonald, owner of the 66 Drive-in Theatre in Carthage, Missouri, found that corona restrictions

2. For this claim, see https://time.com/5811387/drive-in-church-coronavirus/

3. https://www.npr.org/2014/03/03/285278319/roadside-service-drive-in-church-brings-god-to-your-car?t=1589661905100

4. For more details of all their activities, see the church's website https://www.driveinchurch.net/

5. See the report "'Come as You Are in the Family Car.' Drive-in Church Services Are Taking Off during the Coronavirus Pandemic" by Andrew R. Chow, March 28, 2020: https://time.com/5811387/drive-in-church-coronavirus/

prevented him from screening movies, he offered the venue to local churches, and quickly became fully booked: "This Sunday, I'll start at 8:30 in the morning, and then we have slots back-to-back-to-back until 7 at night. I give each pastor an hour, and leave myself 30 minutes in-between to make sure they all get out, or if I have to clean up anything." I make that seven separate churches holding drive-in services, or even eight if 7pm is the start of the last slot, rather than the end of the 5.30pm one. *Time* suggested that for McDonald, "these services represent both a good deed and a shrewd business move, even though he is not charging the churches: 'If this thing carries into the summer and my business is still not operating, I'm supporting the community—and the community will turn around and support me.'"

For other churches, this goes right to the heart of the American Constitution. According to the report "Owensboro Pastor Cites 1st Amendment in Drive-up Communion Service" by Michael Doyle in the *Evansville Courier & Press*,

> In Owensboro, Kentucky, the congregation of HIS Church participated in a drive-up church service complete with communion. Hands raised from the open windows of about 100 cars, horns honked in lieu of "amens" and people sang along to the praise songs being performed. For senior pastor Brian Gibson, it was more than an unconventional church service, it was a call to action on First Amendment rights. Gibson said while the church had been asked to forgo the communion part of the service by the Green River District Health Department, church leadership made the decision to go ahead with it anyway. "I feel like churches and religion have been targeted by these policies," Gibson said. "You see that McDonald's over there? There's teenagers putting french-fries in cardboard boxes and handing them to people through a window. There's a liquor store right there selling liquor to people through the window. So I don't understand why we shouldn't be able to give people communion through a window. . . . [T]his is America, and our freedoms are what makes it America. Tonight, I'm thankful for those attorney generals for working to protect our freedom of religion, and I'm thankful to the Constitution that gives us that freedom! How about making some noise for the Constitution?" he said to a chorus of horn honks.

Michael Doyle, the reporter, also noted that "Prepackaged communion elements were passed out by masked and gloved staffers—who also wore T-shirts bearing the slogan 'Church is Essential.' Social distancing was observed during the service also." He then interviewed members of the church who were very positive about it: one with four children, popping up through the car's sunroof, said, "We loved it. We can't wait to be back in church. We just love being with God's people, in God's house. So this was awesome." Another long-time member of the church said "he was excited to see his fellow churchgoers for the first time since the COVID-19 crisis began: 'It felt good to come here tonight. We've been doing the online services, and that's fine, but to actually come out to the church and see everybody, even if it was just sitting inside the car, it was nice.'"[6]

Significantly, HIS Church, a nondenominational church, also has campuses in Amarillo and Dumas, both in Texas. So it is perhaps not so surprising that the Episcopal bishop of Texas, the Rt Rev'd Andy Doyle, should have devoted part of his paper to drive-in and drive-by services. However, for him, such services "undermine the very core of the interactive, physical presence that we have already spoken of. They are not about our reunion, our ingathering, or our labor. They do not allow the kind of interactivity that is meant as the regular part of making Eucharist."[7]

We have already seen in our consideration of both solitary communions and concelebration in chapters 3 and 4 above the important criteria and requirements that the people are not only present around the celebrant, but also perform their task of inviting the president (who must be a duly ordained and properly authorized priest or minister) to celebrate for them. One problem that arises from using old drive-in movie theatres and following that model is that, even in a cinema, watching a film is essentially a *passive* event for an individual, and anyone else with whom one has come; being shut up in a car, which is essentially a tin can, separate and cut off from those around you, is hardly a model for a Christian church. In contrast, being a eucharistic community requires the people to be active and to participate, at the very least in singing the hymns, psalms, or songs, joining in the prayers, and—if the liturgists we studied in the last chapter, like Dom Gregory Dix, Myers, Hatchett, and Weil are correct—in allowing, permitting, or even inviting the president to celebrate on their behalf.

On the other hand, it seems that drive-in church services may actually be less passive than we might imagine: the *Time* survey noted "As always, Genoa's service included choral music; the audience was still audible as they sang along in their cars. 'We could hear some of them singing. A

6. See the report by Michael Doyle "Owensboro Pastor cites 1st Amendment in Drive-up Communion Service" in the *Evansville Courier & Press*, 30 April 2020: https://eu.courierpress.com/story/news/2020/04/30/owensboro-his-church-holds-parking-lot-communion-first-amendment-protest-henderson/3054112001/

7. Doyle,   https://www.epicenter.org/resources/covid-19-hub/virtual-liturgies/#holy-eucharist, p. 8.

couple of them, I wish I couldn't hear,' Carl says, laughing." And certainly one worshipper, Yolanda Obaze, interviewed at Bethel Church in Evansville, Indiana, very much appreciated being in her community: "It wasn't just one person sitting in a house, looking at a screen. There was that feeling again of having a family. . . . It felt good to know you had people around you. It was exhilarating. . . . I'm a single person here in Indiana—I literally have almost no one. To know that a church is saying, 'In spite of what's going on, we are going to do as much as we can and are thinking of you—that says a lot.'" Her pastor agreed: "We recognize there's a real mental health component to this. With isolation comes depression, anxiety, and fear. While we may not be able to shake hands or give each other hugs, it's still important to get as close to the community as we can, for people's health and well-being."

Meanwhile, back in 2014, NPR's Amy Kiley was also careful to interview some 'parishioners' of the Daytona Beach Drive-in Church, for whom life was not all Florida sunshine and open-top convertibles.

> When Shirley Oenbrink was battling stage 4 cancer, attending church provided her with strength through her illness, she says. But during her year of chemotherapy, she says she could barely get out of bed, let alone into a church pew. Now that she has beaten the cancer, having a private space during worship helps her cope with the emotional ups and downs of recovery. "It's the time to let the tears flow and you don't get questioned," she says. "I don't like for people to feel sorry for me. And when I cry, my eyes get big, my nose swells up. . . . I need to stay in my car."

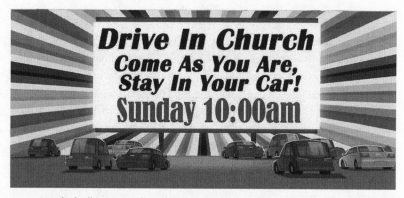

Similarly, "For Russell and Teresa Fry, who are legally blind, the ability to walk to the church and hear the service through speakers is important. They say they both carry wounds from discrimination at churches they've attended in the past. . . . The Frys say the church is a safe place for people who need privacy and healing, and that the congregation readily accepted them." As for congregational participation, "At the service's close, things get even livelier when people use their car horns to 'clap'!" In fact, some have gone so far as to devise a list of possible actions in a car to signal, literally, the worshipper's participation, as in the illustration below. Turning on hazard lights is a real invitation to those in cars around to pray for this one's occupant.[8]

DRIVE-IN CHURCH WORSHIP GUIDE

PARKING LIGHTS ON	HONKING
I am ready to worship	Preach it/amen/right on
HEADLIGHTS ON	LEFT TURN SIGNAL
I am singing along	I want to ask for forgiveness of my sins
RIGHT TURN SIGNAL	
Raising one hand in worship	HAZARD LIGHTS
	I am in need of prayer
WIPERS ON	
Lifting both hands in worship	SPRAYING WASHER FLUID
	I would like to be baptized

Before coronavirus, this Florida church also offered worshippers who could get out of their cars the opportunity to gather in the fellowship hall, which used to be the movie theatre's concession area. As Kiley's NPR broadcast concluded, now "it offers a Christian tradition that transcends even locked cars: doughnut hour!"

Today, however, in such "contagious times", the slogan for a drive-in church may have been transformed into a 'socially-distanced' version, "Come as you are—but stay in your car,"[9] but it is far from clear that the drive-in congregation is any less Christian than all the individuals and households confined to their homes watching services being livestreamed on their lap-tops and tablets under the various versions of 'lockdown' that were imposed around the world during the coronavirus pandemic.

And before we criticize such drive-in congregations 'shut up in their tin-cans' and not meeting anyone, we would do well to consider the great tradition (which is still continuing up and down the land) of the Church of England's weekly 8am Holy Communion service according to the 1662 Book of Common Prayer, attended by a small, but faithful, group of individuals who would sit in separate—and in some churches, even boxed-in—wooden

---

8. I am grateful to Bishop Pierre Whalon for alerting me to this interesting article which contains the illustrated list of car actions: https://www.relevantmagazine.com/faith/church/this-drive-in-church-worship-guide-is-somehow-real/

9. See for example, https://www.facebook.com/events/christ-church-baptist-fellowship/come-as-you-are-but-stay-in-your-car/910205196060546/

pews around the large, empty, and cold church as far from each other as possible, who would go up quietly into the chancel to 'make *my* communion' and then leave at the end of the service as quickly as possible, lest anyone should attempt to speak to them!

So, admittedly to my own amazement, I find myself at the end of this brief study gradually realizing that it would be unfair to label all such drive-in congregations as somehow defective or even un-Christian. Yes, there are perils to watch out for, and pitfalls to avoid, such as encouraging a passive attitude in an 'audience', passively watching a 'superstar preacher' or professional worship band 'performing' up at the front, and going away not having met or communicated with anyone else, as they are also in their self-contained vehicles, but such temptations and distractions are not necessarily intrinsic to this drive-in format—nor confined to it; they apply equally to all Christian churches, cathedrals, and congregations, especially those with a well-respected preacher or a famous choir with stacks of CD-recordings or BBC broadcasts behind them. Equally, the technology of much contemporary worship with its multiple screens, rows of microphone stands, instruments all set up, amplifiers and loudspeaker stacks providing a 'wall of sound', can become as much a barrier as any Orthodox iconostasis or mediaeval rood-screen, preventing the faithful from observing the holy mysteries practised by the clergy alone.

And during "contagious times" when the faithful are chained to their laptops, tablets, and phones, and being self-isolated behind locked doors, just like the apostles on the first Easter Sunday, a drive-in church following proper social distancing and the advertised health precautions might actually permit those same faithful to get out of their houses and watch worship through their windscreen rather than a computer screen, and to hear the word of God being read and preached through their car radio, to join in singing God's praises with all those in the other vehicles around—and yes, just maybe, yes, to be able to receive the bread and wine, the body and blood of our Lord Jesus Christ, consecrated before their eyes by their own priest or pastor, assuming, of course, that a safe way is practised of it being brought intact to their car window.

DRIVE-UP, DRIVE-BY, OR DRIVE-THRU COMMUNIONS

However, can the same be said of that quintessentially American practice, the 'drive-by', or, even worse, 'drive-thru'? Unlike the drive-in movie theatres perhaps, this way of obtaining or purchasing food, drinks, or other 'necessities' has become widespread everywhere. However, here there are at least two aspects that are intrinsic to the format that should give us pause before accepting it for Christian worship and much less, receiving the eucharist. The first is that *speed* is of the essence, with 'fast-food' outlets priding themselves on having your order prepared and ready to be collected at the exit, all done during the brief interval since it was placed, while you have been paying for it. The other, perhaps less obvious but even more inimical, aspect is the essential and thorough-going individualism of making your own choice, tailored to your personal tastes and desires. This cartoon encapsulates it beautifully:[10]

©Chris Morgan 1994   cxmedia.com

Of course, one might expect such drive-thru communions to be offered by the independent evangelical churches found all across the USA, especially in the so-called 'Bible-belt' in the south. One example is Freedom Church in Carrollton, Texas, which is pastored by Kendall and Starla Bridges, a couple who met in Bible College in 1981 and who now have four children and nine grandchildren, which is one way of growing a church! On March 21, 2020, when lockdown measures were beginning to take effect,

10. Taken from http://www.cxmedia.com/CWC10C?subject=5. We are extremely grateful to Chris Morgan for permission to use this cartoon.

they were "excited to announce our first Drive-Thru prayer and communion starting this Sunday. Drive up to the Freedom carport, remain in your car and you will be served communion elements and prayed for. No worries . . . our team will be wearing gloves and sharing pre-portioned, sealed, communion cups."[11]

However, this is not confined to such independent evangelical churches. On Sunday 15 March 2020, St. Thomas African Episcopal Church in Overbrook Park, West Philadelphia also allowed congregants to drive through their car port to receive a blessing and communion without getting out of their cars. This was in response to heath officials' recommendations to practice social distancing and to avoid large crowds during the coronavirus outbreak. The church asked anyone under self-quarantine or who did not feel well to stay home. The Very Rev'd Martin Shaw sanitized his hands between each congregant and parishioners were also required to sanitize their hands before accepting the sacrament.[12]

The *Philadelphia Inquirer* ran a wonderful sequence of photographs depicting cars queuing up in front of a robed acolyte with a large processional cross, while other acolytes processed the church's streamers around the street corners; the verger Lisa Stewart and Karen Ragland, both robed and wearing plastic gloves, squirted hand sanitizer on congregants' hands proffered through their car windows, while two churchmen "squeegied the

11. Taken from https://findfreedom.church/coronavirus/2020/3/21/the-drive-thru -is-open

12. See the report for Fox29 by Kelly Rule, "'Drive-thru Sacrament': Places of Worship Hold Alternative Services amid Pandemic" March 15, 2020: https://www.fox29. com/news/drive-thru-sacrament-places-of-worship-hold-alternative-services-amid-pandemic; see also @fox29philly pic.twitter.com/actf1wz31t and @kellyruletv.

front windshields of the cars as a sign of passing the peace of the Lord and as a symbol of clearing your vision for the days ahead"; several photos depict Father Shaw putting communion wafers into communicants' hands or on their tongues (with one woman giving him an extraordinarily hard stare!), followed by Father Gerald Collins using a traditional aspergillum and stoup to sprinkle holy water onto the vehicles and to give the occupants a final blessing.[13]

A similar approach has also been suggested as one way forward for Roman Catholics. For Catholics, regular attendance at mass is considered a sacred obligation. However, that same Fox29 news item also reported that bishops in numerous dioceses announced that they were "cancelling all public worship services, . . . in some cases indefinitely."[14] Among the Catholic bishops temporarily dispensing with the requirement that parishioners attend mass were the archbishop of Philadelphia, Nelson Pérez,[15] the archbishop of Los Angeles, José Gómez, the president of the U.S. Conference of Catholic Bishops, and Bishop David Zubik of Pittsburgh, who also urged parishes observing the locally popular tradition of parish fish fries during Lent to offer the fish only on a take-out basis, with no eat-in option! Similarly, the archbishop of Washington, Wilton Gregory, "issued a sweeping order indefinitely cancelling public Masses", along with the bishop of Salt Lake City, Oscar Solis, and the Archdiocese of San Antonio.

However, the Roman Catholic bishop of Beaumont, the Most Rev'd Curtis J. Guillory, SVD DD, wrote to his diocese in south-east Texas on May 1, 2020 to say that he was "easing some restrictions" that he had imposed in March. It is interesting to note that while the "suspension of liturgical/sacramental celebrations and public assemblies remains in effect throughout the diocese" along with the understandable "dispensation from the obligation to attend Mass on Sundays & Holy Days" continuing, none the less Bishop Guillory pronounced that "Pastors may set days and hours when parishioners may drive through a designated area of the parish to receive Holy Communion (only in the hand, no chalice) while inside their vehicles.

---

13. Michael Bryant, "Church Offers Drive-through Communion during Coronavirus Pandemic," March 15, 2020; https://www.inquirer.com/photo/drive-through-communion-service-20200315.html. I particularly encourage you to visit this web report and look at the set of twelve excellent photographs, taking you through the whole experience from driving in to the final blessing from Fr Collins peering through the car window!

14. https://www.fox29.com/news/drive-thru-sacrament-places-of-worship-hold-alternative-services-amid-pandemic

15. https://www.fox29.com/news/archdiocese-of-philadelphia-excuses-obligation-of-attending-sunday-mass-amid-coronavirus

Parishioners are encouraged to 'attend' a streamed Mass on the day they receive Communion."[16]

REFLECTIONS

It might help if we start with a comparison with another sacrament being offered for 'drive-by' in the situation of "contagious times", namely the sacrament of reconciliation, the practice of making an individual confession confidentially to a priest in order to receive absolution from God through him. According to the official publication of the Archdiocese of Dubuque, Iowa, *The Witness*,

> The coronavirus pandemic has led to a new spiritual innovation similar to the concept of a drive-thru car wash. Instead of cleaning vehicles, however, clergy around the world, including in the Archdiocese of Dubuque, are adapting the idea to help people cleanse their souls. Father Kyle Digmann, pastor of St. Thomas Aquinas Church and Catholic Student Center in Ames, is among priests now offering the sacrament of reconciliation to people who drive up to him. The participants maintain the recommended social distance while interacting with the pastor. . . .
>
> "Almost everyone that drives up has a smile on their face, partly due to the fact that drive-thru confession is a unique experience but also because they are grateful to still have the sacrament of God's mercy," he explained in an email to *The Witness*.[17]

The point here is that such an individualistic approach is essential, and even intrinsic, to the sacrament of reconciliation, with its focus on an individual's confession, penance, and absolution. Queuing up for a private conversation—"Forgive me, Father, for I have sinned"—through a car window is not really any different from the traditional wait to enter a confessional box to speak to a priest through a screen, and even less so for those who prefer a more face-to-face encounter. However, as we return now to holy communion, we will find, by contrast, that a corporate and participatory dimension is intrinsic to the sacrament, rather than reconciliation's individualism, and it is what which makes the difference.

16. https://www.thevindicator.com/article/news/drive-thru-holy-communion-coming-church-near-you

17. https://www.thewitnessonline.org/vocations/ames-parish-offers-drive-thru-confessions-as-coronavirus-prevention-efforts-continue/; for St. Thomas Aquinas Parish, visit https://staparish.net/

St Pugeot's midnight motor-masses were a huge success.[18]

Given the fact of everyone from independent evangelicals to Roman Catholics in Texas seemingly embracing drive-thru communions, it is not at all surprising, therefore, that the Episcopal bishop of Texas, the Rt Rev'd Andy Doyle, should devote several pages of his pastoral letter to this topic of drive-in and drive-thru communions:

> Both of these methods undermine the very core of the interactive, physical presence that we have already spoken of. They are not about our reunion, our ingathering, or our labor. They do not allow the kind of interactivity that is meant as the regular part of making Eucharist. One may participate in the Eucharistic making without consuming the elements. Christ is present regardless, and grace is administered. We might well remember that when a person does not receive the Wine for whatever reason at the rail, we are enacting this theology.

18. Used by permission, and with grateful thanks to Simon Jenkins.

While the 'drive-by' and the 'drive-in' models are inventive and creative, they undermine the essential participatory nature of Eucharist-making we discussed. By making 'giving the sacrament' an essential part of our life, we undermine the reality that Christ and grace is present and offered through the Gospel, the liturgy of the word, and by even being in the presence of Eucharistic celebration without consuming the Bread and Wine.

The cartoon above—interestingly published on October 7, 2019,[19] and so before anyone had even heard of COVID-19—echoes Bishop Andy's rejection of such drive-thru communion as the answer. For Bishop Doyle, drive-in communions 'undermine' the reunion, ingathering, interactivity, all required in the "essential participatory nature of Eucharist-making". While we argued above that drive-*in* churches could have as much 'participation' and 'interactivity' as many churches—and more than some, such as the individualistic, private 'making *my* communion' BCP tradition at 8 am—this clearly cannot be said of those who drive *up, by,* or *through* to collect communion as though it were the 'fast food' of heaven, which Robin Parry has termed 'McEucharists'![20]

This is essentially individualistic, and even if not tailored to your personal tastes and desires (no option for "would you like fries with that?"!), it reinforces the 'commodification' of the eucharistic bread and wine, 'getting mass' or 'taking communion,' about which Professor Thomas O'Loughlin complained, as we saw in our study of the eucharistic fast in chapter 2 above. While this led O'Loughlin to the eucharistic fast, Bishop Doyle's preferred option—"participate in the Eucharistic making without consuming the elements . . . being in the presence of Eucharistic celebration without consuming the Bread and Wine"—is essentially the 'spiritual communion' that we studied in chapter 3 above.

19. https://www.creators.com/read/for-heavens-sake/10/19/263482. © Michael Morgan. Used with permission.

20. See Andrew Walker and Robin Parry, *Deep Church Rising* (Eugene, OR: Cascade, 2015), 145–47.

Such antipathy towards the fast-food model in which we start with 'drive-up' and '-by', and then 'drive-thru' to collect individualistic communion elements before would-be communicants 'drive-away' as fast as possible, having had no contact with anyone else, let alone with hearing the word of God or pausing to join others in praise and prayer, is clearly correct. However, it is not quite accurate—or even fair—to the examples considered above. For both the Freedom Church in Texas and St. Thomas African Episcopal Church in Philadelphia, those who are encouraged to drive up and through are the regular communicants of those churches; and Bishop Guillory did tell his flock in Beaumont that "Parishioners are encouraged to 'attend' a streamed Mass on the day they receive Communion." However, the separation of the sacrament from the proclamation of the word, through scripture reading and preaching, and also from prayer and praise with others in the ecclesial community means that this can never be part of our solution.

On the other hand, Bishop Guillory's suggestion of 'attending' a streamed mass on the same day might provide a clue towards one way 'drive-thru' might be acceptable—and that is if it comes at the end of a livestreamed celebration in which the word of God was read and proclaimed along with prayer and praise in the ecclesial community of many others who were also participating in watching it. If the eucharist was celebrated as the climax of such a service, with the pre-packaged sealed units of bread and wine also on the altar to be blessed and prayed over in the *epiclesis* for the Holy Spirit to descend also on them and make Christ truly present in them, then people driving up to the church door or porch to put their hands (duly sanitized or clad in a protective glove, of course!) out of the window to receive them with thanksgiving is not so different from queuing up before the altar at the distribution. If the church has a large enough parking lot, and perhaps even some local wi-fi installed, communicants could participate in watching the service on their phones or tablets while waiting and queueing for their turn to 'drive-up'.

CONCLUSIONS—AND IMPLICATIONS FOR THE BREAD AND WINE

It is time to draw these reflections together. While for this Church of England priest, at least, such explorations 'boldly going' into the 'strange new worlds' of drive-in/up/by/thru/away communions may have begun with minimal expectation, in fact, the consideration of these practices outside my experience has brought to the fore some significant elements that are pertinent to our search, and that may yet prove useful for the hope of a solution.

First, our journey around drive-in churches revealed the unexpected conclusion that in many ways—for good and for ill—they are just like other churches, equally able to climb the heights of heaven and prone to the same temptations and pitfalls to the 'other place'. With regard to celebrating the eucharist, if this is done as the climax of a usual service, with the reading and exposition of the word of God, accompanied by praise and prayer in which the worshippers are encouraged to participate, leading to a celebration of communion before all the people and presided over by a duly trained and authorized minister or representative of the church—thus fulfilling the 'check-list' for a valid or effective eucharist which has been growing through recent chapters—then it is not immediately obvious why this should be invalidated simply because the elements of bread and wine are brought around to people in their cars, rather than in their pews or queuing up at the sanctuary. Of course, the temptations of the superstar preacher or the professional musicians turning what should be a participation in the worship of Almighty God into what becomes merely a passive watching of an impressive show are ever present, but no more or less so than any other church, chapel, or cathedral.

During "contagious times", the protection of being confined within the 'tin-box' of a car (especially if it is *not* an open-top convertible in the Florida sunshine!) may be safer for both the people and the priest or minister than physically sharing the same confined space in a church building, the vast majority of which have been shut down by government instructions or ecclesiastical authority—and with good reason. One example of a church that did not take the drive-in option should serve as a warning, taken from the digital magazine, Joy125.com:

> Virginia pastor Gerald O. Glenn had vowed to hold in-person church services, in defiance of a state public health order, and did so until he contracted the coronavirus in late March. Glenn died just one week later. During his last known in-person service, on March 22, Bishop Glenn spoke about COVID-19: "I firmly believe that God is larger than this dreaded virus. You can quote me on that. I am essential, I'm a preacher—I talk to God!" Now, his daughter Mar-Gerie Crawley says that she, her husband, her sister, and her mother (Glenn's widow) all have the coronavirus.[21]

21. https://joy105.com/4-family-members-of-pastor-who-died-of-covid-19-after-holding-services-caught-virus/

On the other hand, our consideration of drive-up/by/thru/away communions based upon the fast-food model of arriving by car to collect an individually chosen meal of food and drink and getting away as quickly as possible ('McEucharist') was immediately shown to be completely unacceptable. Not only does it come under Professor O'Loughlin's strictures about the commodification of 'getting mass' or 'taking communion', it completely fails Bishop Andy Doyle's requirements about the partnership between priest and people, with both clergy and laity participating fully in the celebration of the president on behalf of, and even at the invitation of, the people. It also separates the "proclamation of the Lord's death until he comes" (1 Cor 11.26) in the sacrament from the same proclamation of the same Lord's same death through the reading and preaching of the word—not to mention that it does not provide any opportunity for the people to respond to God's invitation and gift of himself in praise and prayer, nor to meet others and share fellowship, thus taking the *community* out of the *communion*.

We concluded the previous chapter on the possibility of lay presidency by adding a *third* requirement that the *presiding celebrant must be an ordained priest or minister* authorized so to preside at holy communion to our *two previous criteria* that at least one, and preferably *several people should be present* and receiving in addition to the celebrating president, and also that the *laity must be present* to exercise their role in participating with, or even inviting, the celebrant to preside. If the irony of the previous chapter was that a consideration of lay presidency led to the requirement of having an ordained celebrant, it is perhaps similarly ironical that this discussion around drive-in churches and drive-thru communions has led to a new, *fourth criterion*: we have seen that it is essential that *holy communion takes place in the context of, and preferably is the climax of, a full usual church service* preceded by the reading and exposition of the word of God, accompanied by praise and prayer in which the worshippers are encouraged to participate, and including an opportunity for general confession and making or celebrating peace with one's fellow worshippers. It is *this* criterion and requirement that has led us to the, perhaps surprising, conclusion that 'drive-in' churches can be just as much a valid expression of church as any congregation gathered in a building, and may face the same challenges and pitfalls. Equally, this criterion means that a 'drive-up' communion, where a worshipper in a car merely 'drives-thru' the church lot in order to collect a pre-packaged communion set, without having previously experienced any ministry of the word, or praise and prayer, and then 'drives-away' without any opportunity to meet and share fellowship with their sisters and brothers in Christ , belongs to the fast-food industry of a 'McEucharist' rather than to the church of our Lord Jesus Christ.

However, having said all of that, in "contagious times" when normal church services are not possible and God's people 'look hungry and are fed up' (rather than the proper 'look up and are fed'), perhaps there may be a place for some form of drive-up and collect communion, provided it satisfies this fourth requirement, as well as the other three. Therefore, any such 'drive-up' collection of communion elements must come in connection with (and preferably after) a full liturgical service incorporating praise and prayer, the reading and exposition of God's word, and all the communion bread and wine packages must be properly consecrated all together and at the same time by the duly ordained, trained, and authorized priest or minister.

Careful thought also needs to be given to how they can be reverently and safely distributed and consumed in accordance with whatever health regulations are currently in force, as well as any vessels or packaging dealt with appropriately afterwards. In fact, there are plenty of options available online, mostly based around a small sealed cup of the sort used for milk or coffee creamer in hotel bedrooms, trains and aeroplanes, and many coffee shops, but with a wafer in the lid separately on top.[22] Not surprisingly, the *Baptist Standard* reports a significant increase in sales of such pre-packaged communion units with one executive even claiming "a ten-fold increase".[23] Of course, with the Baptist tradition of using non-alcoholic grape juice and individual cups, it is understandable that they have been leading the way in producing these pre-packaged elements.

However, these non-alcoholic pre-packaged elements are not acceptable for Catholics, Anglicans, and many others, for whom it is also a further, *fifth*, requirement of canon law that the communion or altar wine should be the "fermented juice of the grape", and thus *alcoholic*. Roman Catholic priests must have "valid matter" to consecrate for a sacramentally valid mass, and Canon Law No 924 is clear that such "valid matter" must be bread made from wheat and wine

22. See, for example, the various options like the Fellowship cup available from Amazon, or for helpful instructions on how to open the wafer and the grape juice, https://www.celebratecommunion.com/prefilled-communion-cups.html

23. https://www.baptiststandard.com/news/faith-culture/sales-up-for-prepackaged-lords-supper-elements/

made from grapes; in addition, the bread must be "unleavened" according to Canon 926, while the wine must be pure and not corrupted into wine vinegar, or adulterated either with extra sugar, or fortified with brandy or other spirits as in port.[24] For a priest knowingly to use any other substances at the consecration would be an offence, and he and those who received such a sacramentally invalid communion would be in spiritual peril, as well as not having fulfilled their eucharistic obligations.[25] Interestingly, Quentin Letts wrote in the *Telegraph* some twenty years ago that in canon law, "there is nothing about making it 'sweet as fudge.'"![26]

For Anglicans, Canon B 17, paragraph 2, of the Church of England states: "The bread, whether leavened or unleavened, shall be of the best and purest wheat flour that conveniently may be gotten, and the wine the fermented juice of the grape, good and wholesome." In response to a query about so-called 'non-alcoholic' or 'low-alcohol wine', which can contain up

to 0.5% alcohol, the Legal Advisory Commission of the General Synod of the Church of England decreed that "wine from which all the alcohol has been removed would be contrary to the canon law and its use during Holy Communion contrary to ecclesiastical law. If, however, some alcohol remains, such wine may legally be used."[27] This requirement for the wine to be alcoholic means that there are fewer options for pre-packaged communion elements, although the TrueVine prefilled Chalice (illustrated) does provide an

24. See https://canonlawmadeeasy.com/2017/09/14/canon-law-and-simulating -the-mass/ and https://canonlawmadeeasy.com/2011/01/06/the-eucharist-and-sac- ramental-validity-part-ii/; see also the Redemptionis Sacramentum No 50, quoted in https://www.ewtn.com/catholicism/library/table-wine-for-mass-4460

25. It would be interesting to know from where or how Bishop Guillory expected to get large numbers of pre-packaged communion elements of bread (only wheat) and wine (including alcohol) that satisfied canon law for his suggested 'drive-up' collections of communion for the Catholics of Beaumont, Texas.

26. https://www.telegraph.co.uk/foodanddrink/wine/3296516/Almost-left-crying- at-the-altar.html

27. For a downloadable pdf of the LAC's report with the canon laws and their decision and reasons, see https://www.churchofengland.org/sites/default/files/2017–12/non-al- coholic wine and gluten free bread.pdf; similarly, the Legal Advisory Commission also decided that Type 1 wafers in which a minimal amount of wheat gluten remains may be used, but not Type 2 made entirely from non-wheat products; for the distinction, see http://www.coeliac.org.uk/gluten-free-diet-lifestyle/the-gluten-free-diet/communion -wafers; https://www.coeliac.org.uk/document-library/1191-communion-wafer-list/

alternative with fermented wine.[28] An interesting discussion can be found in the *Drinks Business!*[29]

Furthermore, for those who believe in some form of Christ's real presence in the bread and wine, there is the additional issue of the ablutions, literally meaning, of course, the 'washing up'. For such Anglicans and catholics (of all 'c's), it is vital that any consecrated bread and wine is 'reverently consumed' at the end of the service, followed by what can range from a simple swilling out of the vessels with clean water, to quite an elaborate ritual involving both wine and water over several stages; in each case, any water, or wine, used must be also reverently consumed by the priest to avoid leaving behind 'fragments of our Lord' or 'drops of his blood'.[30] There are suggestions in some of the web articles about such drive-thru communions that there might be large refuse bins or trash cans by the exit where the cars drive out in which the worshippers can place their empty little cups and packaging to be recycled. For those concerned about elements of the real presence of Jesus remaining therein, the traditional options for the contents of such bins are of 'returning it to ground' by burying or burning it.

I little thought of including a chapter on drive-in/by/up/thru communions in this book, and even when I started writing it, the idea that it might end up being one of the longer chapters would have seemed preposterous. However, consideration of these practices has in fact led to a number of conclusions that are directly relevant to our search for a solution about how to celebrate holy communion in "contagious times" and helped us to develop significantly further our growing 'check-list' of the criteria for what constitutes a valid and effective eucharist by stressing as a *fourth* requirement the importance of *a full service of word and sacrament together*, including confession, praise and prayer. It has also produced a further, *fifth*, requirement, at least for Anglicans and Catholics, that according to canon law the *bread must be wheat and the communion or altar wine must be alcoholic*.

There is one more proposal in the everyday world that we need to consider before we can draw all these threads together, and finally venture into the so-called 'virtual', or preferably digital, world of online communions in Part II.

---

28. See https://www.truevinecommunion.com/ for both grape juice and wine options

29. https://www.thedrinksbusiness.com/2016/02/communion-wine-now-available-in-a-packet/

30. See our discussion of this in chapter 5 above and Bishop Mark Santer's somewhat facetious comment that "if Jesus can get himself *into* the bread and wine, he can presumably get himself *out* again!"

8

Proposal 7

Extending Further Extended Communion
for the Housebound and Sick Communions

THE SOUND OF THE post-communion anthem from the large, nation-
ally renowned choir began to swell perceptibly in volume as the last pair
of sides-men and -women turned from the altar rail, and made their way
slowly but steadily back to their pews, their tricky job of directing the traffic
of several hundred communicants up the centre of the nave, through the
chancel (running the gauntlet of the choir still singing *sotto voce*, but burst-
ing to be let loose *fortissimo* any moment), to the altar rails before the main
altar and the side chapel, and then back down the sides of the church having
been once again successfully performed—except, of course, for the one or
two usual suspects who insisted on going against the flow of the well-known
and obvious one-way system. As the fairly newly ordained curate in my deacon's year, 1985–86, and therefore still on my 'L-plates'[1] and not yet able
to preside at the eucharist myself, I brought the remains of the consecrated
bread and wine from the side chapel altar, where I had been distributing
communion, to my training incumbent, no less than the vicar of Bromley
Parish Church himself, resplendent in full eucharistic vestments and cope,
standing behind the main altar.

In front of him on the altar were half a dozen small portable communion sets for the ministry to our sick or housebound parishioners who

---

1. In the UK, 'Learner' drivers have to wear L-plates on a car when having lessons
before they pass their driving test and get their driving licence.

could not join us celebrating the great parish communion. After he had checked that each individual set had the right number of wafers in its pyx (a small circular container for the bread) and sufficient consecrated wine in its small bottle, he nodded to me—the usual sign for me to clear the rest of the table, take it all to the side chapel altar, and do the washing-up (officially known as 'ablutions', but which is only Latin for 'washing away'), reverently consuming any left-over consecrated bread and wine, perhaps with the assistance of the teenage sacristans (usually more interested in finishing up the wine than the rather dry wafers, it has to be said), while he got on with the important business of the climax of the service—the parish notices and the recessional hymn.

At the end of the notices, he asked everyone to be quiet and prayerful, as he read out the names written in front of each communion set praying for these absent members of our community in their different trials and tribulations. Then the various (appropriately trained and licensed) lay people, each collected the relevant set, and started solemnly to lead the procession, followed by the choir, inspired by the organist's shift up a gear now from merely 'fff' to 'beltissimo', out through the congregation. Sometimes they could go straight to the sick person's house or residential care home, though the latter's rules often meant waiting until after the Sunday roast had been served.

We have already noted in chapter 3 above, with regard to 'spiritual communion', the provision for both *the Visitation* and *the Communion of the Sick* in the 1662 Book of Common Prayer, complete with its interesting and important rubrics. This service was a self-contained, if somewhat shorter, service of holy communion conducted in the home, or even at the bedside, of the sick person. As we noted, Cranmer's rubrics required that usually several other people were present (giving us the criterion and requirement for *lay involvement*, noted in chapter 3 and 4 above), unless the sick person was so infectious that only the poor priest was permitted to share communion with them—at great risk to themselves. As the 'parish communion' movement in the earlier part of the twentieth century brought regular or weekly communion back into Anglican Sunday worship ("the Lord's Supper for the Lord's people on the Lord's Day" was its slogan), pressure began to grow for a greater sense of inclusion of the sick and housebound within church congregations, rather than these individual atomized services at people's bedsides. This fits in with another of our emerging criteria and requirements for a valid and effective eucharist, that it takes place *in the context of a full church service*, including the ministry of the word, praise, and prayer, with the opportunity for fellowship with others, as we just saw in the last chapter.

The move towards this kind of 'take-out' communion for the sick and housebound was helped by the patristic precedent of deacons taking communion out to sick members of the early Christian assembly, as we can see in the account by Justin Martyr (c. 100–165): "And when the president has given thanks, and all the people have expressed their assent, those who are called by us deacons give to each of those present to partake of the bread and wine mixed with water over which the thanksgiving was pronounced, *and to those who are absent they carry away a portion*" (Justin Martyr, *First Apology*, §65, my emphasis).

However, the careful reader might well be justified in asking how such a 'take-out' communion can be justified, given our strictures against 'drive-thru' communions in the last chapter. There we noted the importance of communion *within the context of a full liturgical service*, including the ministry of the word, praise and prayer, and the opportunity for fellowship, and the requirement for it to be celebrated by a properly trained and duly authorized minister. First, with regard to the latter point, our communion-by-extension could only be taken to the sick and housebound by certain lay people, who had received some training and who had been authorized by the bishop as 'eucharistic ministers'—plus, of course, the fact that the actual eucharistic elements of bread and wine had been previously consecrated by not just any old priest, but the parish priest himself!

Secondly, these home communion visits were certainly not fast-food experiences or 'McEucharists'. I still have to this day a copy of the 1662 Book of Common Prayer (stamped inside with "Bromley Parish Church—do not remove"!) with all the various relevant parts of the communion service marked up to be read at the communicant's bedside, including the general confession and prayers of intercession. I used to marvel how many of the more elderly parishioners, including some moving into the lost world of senile dementia, would respond to the long-familiar cadences of the 1662 Book of Common Prayer; it was moving to see even those who usually had difficulty speaking easily forming the old words with their lips, words that I as a modern youngster would stumble over, such was the power of their memory, hallowed by years of regular worship. Furthermore, we would always include a Bible reading, often the passage set for that Sunday, and a word of encouragement, or repeat the main point of that morning's sermon, to ensure that both ministries of word and sacrament were combined.

Finally, the housebound and isolated individual was made to feel included as part of the main eucharistic community as we would remind them that their names had been read out and that everyone had prayed for them at the end of our main Sunday service. 'Fast' it was not, but 'food' it most certainly was—and the custom of using accredited lay eucharistic ministers (stalwarts of the church who had probably known them for decades) meant that often they would be able to spend more time with the housebound than the over-worked clergy could have managed. I was, therefore, deeply touched at my farewell service on leaving the parish at the end of my curacy to be presented with a pewter and silver home communion set, with a small chalice and paten, pyx, and two small bottles for wine and water, and even a small spoon for dribbling the 'blood of Christ' into mouths that could no longer drink from a cup, all duly and beautifully engraved—and I still use it regularly today.[2]

So the obvious question that arises from this story is what, if anything, we can learn, or even borrow to help us with holy communion in "contagious times", especially in a situation in which everyone is 'housebound' because of a lockdown. I know of many instances in the early days, at least, of the coronavirus pandemic, when use was made of this tradition of such housebound or sick communions. The eucharistic elements of bread and wine—which had been previously consecrated in a small service in the local church by a priest, with, of course, a few lay people present (to fulfil another of our criteria)—were subsequently distributed by those laity in addition to the priest around the parish to those who were self-isolating, so that they did not need to have a 'eucharistic fast' or merely 'spiritual communion' imposed upon them. It also helped to fulfil another of our requirements by

2. Photograph by the author; in actual fact, I have used it at our weekly online communion over the last eighteen months—more than in all my ministry put together!

stressing the importance of the whole people of God, including the sick and the housebound, in inviting the priest to celebrate for them.

Furthermore, I am sure that there must have been plenty of other clergy and parishes doing something similar to ensure that regular communions continued as long as regulations permitted. Therefore, so-called 'extended communion' seems to hold promising possibilities for "contagious times" in which many or most people are in some kind of lockdown. However, before we leap too quickly to pursue this course, we need to step back and consider some of the liturgical and theological controversy that has surrounded this whole question of extended communion—and I am afraid it is quite a long and complex saga.

EXTENDED COMMUNION
IN THREE MAIN UK DENOMINATIONS

Meanwhile, since my curacy in the mid-late 1980s, the waters have become very muddied indeed around the whole issue of 'extended communion', as is made helpfully clear in Phillip Tovey's definitive—but long and detailed— study. He explains the term thus, "Extended Communion may be defined as the distribution of previously consecrated elements to a congregation by a layperson (or a deacon) at *a public service in the absence of a priest*"[3] (my italics for emphasis). This definition makes it clear that he is talking about something different from my curacy experience: "this definition tries to ex- clude rites in support of ministry to the sick, although the use of previously consecrated elements for the sick means that there are some similarities."[4] Tovey candidly admits that "this is only one definition and in this field there is a great fluidity of terms, indeed, this is one of the substantial problems of studying Extended Communion, with over forty different titles being found for the phenomenon."[5]

In the last decades of the twentieth century, the three largest churches in England provided liturgies or orders of services for extended commu- nion, the Roman Catholics in 1988, the Methodists in 1999, and the Church of England in 2001. For the Roman Catholics, this has been driven by the

---

3. Phillip Tovey, *The Theory and Practice of Extended Communion* (Farnham, UK: Ashgate, 2009), 1.

4. Tovey, *The Theory and Practice of Extended Communion*, 1.

5. Tovey, *The Theory and Practice of Extended Communion*, 9; in fact, in his final conclusions at the end of the book, he notes that his original research "discovered *forty -nine* terms for the phenomenon under investigation, indicating its newness and insta- bility"; my emphasis.

increasing shortage of priests, leading to the publication in 1988 by the Sacred Congregation for Divine Worship of a 'Directory' allowing various Episcopal Conferences in different countries to produce liturgies for 'Sunday Worship in the absence of a priest', often shortened to the delightful acronym, SWAP. This is essentially a service, led by a deacon or authorized lay person, of the reading of the word and prayer, as in ante-communion, leading to the distribution of previously consecrated bread and wine as communion elements. Tovey makes it clear that there is "a clear hermeneutical problem" in relating SWAP to "previous Catholic practices, for example, distributing communion after the Mass, or indeed outside the Mass."[6] He then analyses how this has been developed in France, Germany, the USA, Canada, and the British Isles, and concludes that SWAP is "an innovation in the Roman Catholic Church. This conclusion is reached not least because of the distinctive feature of it being a lay-led service in the absence of a priest, a new milieu for the Roman Catholic Church. The consequences of this are yet to become fully apparent."[7]

This was followed in Britain in 1999 by a new service book from Methodist Church, *Methodist Worship*, which includes a service of 'Extended Communion'. Tovey notes that

> this is an act of worship using elements that have been "previously set apart at a service of *Holy Communion*" (Note 1, p. 229, original emphasis). This then could be seen as used in similar circumstances to those of the Roman Catholic Church, or the Church of England. However, Note 2 clearly says that the service could be led by a presbyter, deacon, or lay person, and even a lay person with a dispensation to preside at the Eucharist. It becomes clear in Note 4 that the recipients are to be those who are in a home or hospital.[8]

Therefore, it is clear that "Extended Communion becomes parallel to Communion for the Sick in the Roman Catholic Church and Church of England. However, even this statement must be nuanced, for we shall see that although the bishops of the Church of England have made a categorical distinction between Communion for the Sick and Extended Communion, in practice it is not so easy to make that distinction."[9] This Methodist service naturally draws on John Wesley's own concern for taking communion from a church service directly to the sick, following the precedent set by Justin

6. Tovey, *The Theory and Practice of Extended Communion*, 9.

7. Tovey, *The Theory and Practice of Extended Communion*, 28.

8. Tovey, *The Theory and Practice of Extended Communion*, 30.

9. Tovey, *The Theory and Practice of Extended Communion*, 30.

Martyr, of which he was aware.[10] If we may return to my 1980s curacy in Bromley for a moment, our parish church was part of a wider 'ecumenical parish' involving both the local URC and Methodist churches, so that we often shared liturgical and pastoral practices (including the Methodist female minister celebrating communion when it was her turn to host our regular ministry team meeting in her church; 'when in Rome . . .') . Tovey refers to this "crossover of practice is going on with Anglicanism, that is, Extended Communion in Methodist terms is becoming Extended Communion in Anglican terms."[11] He then concludes "while Methodists have a service called 'Extended Communion', this is not the same as the Church of England usage, indicating some essential differences in the 'genius' of each denomination. Extended Communion in Methodism is for the sick and housebound."[12]

THE CHURCH OF ENGLAND

Tovey then turns his attention to the Church of England and the Anglican Communion. In order to explain why, and fortify us for the tortuous account ahead, it is worth quoting the opening of his chapter 4 in some detail:

> In 2001, the Church of England produced for the first time an official service of Extended Communion (Archbishop's Council, 2001). This event has been described by David Hebblethwaite, the then secretary to the Liturgical Commission, and a key participant in the process, as, "One of the most controversial and theologically divisive issues in this period. . . . So sharp were the divisions that it was unclear until the Final Approval vote . . . whether it would be authorized" (2004: p. 42).[13] This controversial rite was not published in the main *Common Worship* volume for use on Sundays, but exists as a separate booklet (and is available for download from the Church of England's website). It is an unusual piece of Church of England liturgy in that, although authorized by Synod, it may only be used locally with the explicit permission of the bishop. This is the only liturgy in the *Common Worship* services that has this standing.[14]

10. Tovey, *The Theory and Practice of Extended Communion*, 34.

11. Tovey, *The Theory and Practice of Extended Communion*, 36.

12. Tovey, *The Theory and Practice of Extended Communion*, 49.

13. David Hebblethwaite, *Liturgical Revision in the Church of England 1984–2004: The Working of the Liturgical Commission* (Joint Liturgical Studies; Cambridge: Grove, 2004). In fact, it scraped by with only two votes to spare as we shall see later.

14. Tovey, *The Theory and Practice of Extended Communion*, 51.

As with Roman Catholics, the background for this development came out of the renewed stress on the centrality of (weekly) communion in the context of shortages of clergy, especially in rural areas. However, given that the evangelical liturgist Colin Buchanan recorded one of the early Anglican uses of the phrase 'extended communion' in 1972 as being about communion of the sick, Tovey asks, "in practice, is the distinction between Communion of the Sick and Communion by Extension as clear as is assumed by this policy document?"[15]

He quotes a letter to the *Church Times* in 1979 from Bishop Richard Hanson, then professor of historical and contemporary theology at the University of Manchester, in response to its article "Laity to the Rescue" (by D. Smethurst, 1979), saying that "Extended Communion contradicts the Eucharist as an act of the people through the priest, obscures the truth that the Eucharist is an offering by the local church, and puts an undesirable emphasis on the technical capacity of the ordained to consecrate the elements."[16] It is perhaps significant how Hanson's comments echo our developing criteria and requirements for a valid and effective eucharist in its stress on the role of the laity.

Tovey then charts the equally extended debate—and indeed, controversy—around extended communion in the Church of England during 1980s and 1990s, as documented by Colin Buchanan in his regular pamphlets, *News of Liturgy*; it was opposed by some conservative evangelicals (such as Roger Beckwith), but they were not alone: thus Paul Avis "questions the theological, sacramental and liturgical integrity of the service, saying that evangelicals dislike it because it stressed a magic moment of consecration and Catholics dislike it because it lacks the element of offering to God. From this, he develops his fundamental point that it fragments the integrity of the eucharistic community, not least because the eucharistic president is absent and distantly magical."[17] Once again, we note another echo of our criteria and requirements.

Dr Christina Baxter (later principal of St John's Nottingham and chair of the House of Laity) argued against extended communion at the 1993 General Synod because the word is separated from the sacrament, particularly by not having the narrative of institution, and discussed "a number of alternatives, including ordaining local leaders or lay presidency, possibly

---

15. Tovey, *The Theory and Practice of Extended Communion*, 55.

16. Tovey, *The Theory and Practice of Extended Communion*, 58. Tovey is paraphrasing Hanson here.

17. Tovey, *The Theory and Practice of Extended Communion*, 58–59.

by Readers",[18] she being a reader herself. Interestingly, later Glenn Davies, then bishop of North Sydney but archbishop of Sydney and Metropolitan of New South Wales 2013–2021, argued that "Communion by Extension is a departure from the Book of Common Prayer and there was no attempt to consult the Anglican Communion about this departure. He saw this as a justification for Sydney to go forward with lay presidency."[19] Those from the conservative evangelical tradition, like Sydney, would also have not been at all happy at the use of the reserved sacrament to administer communion by extension, even though the *Final Report* of Anglican Roman Catholic International Commission (ARCIC) on Eucharistic Doctrine comments, "Communion administered from the reserved sacrament to those unable to attend the eucharistic celebration is rightly understood as an extension of that celebration."[20]

Tovey notes that similar debates were taking place around the Anglican Communion and the topic was also raised at several Lambeth Conferences. But for the Church of England itself, there was "a long and tortuous process running over two Synods and with a sub-discussion on lay presidency"[21] required by a Private Member's Motion achieving the necessary number of signatures. In 1993, Christina Baxter "begged the bishops to withdraw the proposals. Her objections . . . used the symbolic terms 'some kind of ecclesiastical take-away', 'eucharist meals on wheels', 'hosts through the post', 'picnic communion.'"[22] Again, we have an echo of our discussion around drive-in and drive-thru eucharists.

In yet another debate four years later in 1997 (by which time I had myself become a member of General Synod, eventually representing the University of London for over twenty years, 1994–2015), the Rev'd Patience Purchas raised the issue of the way the consecrated elements were cared for. Always a colourful character to say the least, she explained that "One of the lowest points in my ministry was one August Sunday morning some years ago. . . . I arrived in good time and went into the vestry, as one does,

18. Tovey, *The Theory and Practice of Extended Communion*, 59.

19. Tovey, *The Theory and Practice of Extended Communion*, 59; describing, not quoting, Davies' argument.

20. Anglican Roman Catholic International Commission, *The Final Report* (London: CTS/SPCK, 1982), 23; quoted in Tovey, *The Theory and Practice of Extended Communion*, 61.

21. Tovey, *The Theory and Practice of Extended Communion*, 63.

22. General Synod of the Church of England, *Report of Proceedings* (London: General Synod, 1993), 904. Tovey has a fuller version of this quote from Baxter on page 66, which distinguishes her objections from what she quotes some people as saying—an important distinction: "Her objections were that it defaces the Eucharist. . . . Some people used the symbolic terms 'some kind of ecclesiastical take-away' . . . ."

to find the churchwarden busy filling the chalice from a large lemonade bottle labelled 'consecrated wine'. Beside her was a Tupperware box labelled 'consecrated wafers'. . . . I asked God's forgiveness and did the best I could do in the circumstances."[23] At the other end of the ecclesiological spectrum, the leading Anglo-Catholic traditionalist Prebendary David Houlding the following year also rejected extended communion, saying, "The Eucharist makes the Church, and only a full celebration of the Eucharist."[24] He thus anticipated Pope John Paul II's 2003 encyclical about the relationship of the church and the eucharist, *Ecclesia de Eucharistia*, which we considered in chapter 3 above. At the 1998 Revision Committee, David Phillips commented that "the call for this service is driven by the falling numbers of full-time clergy. However, it assumes that what matters at the Lord's Supper is whether a Priest has said the magic words over the bread and wine, rather than whether the people of God receive the bread and the wine by faith."[25]

Eventually, the final debate took place in 2000 (no less than the twentieth stage in this extraordinary process!), on *Public Worship with Communion by Extension* in which final approval needed a two-thirds majority in each house.[26] Tovey records laconically, "a number of significant points were made in the debate"[27] before the motion was finally put by Houses requiring a two-thirds majority in each, which was easily achieved in the House of Bishops (28 to 2, the two 'noes' being interesting, given that it was actually their Lordships' report) and the House of Clergy (137 to 34, in which I am sorry to admit that I cannot remember now which way I voted). However, in the House of Laity, chaired by Christina Baxter and historically with more, often retired, evangelical members, it was passed by only 131 to 64; the opponents would have needed only two more votes to defeat it, and it would have fallen completely, despite being passed by the bishops and the clergy. Colin Buchanan commented in his inevitable editorial in *News of Liturgy*, "The last figure caused a gasp. It was a close-run thing."[28] Significantly, David Hebblethwaite, then secretary of the Liturgical Commission, felt it necessary to point out that "this rite is unique as a fully authorized liturgy in

23. General Synod of the Church of England, *Report of Proceedings* (London: General Synod, 1997), 397–98.

24. General Synod of the Church of England, *Report of Proceedings* (London: General Synod, 1998), 80.

25. Tovey, *The Theory and Practice of Extended Communion*, 67.

26. The House of Bishops, *Public Worship with Communion by Extension*, GS 1230C (London: General Synod, 2000); quoted in Tovey, *The Theory and Practice of Extended Communion*, 67.

27. Tovey, *The Theory and Practice of Extended Communion*, 67.

28. Colin Buchanan, "Editorial," *News of Liturgy* 308 (2000), 1.

the Church of England, alternative to the provision of the Book of Common Prayer, which is only available for use in a diocese if the bishop gives express permission for it to be used. There are currently some dioceses where it is used and others where it is not."[29] Speaking personally, I find it interesting that I have never been aware of such a service of extended communion being led by a lay person from previously consecrated elements happening in the last twenty years, although admittedly, since I am a priest, it would not have been needed anywhere that I was around.

The Rev'd Dr Paul Roberts, who teaches liturgy at Trinity College, Bristol wrote to me to suggest that: "There are two reasons for reticence over taking this development in the liturgical practice of the Church of England: the first is that issue of the purpose of 'consecrated elements' outside of the actual context of a eucharistic celebration (this is generally the concern of the evangelical end) and the other is the idea that it tends to dissolve the liturgical dynamic of the gathering and dismissal of the Body, which is normally necessary for Christians to celebrate the eucharist. The latter issue is a particular problem, as the gathering and dismissal of a physical fellowship is a key link to Pauline eucharistic teaching in 1 Corinthians."[30]

We have spent quite a bit of time and space on recounting this elongated tale, not least because it touches on so many of our developing *list of criteria and requirements* for a valid and effective eucharist, from lay presidency to the relationship of the laity to the priest, especially in permitting or inviting a priest to celebrate communion, as well as ideas about the 'magic' role of the eucharistic words of the institution of the Lord's Supper, not to mention descriptions of "ecclesiastical take-away" and "eucharist meals on wheels", along with concerns about transporting the sacrament in plastic bottles and boxes, more redolent of our recent discussion of 'drive-in churches' and 'drive-away communions' in the previous chapter. If you still want yet more information, see Tovey's detailed account in chapter 4 of his definitive book.[31]

FURTHER RESEARCH AND REFLECTIONS

Tovey concludes his analysis of the provision for extended communion in these three churches, by noting "a gap in the meaning of the term 'Extended

29. David Hebblethwaite, *Liturgical Revision in the Church of England 1984–2004: The Working of the Liturgical Commission* (Joint Liturgical Studies; Cambridge: Grove, 2004), 43; quoted in Tovey, *The Theory and Practice of Extended Communion*, 68.

30. Personal email of April 25, 2020; quoted with his permission.

31. Tovey, *The Theory and Practice of Extended Communion*, 77.

Communion' between Anglicans and Methodists in theory, but some merging of practice (in a few incidents). There is a commonality between Anglicans and Roman Catholics in that one of the key driving factors is a shortage of (or uneven distribution of) priests. A saying in received wisdom is that Extended Communion is a liturgical solution to a ministerial problem (cf. Huck, 1989)."[32] He continues a few pages later by turning to the "relationship of Extended Communion to ministerial provision: from a problem-solving perspective, Extended Communion may be a short-term fix to a longer-term problem (Mitchell, 2002). The problem is that of providing adequate numbers of ministers to lead Holy Communion."[33] However, he does not "accept the situation as a straight choice between Extended Communion or more priests. The overwhelming argument of liturgical scholars is that Extended Communion should be prohibited."[34]

Therefore, Tovey describes in Part I a detailed "qualitative enquiry into the practice of Extended Communion in the Archdeaconry of Berkshire in the Diocese of Oxford,"[35] which he undertook in 2003–5 against the background of "the prevailing story of pastoral reorganization in response to declining numbers of stipendiary clergy."[36] This study included all our usual suspects, such as the contrast between rural and urban settings, continuing opposition to the ministry of women priests, the development of a new form of lay ministry, including the arguments again about lay presidency, the "connection of the Word and the Sacrament of Communion",[37] and the use of "seemly containers for the consecrated elements",[38] most of which have been appearing in our discussions so far, as well as in our developing criteria and requirements for a valid and effective eucharist.

Also relevant for our concerns is the unnamed bishop who

> justified Extended Communion by the doctrine of economy: 'I can see how with fewer clergy . . . [this] will become a more widespread practice, and I think we have to somehow get the message across that this should not become normative, and that this is an interim arrangement and something to do with the

32. Tovey, *The Theory and Practice of Extended Communion*, 75, quoting G. Huck, "Why Settle for Communion?" *Commonweal*, January 27, 1989, 37–39.

33. Tovey, *The Theory and Practice of Extended Communion*, chapter 5, 76, quoting N. D. Mitchell, "The Amen Corner: Short-Term Solution or Long-Term Problem?" *Worship* 76.5 (2002), 456–66.

34. Tovey, *The Theory and Practice of Extended Communion*, 77.

35. Tovey, *The Theory and Practice of Extended Communion*, 165.

36. Tovey, *The Theory and Practice of Extended Communion*, 117.

37. Discussed in Tovey, *The Theory and Practice of Extended Communion*, 147–48.

38. Discussed in Tovey, *The Theory and Practice of Extended Communion*, 146–47.

doctrine of economy. . . . [I]t is better than . . . not being able
to receive communion at all and it is a way of the Eucharistic
community being together and receiving communion. But that
we really need to think more deeply about ordaining people to
celebrate the Eucharist and encouraging local vocations.[39]

And finally, Tovey noted once again "the issue of the boundary between Extended Communion and ministry to the sick, and there is sufficient evidence to show that in practice the distinction between the two is
misunderstood."[40] This is exacerbated by the wide range of other titles and
descriptions being used, as well as a wide variety in practice on the ground
between and even among the three denominations, all of which are grap-
pling with the decline in clergy numbers. Relevant to our concerns about
the crisis facing holy communion in "contagious times" are his final points:

> The conclusion of this book after in-depth research, both
> theoretical and practice, is that Extended Communion may be
> appropriate in emergency situations . . . and its authorization
> needs to be set within a long-term plan of ministry develop-
> ment. . . . However, the empirical investigation suggests that this
> will need critical ongoing assessment of both the practice and of
> policy, if an emergency is not to become a norm.
>
> Extended Communion is a post-war development of a
> number of Churches in Britain (and across the world). In light
> of the shortage of ministers, Churches have allowed lay-led ser-
> vices with the distribution of previously consecrated elements.
> This new occurrence is a controversial theological and practi-
> cal development. New forms of ministry are emerging with lay
> teams and lay ministers of Extended Communion. The new
> liturgical practice threatens theory and practice developed from
> Vatican II and the Parish Communion movement, perhaps re-
> turning to older models of receiving 'my communion' and of
> the elements 'as a thing'. Ecclesiologically new models of parish
> are emerging that are lay-led, with clergy overseeing a number
> of such parishes. Extended Communion is one area in the life
> of the Churches where practice challenges espoused theology,
> not always in desired ways, and if nothing else, this book dem-
> onstrates the significance of liturgical practice as a location of
> theoretical development.[41]

39. Tovey, *The Theory and Practice of Extended Communion*, 159–60.

40. Tovey, *The Theory and Practice of Extended Communion*, 165.

41. Tovey, *The Theory and Practice of Extended Communion*, 176, 178.

This consideration for further extending ideas of 'extended communion' or 'communion by extension' (choose your own term) may have itself been extended too far for some readers (sorry!), but it has actually proved both helpful and salutary. It has brought together several threads running throughout this book so far, including the widely felt 'need' for *regular communion* (further implying that neither the *eucharistic fast* nor *spiritual communion* are sustainable solutions, particularly in the long term), the importance of *priestly consecration*, rather than *lay presidency*, together with the necessary *full involvement of the laity*, especially a housebound lay person's *expressed and signified desire to receive the body and blood of our Lord Jesus Christ* in the context, not of an individualized solitary or private communion, but as part of the *wider worshipping eucharistic and ecclesial community*, holding together *both word and sacrament together* with prayer and individual concern and support.

Extending Further Extended Communion even further[42]

In addition, it has also raised other issues, ranging from the importance of *'seemly' vessels for the storage and transport* of the previously consecrated elements to concerns about the *health and safety* of both the ministers and those receiving communion. Finally, it confronts us with a warning about the potential dangers in making decisions and undertaking practices in extreme times of pressure and contagious infections that could have unfortunate implications for the longer-term future of the church and her sacraments, as, when, or if, anything like 'normal services' are eventually restored. Paul Roberts echoes this warning: "I wonder whether the Church of England would regard the practice of Extended Communion as a defining practice of its eucharistic theology? I suspect its use falls more into the

42. Cartoon drawn especially by Simon Jenkins, to whom we are very grateful and for permission to use it here.

category of a rubric of permissibility, rather than a practice which defines our theology."[43]

However, the possibility that it might furnish one possible solution to the difficulty of celebrating holy communion with large congregations in churches was, in fact, soon stopped when the Church of England's hierarchy decided to shut down parish churches even for the small livestreamed eucharists,[44] which were actually permitted by the British government's Statutory Instrument of the day before.[45] In addition, the restrictions later imposed in the UK on 'essential' workers of leaving deliveries on the door step and standing back the six feet required by 'social distancing' would have made the attempt to spend time on the other aspects of the service, such as prayer and the ministry of the word, very difficult, to say the least.

CONCLUSIONS

Nonetheless, in conclusion, we need to confront the question of whether some form of holy communion by extension, using previously consecrated elements, could in fact possibly contribute towards a solution for our difficulties regarding communion in "contagious times". Clearly, this perceived need for holy communion reinforces our reluctance to retreat to a *eucharistic fast* or *spiritual communion*, and provided that the bread and wine have been *properly consecrated by an ordained and/or duly authorized minister* in the context of a celebration in which the *laity were involved*, containing the *ministry of the word as well as the sacrament*, and opportunities for *praise, prayer, and fellowship*, this does actually fulfil many of our criteria and requirements. Therefore, it is hard to see a good reason for prohibiting it—other than, of course, the obvious issues of health and safety, social distancing, and infection control.

---

43. Personal email of April 25, 2020; quoted with his permission.

44. See the Archbishops' Third Letter of 27 March 2020, which made it clear that they were actually going *beyond* the Government's regulations: '20200327 Letter from Archbishops and bishops_1.pdf', available for download at https://www.churchofeng-land.org/more/media-centre/news/new-reflection-issued-people-who-cannot-attend-funeral

45. Statutory Instrument, The Health Protection (Coronavirus, Restrictions) (England) Regulations 2020, issued on March 26, 2020, paragraph 5.(6): "*A place of worship may be used (a) for funerals, (b) to broadcast an act of worship, whether over the internet or as part of a radio or television broadcast, or (c) to provide essential voluntary services or urgent public support services*"; https://www.legislation.gov.uk/uksi/2020/350/con-tents/made; pdf available as "uksi_20200350_en.pdf"

The Episcopal bishop of Texas, Bishop Andy Doyle, also raised these issues of health and safety concerns, including transmission and infection, in his pastoral letter:

> Another idea was pre-packaged and delivered wafers to parishioners' doorsteps. Also, sending pre-blessed miniature cups and wafers through the mail. Several health professionals in Houston admit that there is not enough science yet on this novel virus, but that it is most likely not a good idea for anyone to add to unnecessary mail. The virus lives on surfaces for different periods—some for more than 17 days. Furthermore, the fact that asymptomatic people pass it to others makes the practice of mailing items (especially items to be digested), not a good idea.[46]

However, one might imagine, for instance, that the original consecration took place in a small service in the local church (when those are permitted by government regulations and instructions from bishops or other senior church leaders or authorities) attended by a few lay people, hopefully recognized as eucharistic ministers. It would also be extremely helpful if the service could be livestreamed in some way or form. Afterwards, the priest and those lay members so permitted, could deliver the consecrated elements (in appropriate seemly and healthily protected containers—perhaps an Anglican/Catholic version of the pre-packaged elements studied in the last chapter, containing alcoholic wine?) in the same manner as other 'essential delivery workers', such as wearing protective gloves (and face-masks?). This might entail placing the elements with due reverence on suitable plates or cups that have left out ready on the door-step by the would-be communicant, and then retreating the safe social distance of six feet or whatever up the path. If the would-be communicants have already participated in at least watching the livestream of the service, then their reception of the bread and wine is merely delayed compared with if they had been in church, but perhaps the delivering minister (lay or ordained) could say some kind of prayer or blessing for them from a safe, 'socially-distanced' position. If the communicants have not been able to participate or watch any kind of livestream, not having a computer or internet access, one possibility might be for someone to phone them at the start of the service, so that they could at least listen to it. But if none of this has been possible, then the delivery

---

46. Bishop Doyle, https://www.epicenter.org/resources/covid-19-hub/virtual-liturgies/#holy-eucharist, p. 2; he also adds a footnote to say "I would add that only the most necessary clinics, food pantries, and essential care services continue with the utmost care."

minister could attempt to read some portion of the scriptures, give a word of explanation or encouragement, and pray for the communicant at the door, before they receive. In such a way *all our various criteria and requirements for a valid and effective communion could be met*—but the practical concerns about health and safety and the necessary avoidance of infection and transmission may just make it impossible.

With this one possibility arising from communion by extension, whatever nomenclature is used, plus the other one emerging from the previous chapter of a drive-up collection of communion elements after a livestreamed full service—both of which still need the issues of health and safety, transmission and infection control properly dealt with, though that is beyond the scope of this book—being about the only feasible options for receiving holy communion in "contagious times" in the everyday, physical world, it is time to pull all these criteria and requirements together, before we voyage into the 'virtual' or digital world of online communions.

9

Summary of Part I Conclusions

OUR STUDY OF THE various possible options and proposals about holy communion in "contagious times" in the everyday, physical world has produced a number of 'criteria' or requirements, which it would be good to collect together before we move to the new so-called 'virtual' or digital world of online celebration.

From chapter 1, we discovered the deep attachment to **celebrating communion in places of worship**, like parish churches, as also evidenced by the direct instructions of the 1662 Book of Common Prayer for daily prayers and regular communion services. While it is clearly possible to celebrate it in the archbishop of Canterbury's kitchen, the general reaction showed that the decision by the (arch)bishops of the Church of England to close churches completely, even for the clergy to pray and celebrate communion as required by the Book of Common Prayer, was definitely a mistake—and it is interesting that some of our brother and sister churches (like the Roman Catholics), as well as places of worship for other faiths like some mosques and synagogues, were able to take advantage of the British government's permission for *prayer and essential services to take place in church under strict social distancing and health directions.*

In chapter 2, we considered the idea of a 'eucharistic fast'. While this is clearly possible, and has indeed been the experience all too often of many Christians under persecution or in remote areas of the world over the centuries, to undertake voluntarily the **spiritual discipline of fasting from communion**, which is the major practice given by God to assist our spiritual life, seemed **illogical and unnecessary** unless all other options have been explored.

The consideration of 'spiritual communion' in chapter 3 reached similar conclusions. While this has again been important in certain situations and circumstances of sickness or isolation over the centuries, the headlong rush to this as a universal 'go-to' solution *does not fulfil the rubrics of the Book of Common Prayer, nor the 'strict conditions' required by those who developed it*, like the bishop of Melanesia in 1916.

Chapter 4 discussed the current permission being given by various bishops in different churches for 'solitary communions', where clergy celebrate the eucharist on their own. Such "imperfect celebrations" were shown to be directly counter to Cranmer's instructions, the rubrics of the Book of Common Prayer, the whole Anglican tradition, and recent Catholic liturgical reforms—and therefore not an option that should be pursued. Instead, for a celebration of communion to be valid and effective, *it must require at least one other person in addition to the celebrant, and preferably at least several more.*

This led us to explore 'con-celebrations' of the eucharist in chapter 5. This practice, especially when connected to a bishop or priest livestreaming their celebrations online (to which we shall return in Part II), does go some way to counter both the unfortunate appearance of a solitary celebrant feeding just themselves, while others feel excluded and go spiritually hungry. However, it only extends the circle of inclusion to other priests who can celebrate communion along with (hence the 'con' in concelebrate) the bishop or celebrating priest, and raises questions about whether it really is a *single* concelebration of the one bread and one cup, or multiple simultaneous, but still individualistic, communions. This led us to another criterion or requirement, that *there should always be the full participation by the laity in the celebration of the one bread and one cup if we are truly to be one body.*

Discussion of the sometimes suggested possibility of 'lay presidency' in chapter 6 took us into a deeper reflection on the various understandings of the eucharist across Christian traditions, from more 'catholic' theologies of the 'real presence' of Christ in the communion elements to purely symbolic or memorialist Zwinglian approaches. It also revealed a range of ideas about the nature of a priest or ordained minister. But whether one believes in a special, indelible character of priesthood, or not, we saw that it is an almost universal requirement of the Christian churches since antiquity that *the celebrant should be a priest or otherwise ordained, authorized, and recognized minister*, and that even those proposing to extend this to some lay people will still require them to be trained and authorized.

An exploration into the 'strange new worlds' (at least for myself as the writer) of 'drive-in churches' and 'drive-thru communions' in chapter 7 actually proved to be surprisingly helpful and productive in developing both our understanding of the church, generally known as 'ecclesiology', and of the proper liturgical setting for receiving communion. This demonstrated that for a valid and effective communion, it needs to be *in the context of a full church service, inextricably linked to the ministry of the word in reading the scriptures and exposition of them, as well as confession, praise and prayer, and opportunities for fellowship with one's sisters and brothers in Christ.* This criterion suggested that it is indeed possible for many 'drive-in' congregations to be real churches, as much as any congregations in a building—and prone to similar temptations and pitfalls. However, unlike the individualist nature of the sacrament of reconciliation, confession, and absolution, where this may be possible, *so-called 'drive-up' and 'drive-thru' collections of previously consecrated and pre-packaged communion elements, which are separate and divorced from the service in which they were consecrated, do not satisfy this requirement,* but belong rather to the somewhat surreal world of the 'McEucharist'.

However, we did suggest that *one real possibility for receiving holy communion in "contagious times"* could be if the people drive up safely isolated in their vehicles to a church at the end of a livestreamed full service, including the ministry of the word, praise, and prayer, which they have followed online, in order to collect the packaged communion elements that had just been consecrated for them—provided that all the health and safety issues, especially regarding transmission and infection control could be resolved. In addition, we also discovered that for those in the Anglican and Catholic traditions, it is a further requirement of canon law that *the bread must be made from wheat and that the wine must be "the fermented juice of the grape"* and therefore containing some alcohol at least.

Our discussion of 'extended communion' and 'communion by extension' in chapter 8 revealed something of a minefield, with many different names being used in various churches for services and activities that differ considerably. My own experience from early in my ministry was of 'extending' the main, corporate parish communion on a Sunday morning, by taking communion elements that had been consecrated therein out to the homes of the sick and housebound, rather than conducting lots of small individual communions at different sick-beds, as envisaged by Cranmer and the 1662 Book of Common Prayer. While this practice continues within the Church of England and in the Methodist Church, both the Roman Catholic Church and the Church of England now use 'extended communion' as a term for 'extending communion' to a service led by a deacon or lay-person through using previously consecrated bread and wine. While the issue of falling clergy numbers, which is what this is designed to help with, is a real concern across the churches, it is just the same in "contagious times" as in normal, so not relevant to our focus in this book. However, if we return to the concept of 'extension' to the sick and housebound, as in my curacy experience, it has some possibilities for a solution in "contagious times" where everyone is housebound in lockdown. Thus we suggested that, rather than the grand affair of the great parish communions in Bromley, a small service of celebrating holy communion in a local church could still fulfil the criterion and requirement of *a full church service, inextricably linked to the ministry of the word in reading the scriptures and exposition of them, as well as confession, praise, and prayer,* culminating in the celebrant and the few, but necessary, lay people present, who could then 'extend' the service out to people's homes, delivering the consecrated elements to *those who had shared in the service* either online, or at least by listening on a telephone, or by providing *a brief ministry of the word and prayer from the safe social distance* of six feet up the garden path.

However, both these 'real-world' possible solutions of, first, a drive-in full communion service or drive-thru collection of the elements immediately after a livestreamed service and secondly, extending a full communion service beyond the walls of a local church to the housebound by taking them the consecrated bread and wine afterwards, raise real concerns of *health and safety*, both for the clergy and eucharistic delivery ministers on the one hand, and for the communicants on the other regarding transmission and infection, which need detailed attention lest the sacrament of health and healing lead to sickness and death.

****

Given that significant possible danger in the 'real', physical world, it is time to turn to other suggested ways of celebrating communion in the 'virtual', digital world. However, our considerations of various proposals for holy communion in "contagious times" have very helpfully produced a kind of 'check-list' of the criteria and requirements for something to be considered a valid and effective celebration of the eucharist, which we have just gathered together in the conclusions above. It has also demonstrated that under the severe lockdown conditions of "contagious times" it is very difficult or indeed impossible to satisfy these conditions in the physical, everyday world. So that forces us to take our exploration in Part II into the 'virtual' or digital reality of the online world in celebrating holy communion in "contagious times" through our computers, laptops, tablets, and smartphones.

PART II

Holy Communion and Technology in the Digital Online World

10

Background 1

The Internet and the Rise of 'Cyber-church'

IF EXPLORING 'DRIVE-IN CHURCHES' and 'drive-thru communions' in chapter 7 felt like entering *Star Trek*'s 'strange new worlds', then the 'virtual world' of online communications is not just on another planet—it is in a completely different *universe!* Being asked to visit the world of the internet can seem very alien, let alone joining in activities there, and it feels significantly different from all that we know in the everyday or physical world. Of course, reactions to it among different Christians around the various churches can be very mixed, just like those from anyone else. Some embrace it completely, spending huge sums on the latest toy as soon as it emerges, others are more circumspect, and perhaps more than a few are too worried or anxious to go anywhere near it. It is worth, therefore, spending a little time considering how and why we got here. Please note, therefore, that in this chapter we are not considering any fresh proposals but stepping back to take a look at the wider background issue of the development of the internet within the history of communication and how it has come to dominate our lives—and also how the Christian church has reacted to it. This is important for the discussions about the possibilities for holy communion online that follow.

THE DEVELOPMENT OF THE INTERNET
AND THE WORLD WIDE WEB

Human beings have always tried to communicate with each other across distances, from smoke signals and waving flags, through using carrier pigeons and developing alphabets and writing, to the ability to exchange letters and send and receive messengers. The Roman Empire's network of roads and sea routes certainly allowed imperial bureaucracy to function efficiently, but, in what Michael B. Thompson nick-named "the holy internet",[1] it also enabled early Christian apostles like St Paul to communicate with their churches across the known world and eventually to turn it upside down. A letter from the emperor at Rome, through the medium of the imperial messengers' relay system of fast horses and selected sea routes (prevailing winds enabled news to travel from west to east much more quickly than the other way), could reach the commanders on the far-flung frontiers of the empire like the auxiliaries on Hadrian's Wall or the legions in Syria, keeping out the Scots and the barbarians of the east, in forty days. The news of the death of the Emperor Tiberius in AD 37 reached the legate of Syria (the commander of the legions) within five weeks, according to Tacitus' *Annales*, VI.50. Thompson suggests that "news from Ephesus and Corinth . . . where Paul extended his visits, could reach Rome and Jerusalem in a month or less, if conditions were favorable."[2]

The expansion of technology in the nineteenth century led to the inventions of *tele-graphy* (literally '*far-writing*' in Greek) in the 1840s, essential in opening up America to the west, and the *tele-phone* ('*far-voice*'), emerging from different experiments by various people leading to Alexander Graham Bell's fateful phone calls in the summer of 1875. A similar process of experimentation with electromagnetic radiation led to Marconi's famous radio transmissions in the 1890s, followed by a couple of decades' work on *tele-vision* ('*far-seeing*'), which led in turn to John Logie Baird's extraordinary demonstrations on March 25, 1925 at Selfridge's (of all places). It only merited a small report by the prestigious journal *Nature*, on its second page of 'current topics' on April 4, 1925, with the laconic, if prophetic,

1. Michael B. Thompson, "The Holy Internet: Communications between Churches in the First Christian Generation," in Richard Bauckham (ed.), *The Gospels for All Christians* (Grand Rapids: Eerdmans, 1998), 49–70; see also in the same volume, Loveday Alexander, "Ancient Book Production and the Circulation of the Gospels," 71–111, and my own contribution, Richard A. Burridge "About People, by People, for People: Gospel Genre and Audiences," 113–45.

2. For statistics about the rapidity of communication across the Roman Empire, see Thompson, "The Holy Internet," especially 60–65, including his helpful diagrammatic map; quotation taken from p. 68.

note that "Mr Baird has overcome many practical difficulties, but we are afraid that there are many more to be surmounted before ideal television is accomplished."[3]

The historian of the internet Ian Peters claims that "in 1863 . . . futurist Jules Verne, without a doubt the king of science fiction writing, told us of a future world where 'photo-telegraphy allowed any writing, signature or illustration to be sent faraway—every house was wired'. Now that's as good a description of what was to come as you can get! Jules Verne also anticipated the first trip to the moon, so he often talked of events and inventions well before they happened."[4]

Over the last quarter of a century, the rapid growth of the internet has transformed all our lives across the globe. Its origins are lost in the mists of (admittedly only recent) time, not to mention the inevitable conspiracy theories about secret military operations and clandestine corporate business, "fuelled largely by the PBS television series 'Triumph of the Nerds' some years ago, and by the earlier writings of Silicon Valley gossip columnist Robert Cringely in the beautifully titled 'Accidental Empires—how the boys of Silicon Valley make their millions, battle foreign competition, and still can't get a date' (Penguin, 1992)," as Ian Peters notes.[5] In fact, probably there is no single moment of birth for the internet, but rather, as with all the advances above, experiments by scientists, large corporations, and, yes, military scientists, tried to explore developing long-range communications under the twin pressures of the Cold War and growing international business through trying to link, or 'network', early computers together.

Here too the invention has English origins, as Ian Peters notes sardonically in an all-too-typical story of British research and American money: "In 1965 . . . an Englishman called Donald Davies had proposed . . . in the United Kingdom the NPL Data Communications Network. It never got funded." As someone who has spent his life working and ministering in higher education in England, those last brief, but stark, four words come as no surprise to me whatsoever! However, "Donald Davies did develop the concept of packet switching, a means by which messages can travel from point to point across a network. Although others in the USA were working on packet switching techniques at the same time . . . , it was the UK version

3. "Current Topics and Events," *Nature* 115 (1925), 504–8, quotation from p. 505; https://www.nature.com/articles/115504a0#article-info;   https://doi.org/10.1038/115504a0

4. See Ian Peter's fascinating history of the internet; this quotation is taken from his first page on so-called 'prehistory'. https://www.nethistory.info/History%20of%20the%20Internet/prehistory.html

5. https://www.nethistory.info/History%20of%20the%20Internet/origins.html

that Arpanet [Pentagon's Advanced Research Projects Agency Network program] first adopted" in 1969.[6]

The involvement of the Pentagon, of course, is the green light to any conspiracy theories, and you can take your pick, but everyone agrees that it was another Englishman, Tim Berners Lee, who brought this all together and created the World Wide Web. Peters continues the story: "The first trials of the World Wide Web were at the CERN laboratories (one of Europe's largest research laboratories) in Switzerland in December 1990. By 1991 browser and web server software was available, and by 1992 a few preliminary sites existed in places like University of Illinois. . . . By the end of 1992, there were about 26 sites." But unlike the other stories of communications and inventions above, all of which quickly descended into patents, lawsuits, and arguments about intellectual property rights, something amazing happened: "On April 30, 1993 CERN's directors made a statement that was a true milestone in Internet history. On this day, they declared that WWW technology would be freely usable by anyone, with no fees being payable to CERN. This decision—much in line with the decisions of the earlier Internet pioneers to make their products freely available—was a visionary and important one."

Peters also helpfully explains acronyms that many of us use every day but have never even thought about: "Another important building block was the URL or Uniform Resource Locator. This allowed you a further option to find your way around by naming a site. Every site on the worldwide web has a unique URL (such as www.nethistory.info). The other feature was Hypertext Markup Language (html), the language that allowed pages to display different fonts and sizes, pictures, colours, etc." Yet, even without knowing what those funny letters meant, all of this really did begin to change our lives completely. From the twenty-six sites in operation in late 1992, Peters notes that "by the end of 1994, there were a million browser copies in use—rapid growth indeed!!"[7] The digital revolution had begun in earnest, and the world would never be the same again. Those of us born before all of this can only struggle to become fluent in 'digital speak', like a foreign language—as in my lack of understanding of (let alone curiosity about) the meanings of URL and HTML. I had written nearly half of my PhD thesis using the tried and tested technology of a pad of paper and a fountain pen (which I still have, along with some now fading handwritten drafts) when I bought my first computer to type it up in 1985; my first daughter did not follow until 1986, a year later, and one therefore of the first to be born 'digitally native' to

6. https://www.nethistory.info/History%20of%20the%20Internet/beginnings.html

7. https://www.nethistory.info/History%20of%20the%20Internet/web.html

parents with a computer. My godson, born in 2008, was using an iPad tablet long before he was two—and used to get very frustrated with the antiquated television machine, because he simply could not understand why it did not switch channels or pictures when he swiped the screen! (I'm afraid to admit that his boring godfather still prefers to buy him actual, physical books—which, fortunately, he has also come to love.)

THE CHURCH AND CHANGES
IN COMMUNICATION METHODS

Priests and worshipping folk have always been quick to jump on the communications bandwagon. Many of humankind's earliest writings are religious proclamations, inscribed on rocks, stones or monuments, and holy texts, scratched on wood, metal, or reeds pressed together to make papyrus. We noted above how the 'holy internet' of Rome's interconnected road system allowed the early Christians to spread their message—even if sometimes by foot and not at the speed of the imperial messengers' fast horses—and even to capture the empire itself within a couple of centuries. The period that followed is often termed the 'Dark Ages', not because they were particularly 'dark', as in evil or oppressive, but they went 'dark' in that reading and writing were lost to most people, being mainly confined to priests and monks, who were trying to keep safe precious scrolls from the past and were busily illuminating manuscripts, like the *Book of Kells* or the *Lindisfarne Gospels*, and the rest of the Bible, together with all sorts of prayer books. Sadly, when marauders like the Vikings appeared on the horizon, it was the gold and jewels on the book covers that called to them, rather than the beautiful contents and their intellectual and spiritual meaning.

During the mediaeval period, the monasteries' libraries formed the basis for the subsequent Renaissance, literally the 'rebirth', of Graeco-Roman culture and learning. And it was by whole-heartedly embracing the new communications technology of the printing press that the Reformers proclaimed their understanding of God's overwhelming grace in the gospel freely available to everyone, and not just for the *literati* of the scribal class, the 'clerks', whether in 'holy orders' or not. Tyndale famously proclaimed that "if God spare my life, ere many yeares I wyl cause a boy that driveth the plough to know more of the scripture, than he doust", with several variant versions of the saying, in which the "he" is either the pope or a priest to or about whom Tyndale was speaking.

A more modern parallel of the dissemination of information beyond the previous control of church authorities happened in 1995, just after I had become dean of King's College London. I had the privilege and responsibility of organizing Archbishop George Carey's first formal appearance as the 'visitor' of King's, a role that goes back to our foundation in 1829, and, beyond that, back to mediaeval communities and universities. This was made doubly daunting since he was an important alumnus (having done his PhD through King's), so I did my best to lay on a fascinating and mixed day for Archbishop George and his chaplain, visiting science laboratories, meeting academic staff in theology, a round table with the KCL Student Union sabbatical officers, leading to a conversation with all the leaders and committees of the student Christian societies.

However, I was completely taken aback by what turned out to be the highlight for Archbishop George himself as we were robing in my office for Evensong in chapel at the end of what I was beginning to dare to hope had been a successful day—namely, when he saw the computer on my desk with not only e(lectronic)-mail scrolling across it, but also a live connection to the new-fangled World Wide Web, which even Lambeth Palace did not have yet. I have to confess that we were a bit late for the drinks after chapel, because the archbishop insisted on spending some time playing on it while unrobing before dinner! I think Lambeth Palace had an early version of its website up and running within a couple of weeks afterward . . . .

THE SHIFT TO THE ONLINE WORLD
—AND SOME RESISTANCE

However, my generation, and the current generation of bishops and church leaders—no matter how 'digitally-fluent' we manage to learn to be—can never really understand the internet and the World Wide Web in the way that my children and godchildren can, born as they were after their parents first acquired a computer, and thus digitally-native. And what we do not understand, we are naturally suspicious of—is it safe? The internet is certainly *quantitively* different from what went before: whereas handwritten scrolls might be read by *hundreds* of people at the most, the printing press could enable *thousands* to have a copy, and the various tele-graphs/-phones/-visions could reach *millions* of people, the internet touches *billions* of lives in so many ways that they—or we—are not even aware of. But is it, perhaps, not also *qualitatively* different from the other communications revolutions; they are all linked by that little Greek word 'tele', meaning 'from afar', or 'far off'. Unlike tele-graphy, -phones, and -vision, we do not just have a '*tele*'-net, reaching us from far away, but the '*inter*'-net, which binds us together internally and internationally into a network, whether we like it or not.

Hence, there are all the quite justifiable concerns about the internet and its safety and security, as scams proliferate and the shadow of Big Brother gradually increases if we are not very careful. On the other hand, during the coronavirus pandemic lockdown, practically everything moved online, from government meetings to TV chat shows, from ordering your groceries to keeping in touch with your family, whether the other side of the world or just in the next street along. If you did not have the internet, then you could not order food or drink, medication or clothing, talk to your friends or see your grandchildren. Breadwinners were lucky if they could 'work from home' on their computers, rather than being furloughed or losing their jobs altogether, while households with only one device had to deal with children squabbling over 'screen-time' to do their schoolwork at home.

Prior to the pandemic, I had just moved from London to an area outside Manchester where we knew literally no one. To my delight, I found some music studios in our village High Street where I could have guitar lessons, join a classical music appreciation class, and participate every Friday evening in a concert with the opportunity for 'open-microphone' participation. I also started going to the small mid-week communion service with a nice group of mostly retired folk in the local parish church, there was a good local pub a few minutes' walk away, and I had started to check out the nearby golf courses when suddenly the lockdown closed all of these. Obviously, there was nothing that could be done about the pub and the golf courses, but I was fascinated that the music studios with all their equipment soon migrated everything online using webinar technology. So I moved to having two individual lessons a week with my guitar teacher (one classical, and one folk or electric) and I still met the same group at the classical music appreciation class to discuss and listen to music, but all online—and on Friday nights anything between twenty-five and forty of us crowded onto a computer screen to play instruments, sing songs, or read poems to each other, while enjoying a glass of wine or whatever in the privacy of our locked-down homes.

But what about the communion service in the local church that I had just started going to? Zilch, nada, nichts, sweet Fanny Adams! I spoke to the priest, but she did not think many of that particular congregation even have a computer, and so they were trying to stay in touch by telephone instead. And so I started instead a small online communion service with various friends (what will become the topic of chapter 15)—and then we ran straight into all the official debates with the proclamations from archbishops and bishops and other members of the church hierarchy all saying that we *should* not be doing things like holy communion online—with some even going further to argue that, whatever it might look like, we *could* not actually be celebrating communion in this way since it was just impossible—physically, theologically, sacramentally.

It is too cheap and easy of course just to respond that every technological advance has been met with opposition from those who will have to face change, or who feel genuinely threatened for themselves, their families, and their livelihoods. This charge—generally known as being 'Luddites'—goes back to certain poor English textile workers who took violent action in smashing new machinery, which threatened their jobs and livelihoods in the desperately poor conditions during the Napoleonic Wars, starting on March 11, 1811 and continuing for the next few years. Although the story that they served an imaginary General Ludd in Sherwood Forest was as mythical as Robin Hood, these 'machine-wreckers' were sufficiently organized and committed to their actions that they were met with the full force of the British army, where according to Hobsbawm, "the 12,000 troops deployed against the Luddites greatly exceeded in size the army which Wellington took into the [Iberian] Peninsula in 1808."[8]

Whatever or wherever the name 'Ludd' came from, it has remained as a term for those who oppose technological advance. In our own time, according to *Le Monde Diplomatique*, it was applied to a "new political force in the United States political scene . . . , seeking to popularize the idea of a new Luddism. In the words of a manifesto for the Second Luddite Congress which took place in Ohio last April [1996], it is 'a leaderless movement of passive resistance to consumerism and the increasingly bizarre and frightening technologies of the Computer Age.'"[9]

So, in one sense, that is why I am trying to write this book, examining these various proposals and options about what makes for a 'valid and effective' celebration of the sacrament of holy communion. When I try to explain why I am spending all hours of the day and night writing this volume to members of the younger generations, our children, godchildren, and grandchildren, the very ones to whom the future of the church and our civilization belong and on whom it depends, I'm afraid that they simply do not 'get' these sorts of concerns and debates, and look at me like 'the old man has finally lost it'! They just do not comprehend things like the bishops' opposition to communions on the internet, any more than my eighteen-month-old godson could understand why that battered, old machine in the corner of the living room needed him to push certain buttons before

8. E. J. Hobsbawm, "The Machine Breakers," *Past & Present* 1.1 (1952), 57–70; quotation from p. 58. doi:10.1093/past/1.1.57

9. See https://web.archive.org/web/20020630215254/http://mondediplo.com/1997/02/20luddites

changing what was on its screen—and even then, there seemed to be only a few choices of TV channels. Clearly, it was nowhere near as much fun as his mother's iPad . . . .

The younger, 'digitally-native' generation do not understand why we need to push certain theological buttons before we can get the TV to change channel or gain access to holy communion online. For them, it is all too tempting to compare some of our current debates to mediaeval scholastic controversies about how many angels can be balanced on the head of a pin. After all, I demonstrated earlier in this chapter that I did not need to know what the acronyms 'URL' and 'HTML' actually stood for in order to use them to be able to visit all sorts of web pages online; I do not have to understand *how* a computer works, to know *that* it does—which is just as well, as these machines become more and more complex with each new development. Back in the 1970s I could change a head gasket and re-bore new valves into the engine of my car, an old Ford Cortina Mark I, and even in the late 1980s I could rewrite my early Amstrad computer's software to teach my dot matrix printer how to draw characters from the Greek alphabet for my PhD. To try to dive into the innards of complex machines like car engines and computers today would be as foolish as it would be pointless, to say nothing of being dangerous and expensive, invalidating any warranties!

THE CHURCH EMBRACES THE ONLINE WORLD

And yet, we go on buying the newest car and the latest computer, rejoicing in all the new bells and whistles. And to be fair, so has the church, for the most part. Like the first Christians with the Roman roads, or the reformers with the printing press, the immediate and generally overwhelming response of the church to the online digital revolution and the so-called 'virtual' world has been to embrace them fully and to use them to further the gospel.

When writing a book about the internet, it is only right at times to consult the oracle of the blessed Wikipedia, even though normally I would criticize any of my students for doing so. It is perhaps one consequence of writing under lockdown without being easily able to pop into libraries. For its writers, the terms "'internet church', 'online church', or 'cyberchurch' refer to a wide variety of ways that Christian religious groups can use the internet to facilitate their religious activities, particularly prayer, discussion, preaching, and worship services." The term 'internet church' itself may be defined as "a gathering of religious believers facilitated through the use of online video stream, audio stream and/or written messages whose primary purpose is to allow the meeting of a church body of parishioners using the internet."[10]

Like Archbishop George Carey after his visit to my office at King's, the first reaction of Christians was usually to build a website, which meant developing web pages using HTMLs and acquiring a URL to put them on (even if no one knew what these *sacra nomina*, or 'holy names', actually meant!). The early computer name 'bulletin board' gives the clue; we are used to news bulletins, school bulletins, hospital bulletins, and, in the USA, church bulletins, although these are perhaps more generally known as the 'pew sheet' or the 'notices' in Britain. The point is that these first church websites were all about giving information out, reaching more people with details of the church's activities—and fairly soon, in trying to give instruction in the faith, or to reach new people in evangelism, giving them the 'good news' of Jesus Christ.

In fact, it is probably accurate to say that the vast majority of the Christian use of the internet is to provide resources for worship and teaching for discipleship, including promoting debate and discussion. But this is essentially a *passive* model, where the originators, in the church's hierarchy or the clergy, instruct the people who faithfully read and receive all this information. It is also still a 'top-down' model, where the hierarchies of the church or the government or business have all the power and knowledge, which they are generously bestowing on the humble reader and internet surfer. However, it does not take long to realize that these 'users' can also be *active*, in writing and distributing their ideas as well. The internet can be as equally 'bottom-up' as it is 'top-down'.

Exactly the same phenomenon happened through the previous communications upheaval. A particular consequence and spin-off of the 'printing revolution', which was perhaps as unwelcome to, as it was unseen by, the church authorities was that anyone with a printing press, or able to pay a small fee to a local printer, could print up their ideas into tracts and pamphlets and distribute them as widely as they liked. The church's control of information, jealously guarded by the 'clerks in holy orders' who often did the reading and writing for their whole local community, was gone for ever—and the centuries of the pamphleteers made sure that controversy was never silent. Wikipedia's judgement is that people like John Calvin and Jonathan Edwards "changed the course of Christianity with their pamphlets".[11]

---

10. Taken from https://en.wikipedia.org/wiki/Internet_church
11. https://en.wikipedia.org/wiki/Pamphleteer

Equally Thomas Paine's pamphlets, especially his call to action in *Common Sense*,[12] were influential in the history of the American Revolutionary War, or War of Independence (depending upon your choice of nomenclature!); later, during the French Revolution, Paine joined other pamphleteers who were highly active in attempting to shape public opinion. It is generally considered that the practice of the pamphleteers led to what we term 'the Press'—and that very name is itself instructive, referring to the printing press at the traditional heart of newspapers.[13] In 1840, Thomas Carlyle noted that "[Edmund] Burke said there were Three Estates in Parliament [clergy, nobility, commoners];[14] but, in the Reporters' Gallery yonder, there sat a Fourth Estate more important far than they all."[15] Following the development of all the '*tele-*'s—*telegraphy, telephone*, and *television*—the Fourth Estate came to be known more widely as not just the 'Press', but *the 'media'*, so as to include these others, since plurality is of the essence of the media in all its/their forms.

Therefore, it did not take long for ordinary Christians to start posting their views on early bulletin boards or 'web-logs'. The latter phrase quickly shortened into 'blogs', with the connected noun and verb, 'bloggers' and 'blogging', and most people now have no idea where the 'b' came from! Some people or sites quickly developed a reputation for being a very helpful and useful 'sounding board' to go to for comments about all the latest news and developments in a particular field. Thus, in my particular academic field of New Testament studies, my publishers are always keen to get some kind of review or mention of my work on blog sites run by people like Mike Bird (Australia), which he posts on patheos.com,[16] the Jesus Research project with Chris Keith and others (USA),[17] Chris Tilling's Chrisendom, or Steve

---

12. For more details, see https://www.thomaspainesociety.org/common-sense

13. See James A. Oliver, *The Pamphleteers: The Birth of Journalism, Emergence of the Press & the Fourth Estate* (Information Architects: Ingram, 2010); see https://www.thepamphleteers.com/

14. The traditional European political model divided society into three 'Estates': first the clergy, second the nobles, and third including both the peasants and bourgeoisie. In Britain this was translated into a bicameral Parliamentary system with the clergy (or at least, the bishops, with clergy not allowed to stand for Parliament until this disqualification was removed in 2001) and nobles sitting in the House of Lords, and all the others in the House of Commons.

15. In his Fifth Lecture, "The Hero as a Man of Letters: Johnson, Rousseau, Burns," delivered on Tuesday, 19 May 1840; see his book *On Heroes and Hero Worship* (Everyman Library; London: Dent, 1908), 392; available at https://www.gutenberg.org/files/20585/20585-h/20585-h.htm#page383

16. https://www.patheos.com/blogs/euangelion/

17. https://historicaljesusresearch.blogspot.com/

Walton's Acts and More (UK)[18] in the hope of getting some free publicity through the large number of 'followers' that they have acquired.

Within the church, various blog sites easily become known as espousing a certain view, such as on the conservative wing of the Anglican Communion;[19] by way of contrast there are more liberal sites, such as Via Media (which is nothing about going 'through the media of TV' etc.), which "aims to bring the historic Anglican perspective of the 'Via Media' [the Middle Way] to debates that are current in the Church of England", although most, if not all, the contributors, and many posts, are known to espouse a liberal attitude to LGBTI issues in the church.[20] On the other hand, the Archbishop Cranmer blog "adopts a Christian conservative and conservative Christian perspective contra the forces of relativism, liberalism and secularism, and lies in the Catholic and Reformed tradition"; it is written by Dr Adrian Hilton, who describes himself as "a theologian, political philosopher, educationalist, lecturer, occasional theatre director and former politician."[21]

Alternatively, other sites act more like a 'clearing house' where, instead of the blog opinions of the author, editor, or contributors, lots of different articles on a particular issue will be posted. Thinking Anglicans provides new pages of lots of relevant links on an almost daily basis, to "actively report news, events and documents that affect church people, and will comment on them from a liberal Christian perspective, . . . a tolerant, progressive and compassionate Christian spirituality, in which justice is central to the proclamation of the good news of the kingdom of God." Rather than just grinding the same old axe, Thinking Anglicans wants to provide "a range of opinions, which contributes to debate, and is legitimate diversity within the Christian faith. . . . In a world where the voices of fundamentalism and conservatism are frequently heard, Thinking Anglicans is a place for a tolerant, thoughtful and understanding exploration of Christian faith."[22]

To return to my discipline of New Testament studies, Mark Goodacre's NT Gateway, for instance, quickly acquired an international reputation as a similar resource for a very wide range of topics and issues arising in biblical research and scholarship,[23] though it also contains Goodacre's own

18. http://blog.christilling.de/ and https://stevewalton.info/

19. The obvious person used to be Kendall Harmon, who ran a blog called Titus 1.9, now at https://sounddoctrineattitusonenine.blogspot.com/; others in that field include https://accurmudgeon.blogspot.com/; https://standfirminfaith.com/home/

20. https://viamedia.news/about-viamedia/

21. https://archbishopcranmer.com/about/

22. https://www.thinkinganglicans.org.uk/65–2/

23. http://www.ntgateway.com/

thoughts in a page that has been going so long that it still uses the full, if old-fashioned, word, 'weblog'![24] However, it has also moved to include the more recent phenomenon of posting so-called 'podcasts', recorded broadcasts, often relatively short, discussing a particular subject.[25]

This extraordinary outpouring of material provoked web-developer Tim Bednar as long ago as April 2004 to compose, and upload, a paper entitled, "We Know More Than Our Pastors"—the ultimate 'bottom-up' scenario—which detailed the blogging movement's influence on the experience of faith up to that point.[26] His main argument is the obvious one that the sum total of information and knowledge now available to such bloggers—and those who read them—is bound to be more than that of any individual pastor, and the intervening years since have witnessed further massive expansion. Another interesting point is that it is thought that this paper contains the first use of the word 'cyberchurch', although as far as I can tell, it occurs only once in his paper.

Of course, there is one final point that needs to be made here. The internet cannot be controlled by the people of power and only used for 'top-down' decrees or bestowing of information; as a 'bottom-up' medium, it is essentially democratic and levelling in that it provides a platform for people to find a voice and publish their personal views, regardless of their own resources, wealth, education, knowledge, privilege, beliefs, politics, axe-grinding, hobby-horse riding, or whatever—beyond, obviously, having the capacity to access a computer linked to the internet. If the control of the scriptures by the 'clerks in holy orders' had been lost by the printing press revolution, allowing Tyndale's "boy that driveth the plough to know more of the Scripture" than the priest or the pope did, the internet revolution allows the ploughboy to talk back to the priest and the pope, and there is nothing they can do to stop him.

This is, however, at once liberating and problematic, in that there is no kind of editorial oversight, or quality control—just the outpourings of people saying what the heck they like. There is no way to assess the accuracy or reliability of what one reads on the net—and the bane of most doctors' lives are patients turning up in their consulting rooms who have diagnosed themselves or their symptoms from reading 'things on the web' and who know that they have some terrible condition and are about to die, unless the doctor can provide them with the latest wonder drug or miraculous

24. https://ntweblog.blogspot.com/

25. https://podacre.blogspot.com/

26. Tim Bednar, "We Know More Than Our Pastors: Why Bloggers Are the Vanguard of the Participatory Church" which is available as downloadable PDF from https://www.scribd.com/document/47331/We-Know-More-Than-Our-Pastors

treatment that they read about! Similarly, academics and teachers now have to be constantly vigilant for the students or pupils who just type their essay question into a search engine and then simply 'cut and paste' whatever they might find, regardless of accuracy, and with no concern about plagiarism. And that is before we get into the question of whether Wikipedia is a trustworthy and quotable academic source. On the other hand, being able to access information across the whole world, and to find answers instantaneously, means that I need to confess that, in a situation like the lockdown, even I have needed to drink from that particular well occasionally . . .

THE INTERNATIONAL DEVELOPMENT
OF ONLINE RELATIONSHIPS AND SOCIAL MEDIA

In addition to providing lots of information about what is going on in the so-called 'real' or material world of human society and the activities of organizations like the church, and giving a platform for everyone to post their ideas and beliefs, there is a third major use and benefit of the online world, namely providing opportunities for fellowship and deepening relationships, especially around the wider community, and even out into the whole world, allowing those who may be physically separated by thousands of miles and different time zones to communicate with each other in real time, if not the same physical space. Neither 'top-down' nor 'bottom-up', this use of the internet is essentially 'side-by-side'.

'Long distance' phone calls used to be expensive, and international ones were prohibitively so. For much of my time as dean of King's College London, the only telephone in my department that permitted international dialling was on my desk—so when we found that the bill included lots of calls being made to Paris around 7am, it meant difficult conversations with the French-speaking cleaner who was responsible for offices across the whole floor. I grew up in the 1960s when having a couple of 'pen-pal's in Europe was pretty *avant garde*; to be able to go and visit them in the 1970s was even more amazing, but several personal relationships that started during those visits, or with international students during my time at university, quickly petered out once I or they went back home.

However, in almost a parable of modern times, an English colleague in biblical studies on an international lecture tour a few years ago met a fellow scholar who was teaching in Australia, and they both sensed some kind of attraction. On the other hand, everyone else, their friends and families, thought it was crazy given the twelve-thousand-mile trip between their respective homes and workplaces, to say nothing of the ten-hour time difference. Nonetheless, over the next two years, the relationship not only continued, but deepened, mainly through video-calls made through media like Skype and Facebook, which are, unlike the old phone calls, free and unlimited, even if helped, of course, by meeting at international conferences plus the occasional, but expensive, plane ticket! As things became more serious, they ended up talking most days, often over a drink or a meal—except that usually one would be having breakfast, and the other dinner; one might be in pyjamas getting up, while the other was having a glass of wine or a nightcap. And then yes, two years later, they were married. Sadly, and paradoxically, the relationship forged over huge distances on the internet did not survive being physically locked down together in one small house for over a year.

Speaking personally for a moment, I have had a similar experience with my first grandson, born in Hong Kong at the height of lockdown both there and in the UK. However during this last year, I have watched his exciting development through (free!) video calls on What's App every couple of days—all those little milestones (yard-stones?) beloved of new parents, the first day back out of hospital, learning to breastfeed, was that a smile—or just wind?, the beginnings of real communication, reactions and reaching out, gurgles and chuckles, laughter and tears, beginning to hold his head up, to sit up, to roll over, to crawl—even perhaps soon, to stand up, and so on. Of course, this developing relationship was helped by a visit in the summer where he and his parents spent almost as much time in quarantine at both ends of the trip, here in England and back in Hong Kong, as they did being free to travel round so many friends and family, times when I felt he really began to recognize his Grampy. Now because of the time difference, my day often begins with a short video call watching him working his way through his first encounters with vegetables and fruit, followed by the inevitable and necessary bath to clean it all off before bedtime.

What is more, unlike my private phone with expensive international dialling only a few years ago, not just the subcontracted French-speaking immigrant cleaner, but increasingly now the poorer in the world have access to one another. Through the development of the smartphone and the internet, developing countries have leap-frogged the decades that it took the West to connect homes with telegraph poles and telephone wires or to lay undersea cables of the sort that allowed Winston Churchill and Franklin D. Roosevelt to converse privately in the dark days of the Second World War, to be able now to enter instant international communication. If Microsoft's vision statement of the 1980s and 1990s was "a computer on every desktop", this has been hugely exceeded by the numbers of people now having a computer in their pocket—and the growth is staggering, and perhaps frightening. These figures are updated daily and I was amazed to discover the difference between the numbers when I did the final edit of this chapter (with 90 percent of the world's population owning a cell or mobile phone, and 80 percent having a smartphone) up from the first draft (65 percent and 45 percent).[27] With it taking fours years for the figures to nearly double from 2016 to 2020, and not quite eighteen months for a similar increase 2020 to 2021, the days when nearly everyone in the world will be connected must be expected very soon.

Meanwhile, these possibilities for general online interaction (and not just finding romance or deepening family ties) have been further expanded through the rapid growth of social media. Perhaps it is appropriate to let Wikipedia comment about this:

> Christians, like many Internet users, are increasingly using social networking sites like Facebook. These sites incorporate much of the technology of blogging but forge more concrete connections between users, allowing them to 'message' each other within the system, connect officially as 'friends', rate and rank each other, etc. These connections may or may not materialize in the real world, but many people now consider online relationships a significant part of their lives, increasing the potential influence of a Christian presence in these environments. Criticism of Christian use of these sites has grown, however, due to prevalence of questionable content and issues of safety.[28]

From humble beginnings in his student room in Harvard, Mark Zuckerberg used to communicate online with his college roommates and fellow students—a practice that he then launched as 'The Facebook' on 4 February 2004. Originally limited to only Harvard students, it was expanded to other colleges in the Boston area, then the Ivy League, and gradually most universities in the United States and Canada, corporations, and by September 2006, to everyone with a valid email address, along with an age requirement of being thirteen and older. In little more than fifteen years, it has grown into one of the largest initiatives on the planet, and made its founder one of the world's wealthiest billionaires. It has also got embroiled in massive controversies about the safety and use of everyone's personal information, not to mention concerns about its use to influence presidential elections in the USA and the Brexit referendum in the UK.

27. The figures are current for Oct 25, 2021. Check it out for yourself in your 'today', dear reader, at: https://www.bankmycell.com/blog/how-many-phones-are-in-the-world; it may be 100% by the time you read this footnote.

28. Also taken from https://en.wikipedia.org/wiki/Internet_church

From being originally a young person's preserve, Facebook is often now seen as old-fashioned and fuddy-duddy, used by retired people like me to keep in touch with family and colleagues, while many youngsters have switched to one of the many proliferating alternatives, like Instagram, Snapchat, Tik-Tok, and so forth—as well as Twitter, of course, all aided by the development of the smartphone, which enables users to share a comment or photograph or video from wherever they are in the world and make it available to any of their friends (big F and small f) that they choose—or make it public for the entire world. And, like any other organization, no church can now afford to be without its Facebook and Instagram accounts, or its Twitter feed, proudly displayed on all its outputs.

Such usages of the internet by churches, even to the extent of being seen as 'cyber-churches', have not been without some critique. Thus, the Roman Catholic Pontifical Council for Social Communication declared in 2002 that "the virtual reality of cyberspace cannot substitute for real interpersonal community, the incarnational reality of the sacraments and the liturgy, or the immediate and direct proclamation of the gospel", while acknowledging that the internet can still "enrich the religious lives of users".[29] Similarly, in his wonderfully entitled book, *Who Stole My Church? What to Do When the Church You Love Tries to Enter the 21st Century*, Gordon MacDonald notes that "Internet churches now exist all around the world; however, they are still criticized for their lack of 'human connection'".[30]

These critiques make a valid point. However, few people are advocating for the *replacement* of 'real-life', embodied-in-space-and-time church with 'virtual' or digital churches, existing in cyberspace only, as we shall see in the next chapters. Rather, the online aspects of church life have, for the most part, been proposed as ways to *support*, enrich, enhance, and expand existing everyday-world communities, rather than becoming *substitutes* for more conventional relationships and churches.

However, the fact that these internet church links and people's use of social media were originally being used more for teaching than for worship and fellowship, and more interested in instruction than in fostering *community* and celebrating *communions*, all changed with the advent of the COVID-19 pandemic in 2020. The enormous use of the internet and social media by individual Christians and churches worldwide, both denominations as a whole as well as particular congregations, did form the important *background* to the pressure for forms of online worship, including holy

29. *Catholic Church. Pontificium Consilium de Communicationibus Socialibus.* (2002). *Ethics in communications. Città del Vaticano: Libreria editrice vaticana.*

30. Gordon MacDonald, *Who Stole My Church? What to Do When the Church You Love Tries to Enter the 21st Century* (Nashville: Thomas Nelson, 2008).

communion, at a time when churches were shut and the clergy and people were alike locked down.

It is, therefore, now high time, as we go forward into (hopefully) a post-pandemic world, that we begin to explore what the options for online services, including holy communion, might actually be, and—at the risk of being accused of hair-splitting and counting angels on pin-heads—to consider what the positive and negative reactions of church leaders have been over the last year or two.

11

Background 2
Voyaging on the 'Ship of Fools' into Digital Space

GIVEN ALL THE PROBLEMS and difficulties facing celebrating holy communion in "contagious times" in the 'real', physical, everyday world, as discovered in the coronavirus pandemic of 2020 and demonstrated in Part I above, it is worth exploring whether possible solutions might be found in the online world, where the only viruses you might catch affect your computer rather than your bodily life—hence our whirlwind tour of the history of communication and the development of the internet in the previous chapter. One of the first options, and a particularly significant example, was the Church of Fools, a project originating in 2004, involving Simon Jenkins, the creator of Ship of Fools.

It is worth spending a little time tracing the history of Ship of Fools in order to understand how the Church of Fools came into being. It had its origins in a satirical Christian magazine that emerged from "a back room in London Bible College" in 1977; Jenkins explains:

> When I was a theology student, I was in the library one day absorbed in a biography of Karl Barth, and came across a letter he wrote in the 1920s to fellow young theologian Friedrich Gogarten. The two of them were planning to launch a radical new journal and were casting about for a name, when Gogarten suggested calling it "The Word". Barth choked on the idea. "Better to call it 'The Ship of Fools'", he quipped, "than this idolatrous encumbrance!" I looked at that passage and immediately thought: that's the name of the magazine I want to edit. It might

be a Barthian cast-off, but it was perfect for what I wanted to do.[1]

He later came across the allegorical poem, *"Das Narrenschiff"*—"The Ship of Fools"—by the German poet Sebastian Brant, published in Basel in 1494, and set on a ship crewed by all the fools of the world. However, even though Jenkins was unaware of it at the time, Brant would have been drawing on the political allegory of a ship with a dysfunctional crew in Plato's *Republic* Book VI, representing the problems prevailing in a political system where, instead of government by experts with appropriate and relevant knowledge, democratic leaders, who need to please the electorate, govern without even listening to the experts.[2]

For Jenkins and his co-conspirators, Ship of Fools may have been a perfect title for an A5 stapled student magazine, subtitled "the magazine of Christian unrest", but this title reveals much more, for it stands in a direct

1. Simon Jenkins, "Rituals and Pixels: Experiments in Online Church", lecture given at the University of Heidelberg, August 2008. I am grateful to Simon for giving me a copy of his lecture script, which is much fuller than the later version published in the *Heidelberg Journal of Religions on the Internet* 3.1 (2008), 95–115.

2. It is worth quoting Plato's description in full, as it is a stunning depiction of the attempt by governments on both sides of the Atlantic to tackle the coronavirus pandemic without following the advice of their medical and scientific advisers: "There's the shipowner, larger and stronger than everyone in the ship, but somewhat deaf and rather short-sighted, with a knowledge of sailing to match his eyesight. The sailors are quarrelling among themselves over captaincy of the ship, each one thinking that he ought to be captain, though he has never learnt that skill, nor can he point to the person who taught him or a time when he was learning it. On top of which they say it can't be taught. In fact, they're prepared to cut to pieces anyone who says it can. The shipowner himself is always surrounded by them. They beg him and do everything they can to make him hand over the tiller to them. Sometimes, if other people can persuade him and they can't, they kill those others or throw them overboard. Then they immobilise their worthy shipowner with drugs or drink or by some other means, and take control of the ship, helping themselves to what it is carrying. Drinking and feasting, they sail in the way you'd expect people like that to sail. More than that, if someone is good at finding them ways of persuading or compelling the shipowner to let them take control, they call him a real seaman, a real captain, and say he really knows about ships. Anyone who can't do this they treat with contempt, calling him useless. They don't even begin to understand that if he is to be truly fit to take command of a ship a real ship's captain must of necessity be thoroughly familiar with the seasons of the year, the stars in the sky, the winds, and everything to do with his art. As for how he is going to steer the ship—regardless of whether anyone wants him to or not—they do not regard this as an additional skill or study which can be acquired over and above the art of being a ship's captain. If this is the situation on board, don't you think the person who is genuinely equipped to be captain will be called a stargazer, a chatterer, of no use to them, by those who sail in ships with this kind of crew?" Plato, *The Republic*, Book VI, 488b–489a, edited by G. R. F. Ferrari, translated by Tom Griffith (Cambridge: Cambridge University Press, 2000), 191–92.

line through several communications revolutions, from Plato at the blossoming of Socratic philosophical dialogue, through the early Reformation protests enabled by the printing press, to the growth of biting satire through publishing pamphlets, which led to what we now know as 'The Press'. The magazine published ten issues from 1977, covering issues as varied as Pope John Paul II's visit to Britain and white violence in apartheid South Africa, until it folded in 1983.

However, the next communications revolution allowed Jenkins and his co-editor, Steve Goddard, to relaunch it online on April Fool's Day, 1998, and reach a much wider audience, as it "very quickly became popular not just as an online magazine, but as a virtual community",[3] attracting thousands of visitors, with access to millions of pages. It provides a marvellous portrayal of the wackier side of Christianity, such as "tacky and tasteless religious merchandise" under the section previously called "Gadgets for God" but now "Junk for Jehovah", such as the "Last Supper musical pillow", embroidered with Leonardo da Vinci's *Last Supper*: when you place your head on it, the cushion plays "Hey Jude" by the Beatles.[4] Alternatively, what makes the "What Would Jesus Do?" boxer shorts truly Christian is, "There's some specially good news for the testosterone-driven young man. The boxers are thoughtfully provided with a closed fly. So in those situations where 'What Would Jesus Do?' isn't reminder enough, access is denied anyway."[5]

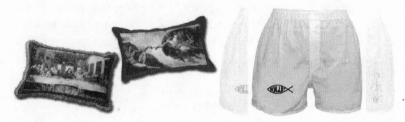

Because of our focus on holy communion in "contagious times" and our discussion about using little individual cups at communion in chapter 7, I was particularly interested in the Quick-R-Filler (presumably based on Toys-R-Us, but the 'R' does not really work, 're-filler'?), which "can prepare as many as forty cups in sixty seconds without making the church kitchen look like a bloodbath—or so boasts the Salem, Ohio, company which makes it.[6]

3. See https://shipoffools.com/

4. https://shipoffools.com/2018/05/last-supper-musical-pillow/

5. https://shipoffools.com/2017/11/what-would-jesus-do-boxers/

6. https://shipoffools.com/2018/07/communion-wine-on-tap/. See the company website at http://www.quick-r-filler.com/

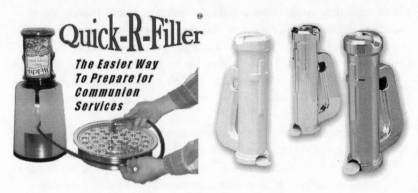

An even more prescient post from September 16, 2017 would be very helpful in the current pandemic: the "Holy Host Dispenser is offered by Purity Communion as a 'touch-free solution' to the problem of raging epidemics being caused by communion services, which as everyone knows happens all the time. 'Germs and viruses have no reverence for holy communion,' says the website."[7] Joking apart, this one could be quite useful right now, or any time we are celebrating holy communion in "contagious times."

Another standard feature is the so-called "Mystery Worshipper", where various anonymous correspondents visit and review different church services and answer the same standard set of questions, leaving a 'calling card' in the collection plate of churches in the real, physical world; now, it even includes a review of the archbishop of Canterbury's famous Easter Day service broadcast from his kitchen at Lambeth Palace, complete with an interesting trail of comments and debate.[8]

FROM WEB-BASED INFORMATION TOWARDS A COMMUNITY

In the previous chapter, we traced how the internet developed from a 'top-down' disseminator of information, through experiencing the same kind of 'bottom-up' use for satire and protest as other communications revolutions, through to being capable of engendering a 'side-by-side' sense of community, especially through the development of more interactive software, such as in social media.

Something similar happened with Ship of Fools. Although it was always 'top-down', in that Jenkins and his 'cronies' decided what information

7. https://shipoffools.com/2017/09/holy-host-dispenser/

8. see   https://shipoffools.com/mystery-worshipper/the-kitchen-lambeth-palace-london/

to disseminate, right from the start, it also had a strong whiff of the 'bottom-up' tendency for satire and protest. However, it quickly developed a community dimension, 'side-by-side', initially through its use of 'bulletin boards', "one of the oldest discussion boards on the Net", claims Jenkins in his paper from 2008: "we have almost 14,000 registered members on our bulletin boards, and we frequently have some 200 of them logged in together, debating, joking, arguing, playing games, arranging to meet up, or just lurking." After beginning with the old standard of a letters page they quickly separated it into various 'forums', each "looked after by a small team of volunteer hosts, who look after their board, monitor it every few minutes for obscenity and libel, and generally keep things on track."

Heaven is the place on the site for people to be creative, make jokes, share ideas, moan about spam, with typical threads like "Favourite Fridge Magnets", "What is the worst song ever written and performed?" or "Christmas presents on a tight budget." *Purgatory* is for serious debate about theology, philosophy, and ethics, including "Legalization of gay marriage", "Is God the God of the universe (or just our galaxy)?" "Muslim headscarfs in French schools." Thirdly, there is *Hell*, of course, for "people who are there to cause trouble, or who sometimes get a bit personal and get into a flame war with someone else" or threads like "Is Mel Gibson one bead short of a full rosary?" "What stinks about being an evangelical", or "My job sucks like a Dyson." *All Saints* is for "community announcements, birthdays and prayer requests", while *Ecclesiantics* deals with the "rite stuff", from liturgy and worship, ranging from thuribles to tambourines![9]

Like all communities, it is the experiences of joy and sorrow, celebration and tragedy that really bring people together: in 2008, Jenkins noted that "there have been six marriages I know about, involving people who first met on Ship of Fools, and I was best man at one of them."[10]

However, he continues, "all communities, even online ones, are shaped by traumatic events", so he outlines two that "had a significant effect on the Ship of Fools community." The first, which became known as "Hurricane Joanne", took place in January 1999, less than a year after the bulletin board was founded, running on very basic board software with no ability to disable postings. Joanne was posting comments from Florida, and she was initially warmly welcomed, but quickly turned out to be a troll, becoming "incredibly hostile" and "heap[ing] personal scorn and ridicule on everyone", posting hundreds of messages in one night, causing Jenkins and the others to shut the board down completely, and relaunch it a week later with properly

9. https://forums.shipoffools.com/
10. The weddings did not take place online, but in normal, everyday world churches.

protected software. "But what had happened was that we had unexpectedly discovered we were a community, and not just a discussion forum. . . . [A] good number of board members had found a sense of belonging and identity in Ship of Fools."

The second event happened in July 2002,

> when one of our members, whose alias on the boards was Miss Molly, was diagnosed with terminal lung cancer. She decided to share the last three months of her life with us, in a thread she posted called "Fields of Gold", named after the song by Sting. . . . After three months, and almost 1,000 posts on the thread, Miss Molly died, just before Christmas. In tribute, we turned all the coloured graphics on the bulletin boards black and white for three days, and a special thread was posted where people could make their farewells to Molly. The Fields of Gold thread is archived on our boards for everyone to read.[11]

Significantly for our purposes regarding holy communion online, such happy and tragic events

> had a very powerful effect in strengthening the bonds of the community. Looking at events such as this, over the nine years we've been running online community, we often asked ourselves if we could ever be a church, or ever run as a sort of alternative church online. But we always reached the same answer of No, essentially because we believed that running an act of worship online would need a greater sense of place than we had. We felt that the key difference would be to have somewhere that felt like sacred space, and which gave a visible metaphor for people meeting together. And that was something we just didn't have.

Now this is not only very interesting, but also highly significant in the light of all our discussions so far in the context of the coronavirus pandemic. We saw in chapter 1 that while churches and places of worship were generally closed down around the world in the lockdown, the British government's Statutory Instrument of March 26, 2020 specifically allowed places of worship to be open for three things: funerals, livestreaming of services, and other essential services. However, the hierarchy of the Church of England specifically went beyond this, and even closed the churches for clergy to enter on their own and pray the daily offices (as required canonically by the Book of Common Prayer) or to livestream their services—hence Archbishop Justin's decision to broadcast the Easter Day communion from his

---

11. See, https://bit.ly/miss-molly

kitchen in Lambeth Palace, rather than his private chapel in the same building, as a sign of solidarity.

The mantra "we haven't closed the church, just the buildings" may
have been repeated *ad nauseam* by the bishops, but without convincing the
majority either of church members or the general public. In fact, the generally negative reaction and things like letters of protest from MPs throughout
the summer and autumn of 2020 demanding that the churches should be
reopened bore witness to this similar feeling among the Ship of Fools community, just mentioned above: despite their shared experiences of tragedy
and celebration all within the context of their Christian faith, "running an
act of worship online would need a greater *sense of place* than we had, . . .
somewhere that felt like *sacred space*, and which gave *a visible metaphor* for
people meeting together."[12]

THE ARK

However, God had a surprise waiting for them when the Ship of Fools embarked on its next voyage of discovery. This arose from a typical speculation
from Jenkins and his crew:

> Have you ever found yourself wondering what it would be like if
> you got some of the best-known characters of the Bible together
> in a bar for a drink or two? How would they get on, these saints
> and sinners, these heroes and villains of the Bible? Would Moses
> compare beard lengths with John the Baptist? Would Eve offend
> Paul with her figleaf costume? It's inevitable that some of the
> great saints would find it hard to spend even a few minutes in
> each other's company.

The obvious background at the time, of course, was so-called 'reality-
TV' shows like *Big Brother*, which was originally conceived by Dutch TV
mogul John de Mol in the late 1990s, and versions of which aired over the
next ten years or more in the USA, UK, most European countries, Brazil,
Africa, India, and Australia—some thirty countries each with their own
show. Quite where the 'reality' is in an artificial environment where a group
of complete strangers are made to live couped up with one another for 100
days watched by millions live on TV, who have the power to vote to eject one
member each week, is anyone's guess. Still, the ratings were good.

12. My italics.

Therefore, the Foolish Shipmates hatched a project called The Ark, and got funding from the UK's Jerusalem Trust, and worked with Specialmoves, a new media agency in London. Jenkins explains how it worked:

> 12 real people, sitting at their computer screens round the world, logging in and playing the role of a biblical saint or sinner, on-board a virtual Ark for 40 days and 40 nights. The divine dozen would play games, complete tasks, overcome crises, discuss the big issues of the day and argue over whose turn it was to muck out the gorillas. All in full view of a global audience, watching them on the Internet. The Ark was quite a large environment, with seven rooms on two floors. Plus two lower decks for storage and animals, which included pairs of elephants, alligators, zebras—and a single T-Rex.

From over 1,000 applicants from around the world, they chose twelve 'Arkmates', six from the UK, four from the US (New York, Washington DC, New Orleans, and California) and two from Canada. They included three priests, two youth workers, a teacher, a psychologist, and an astrophysicist. The contestants all logged into the game to play it live and were in full control of their online avatars. Of course, they could not talk or be heard, so they had to type in what they wanted to say, hit 'return', and their speech appeared onscreen in floating speech bubbles. They could move their avatars around via point and click and do a good amount of gesturing. The Ark was online every day for an hour in the evening over forty days (six weeks) from 20 April to 30 May 2003, although Jenkins does not tell us if it rained all forty days and nights! Some 1.5 million pages on the website were accessed during that time, with up to 4,000 people per day logging into the Ark environment.

And it was certainly a soap opera worthy of any *Big Brother* show, with Simon Peter and St Paul taking an almost instant dislike to each other and starting arguing on the very first day, leading Paul to hide in his cabin to write a third epistle to the Corinthians, Eve setting hearts racing with her skimpy fig-leaf costume, and Joseph being spirited away by God (who operated from the Crow's Nest above it all) to be replaced by either Jonah or Jezebel, depending on the audience vote—and that's just some of the first week's headlines![13] Gradually, the various arkmates were reduced by the regular votes of the audience deciding who should walk the plank this time, until after forty days (and forty nights), John the Baptist, paradoxically the only one *not* to get dunked in the water, finally stepped ashore dry-foot on

13. You can still catch up with the events of each week by week at http://ark.saintsimeon.co.uk/news.php

Mount Ararat to claim the prize of £666 and, to his surprise, a rapturous welcome from all his previously drowned shipmates.

In his lecture reflecting upon it all, Jenkins says that they "learned many things from running the Ark game show, but two really stand out. First was the Contestants' emotional involvement in the game. Their immersion in the 3D world, the relationships between the avatars, and in their own online identity. But it was the second that was going to have the biggest implications for our concerns about services of holy communion in the virtual world:

> The second standout point was when we turned the Ark's spa-cious living room into a chapel every Sunday, and gave three of the Ark mates the task of preparing Divine Service for everyone else to join in. When we saw how this worked, with preaching, Bible readings, prayers and discussion, it planted an idea in our minds which eventually became Church of Fools.

THE CHURCH OF FOOLS EXPERIMENT

We have already noted that after the traumatic events of Hurricane Joanne and the tragic death of Miss Molly and the joy of some weddings, the Ship-mates had wondered about setting up their own church, but concluded that "running an act of worship online would need a greater *sense of place* than we had, . . . somewhere that felt like *sacred space*, and which gave *a visible metaphor* for people meeting together."[14] Almost by accident, during the forty days of the Ark they had stumbled on a possible way of making 'sacred space' online. On the first Sunday of the voyage, April 27, 2003, the Ark's crew worshipped out on the top deck, but the following week, May 4, 2003, they turned the living room into their chapel with the sofas and chairs be-coming pews arranged around an altar table adorned with a cross.[15]

14. My italics.

15. See the transcripts of these Sundays at http://ark.saintsimeon.co.uk/logs/index. php

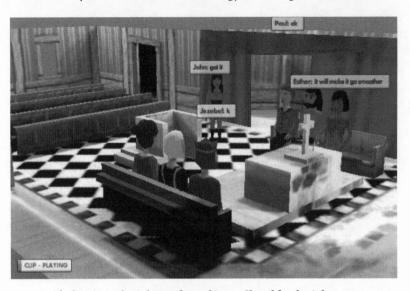

**The lounge in the Ark transformed into a Chapel for the Arkmates
to worship together**

The following year, Jenkins and the Shipmates decided to try to build a
church online with services for a three-month experimental period. Inspired
by the example of John Wesley in taking worship to the people in the fields
and streets of the eighteenth century, they wanted to take church to where
people are now—on the net. Appropriately, therefore, they were able to get
some sponsoring funding from the Methodist Church of Great Britain, and
also from the bishop of London, Richard Chartres. The three aims were "to
translate church into the medium of the net, . . . a genuine experiment, . . . to
find out if online church is a viable way to do church; to create moments of
genuine depth and spirituality, helping people feel they're connecting with
God, themselves and others; and to educate and inform people who would
never darken the doors of a church about Christian worship and fellowship."

This all meant creating a building in the medium of computer games
that would be recognizable as a church, so they went for "Romanesque as
our building style, partly because Romanesque churches were built during
the first evangelisation of Europe, but also because we liked the interplay
between the new medium of the net and this very old-looking architecture."
The interior needed to be fairly traditional, with enough wooden pews in
the nave to accommodate thirty worshippers, with a chancel containing an
altar with a cross, a pulpit, and a reading lectern. They soon discovered this
had to be a locked area to prevent "disruptive visitors" from entering it during services, and especially sermons.

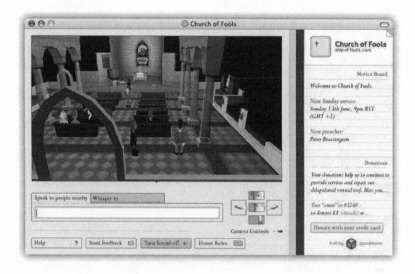

In addition, as Jenkins explains:

> As one of our aims was to help create genuine moments of
> spirituality in Church of Fools, we decided to enrich the envi-
> ronment by adding a modern equivalent of 'stations of the cross'.
> The church was basically designed for corporate worship, for
> everyone to join in, but these stations would offer an opportu-
> nity for individual prayer and reflection . . .with three of these
> stations on [each] side of the nave. Each station had an image
> from the passion of Christ, painted or sculpted by a contem-
> porary artist. The images were taken from an exhibition called
> "Presence" which had toured six English cathedrals earlier in
> 2004. If you clicked on one of the stations, a second window
> would open to show you a large version of the image, plus two
> or three paragraphs of text meditating on it. The stations gave
> us the opportunity to add both visual and verbal content to our
> environment, and they also signalled that we were attempting to
> create a form of sacred space, even if the overall context of the
> environment was cartoon-like and had the feel of a computer
> game.

Those who logged in appeared in the environment as a cartoon-like
avatar, male or female, with a variety of hair and skin colours, and dressed
in different clothes styles. These avatars could talk to each other, walk
around, sit down on a pew or chair, or kneel on the ground. Avatars also had
a menu of gestures, three specifically 'religious' (bless; cross self; hallelujah)

and nine ordinary 'socializing' gestures (clap; hands on hips; laugh; point; pull hair out; shrug; scratch head; shake hands; and wave).

All speech had to be typed in and would appear at the bottom of the screen, while the prayers or sermon of those leading services materialized in speech bubbles over their heads. Jenkins relates how

> The power of gesture and avatar body language was apparent as soon as the environment was opened. On the day the development team was first able to go into the church, we entered the sanctuary as avatars and started to explore. One of the team members came up to me and said, "I think we should pray, as this is a church." I said, "Of course, let's pray everyone." We gathered our avatars by the chancel steps and one by one our avatars knelt to pray. As the prayers started to appear on the screen— "Thank you God for this place"—I immediately knew that this not only felt like prayer, but was actually prayer. Even though it was being done in a virtual space, and we were separated by hundreds and even thousands of miles geographically, what we were doing was authentically praying together. At this point, I knew that our experiment would lead to genuine expressions of spirituality and would be exciting and worthwhile as an attempt to do church on the Net.

Since there was only room for thirty to be logged into the church at any one time as a visible avatar, large numbers of other people arriving later could log in as a 'ghost', with a semi-transparent avatar, whom no one else could see, although the ghosts (who could number 200–300) could see all the visible avatars, their conversations, and everything else that was happening in the church. Therefore, the worshippers would also greet the ghosts and share the peace with them, as in this screen grab.

Jenkins recalls the launch service on May 11, 2004 at the Christian Resources Exhibition just outside London: "The church was full of the avatars of invited journalists from the *Times*, the BBC and CNN, and the bishop of London, Richard Chartres, sat next to me and dictated his sermon, while I rattled it into the environment on a keyboard. In his sermon, he talked about 'setting out into the cyber ocean aware that the Spirit of God is already brooding over the face of the deep.'" They even made a special avatar for the bishop (with a fuller, and browner, beard than normal, so the BBC report pasted a picture for comparison!).

In his report, "In Cyberspace, Can Anyone Hear You Pray?" the BBC correspondent, realized that "As I took my pew, I noticed that not only was the guy next to me wearing the same clothes as me, but we had the same heads on as well. A true 21st Century faux pas."[16] On the ninth day of the project, the church was featured on Slashdot, a website for techies and programmers—and then they recorded 41,000 visits to the church in one twenty-four-hour period, which they reckoned made it the most popular church in the world on that day. On average, there were 7,337 visits per day, and on some occasions there were 3,000 users logged in at the same time. As Jenkins notes, "we were drawing cathedral-sized congregations to our little church." At first, the church was open twenty-four hours a day, with the intention to run one service a week, on Sunday evenings, with a full liturgy, prayers, readings, a hymn, and sermon. But due to visitor demand, they soon started running daily services of morning and night prayer in UK time, and eventually also an evening service for US visitors, and other ad hoc services during the day and night.

An online survey attracted some 2,400 responses, of which 58 percent were male, 50 percent under 30, and 39 percent of visitors were not regular churchgoers—precisely the kinds of people the 'real' church says it wants to attract. The profile also reflects those drawn to computer games—and not all were benign, as the church began to gather attention from trolls and even Satanists, who attempted to occupy the pulpit or disrupt proceedings. Jenkins received a surprising email one day apologizing for the behaviour of their fellow Satanists: "I have been Satanist all my life and would never have pulled any such thing. So, for all the immature twits within the Satanic community, you have my sympathies as I truly hope to see you fix the problem soon. Best of luck, sincerely, Satanist with a heart." Others would try to block doorways, use the 'kneeling' button to suggest oral sex, or worship the vending machines, so the church wardens had to be equipped with a 'smite' button, which would exercise their traditional power to 'keep the peace' since mediaeval days and remove the avatar from the church!

However, many others who entered the church thinking that the whole thing would be trivial found themselves surprised, perhaps even by God. "Church of Fools is an oasis in my day", said one regular visitor from Georgia in the US. "I often leave my 'ghost' alone, kneeling at prayer in the church while I work nearby", while another from North Carolina wrote "I have a friend who had a crisis this week. No way would he ever go to a real church. But he went to yours and said his first prayer in many years. You are providing a valuable site for him and others who might never go to a traditional house of worship."

16. For a full report, with more photographs and an interesting trail of comments, see Giles Wilson, "In Cyberspace, Can Anyone Hear You Pray?" http://news.bbc.co.uk /1/hi/magazine/3706897.stm

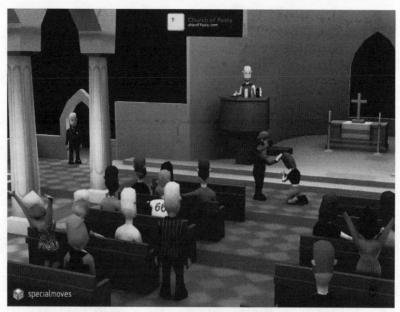

A service taking place in the Church of Fools showing how avatars could perform actions like laying on of hands". It is taken from http://www.stpixels.com/

ST PIXELS

When the Church of Fools closed its doors in September 2004 (a month longer than the originally planned three-month experiment), they discovered that, although the project had started with technology in the virtual world, a small community had grown around it, which continued after the technology could no longer be sustained at that level. However, worship continued in a conventional 2D chatroom, and in May 2006 they changed the name (perhaps inevitably) to St Pixels, with a multi-media chatroom that had been developed by members of the community, including a virtual pulpit in a separate window. The St Pixels website reflects on this period:

> To some of us, the 2D period felt a bit like an exile. But it was during this time that we reflected on our experience and became much more of a stable, welcoming community. We learned to learn from each other and our different backgrounds, in bible study and general discussion—which did sometimes get heated. We began to care and pray for each other. We found authentic ways of worshipping in our regular chatroom prayer services.[17]

17. See http://www.stpixels.com/ for a fuller history of both Church of Fools and St Pixels itself, complete with various comments from different avatars.

In April 2009, St Pixels parted company (amicably) with Ship of Fools, and St Pixels Ltd came into operation—a company owned by its members, registered in the UK, with membership worldwide. In May 2010, they again moved to new software offering greater flexibility in live worship as well as some new features on the website. They also introduced Peer-to-Peer Discipleship groups. In 2012, they finally relocated to a new home on Facebook, as "an opportunity to reach out to where people were already gathering." However, for reasons unexplained on their website, St Pixels conducted its last service on Facebook on November 22, 2015 and the company was wound up in January 2018, although "its community stays in touch via Facebook and Twitter."

As if to make this point, the brief comments on the website are very moving in their honesty: (J) "I have this community—past and present—to thank for my sanity. Thanks for being there when things were darkest, and there to celebrate at their brightest." (P) St Pixels "broadened my spirituality more than I think I ever will realize." (C) "So many happy treasured memories all the way back to the Church of Fools. Friends for life, most of them friends never met in real life." (M) "St Pixels was for me a very safe place." (W) "I gained so much from St Pixels, Some wonderful friends and a lot of insight. I seem to have grown a great deal."

CONCLUSION

Both the Ship and the Church of Fools, as well as St Pixels, show that it is in fact possible to build real and lasting relationships in the digital world of online communities, and even to go further—to experience authentic spirituality, prayer, and fellowship. Another similar project, which has managed still to continue, is *i-church*, which was founded by the Diocese of Oxford also in 2004 as an experimental online community in the Benedictine tradition.[18] It is also a registered charity and a limited company; there is a priest-in-charge, who is licensed by the bishop of Oxford, and it is supported by a council chosen from the core community and key volunteers authorized by the trustees.[19] It is text-based and contains a number of areas:

- The *Gatehouse* provides information and resources about Christianity for everyone to use

- The *Courtyard* gives access to a number of open forums where visitors can join in various discussions, read blogs, or post prayer requests.

- There used to be a *Chapel*, a chat room where people could join in live services, although that appears not to be functioning at present, so visitors are referred instead to the Prayer Forum.[20]

- The *Core Community* pages are private for those "who are committed to the long-term future of i-church and for whom i-church is an integral part of their faith journey", although those who might wish to become members are encouraged to contact the priest-in-charge for further conversation.[21]

What these different experiments all demonstrate is that not only are real and lasting relationships to be found in the digital world of online communities, but also that information-sharing and supporting others online can take us further, to experience authentic spirituality, prayer, and fellowship. Significantly, these are all some of the marks of our criteria and requirements for a eucharistic community and for a valid and effective celebration of the sacrament, which we developed through the first half of this book. What is both interesting and significant about it all, however, is that I have not found any examples or discussion of holy communion or the sacraments in this material about the Ship or Church of Fools, nor St Pixels. For that we now need to visit the online world of Second Life.

18. https://www.i-church.org/gatehouse/
19. https://www.i-church.org/gatehouse/home/information/4-community
20. https://www.i-church.org/courtyard/viewforum.php?f=8
21. https://www.i-church.org/gatehouse/home/information/5-core-community

12

Proposal 8

'Second Life', the Anglican Cathedral, and Sacraments for Avatars

VISITING SECOND LIFE

HERE WE 'BOLDLY GO where no theologians have gone before', not into outer space, but into 'virtual space', the digital area in cyberspace known as Second Life (SL) to distinguish it from the 'First Life' of physical existence. Second Life is an online world, owned by Linden Lab in San Francisco and launched in 2003 with a thousand members. Within a few years, there were one and a half million users and 50,000–100,000 are usually logged on at any time. Users create avatars, to explore the digital world, interact with places and objects, meet other 'residents', socialize, participate in group activities, build, create, shop, and trade virtual property and services. SL time is Pacific Central Time as in San Francisco, and the currency, Linden dollars $L, is linked to real US dollars.

Before starting writing, I joined SL freely and easily, chose an avatar 'off the peg', and started exploring 'Learning Island'. Other avatars approached me, mostly with female names, such as Dolly, Stella, and Marg. Locations were marked G (for General) or M (Moderate, or previously 'Mature'), while the A-Adult places were not open to my level. The search facility did not like 'religion', but 'spirituality' listed a variety of Christian sites, plus other faiths like Judaism and Buddhism, even including Mormon sites and a seminary training ministers in pagan Wicca!

I managed to 'teleport in' to Dornoch Cathedral, which, although based on that place in Scotland, had more beautiful hanging lights, gorgeous marble floors, and a massive pipe organ. It proclaims to be "open to the public for quiet contemplation, worship services and both Christian or non-denominational weddings." I could make my avatar walk, stand, sit, and pray—and was greeted by a message, "Resident, welcome to the Dornoch Cathedral. May the peace of the Lord be with you." Otherwise, it was empty, and having sat, stood, and prayed, I grew tired of how slow and clunky everything seemed, and the effort needed simply to make my avatar move, reminding me of computer games I used to play in the early-mid 2000s.

The self-styled 'Evangelist of the Metaverse', Theodore Wright, had worked as a computer programmer before finding a cyberchurch on SL in 2006, run by a pastor in the physical world. "I asked him if I could rent space on his simulation from him and be the church evangelist there, such as I do in life. It was there I ran a virtual café and started doing evangelism in Second Life."[1] He also created a 'SL Bible', freely available, as he sat with his SL Bible T-shirt in his digital café, called '*dokimos*' (meaning 'approved' or 'excellent' in the Greek New Testament). It was also the name of his original website with flashing colours and canned music, to say nothing of its conservative politics and anti-Catholic articles, now linked to his newer website, maverickchristians.com.

1. Theodore Wright, "CyberChurch in Second Life" http://www.dokimos.org ; http://maverickchristians.com/2014/11/08/evangelist-of-the-metaverse/; Use of Linden Labs in plural is *sic* in Wright; normal use is singular.

Wright's story illustrates what happened with SL: in a 1992 sci-fi novel, *Snow Crash*: "author Neal Stephenson imagined a collective virtual reality called the Metaverse, where user-controlled avatars hung out in 3D bars and nightclubs. . . . There was the distinct possibility of the internet truly going 3D because even major corporations were investing into the creation of simulations representing their businesses in Second Life. The year 2007 was a boom year for Linden Labs, the creators and host for Second Life."

However, "2008 was the start of the decline of the mass popularity of SL. Linden Labs came up with restrictive policies that disfavored businesses in SL, which discouraged investors. Metaverse Meetups were still going on during this time while Camelot had fallen." This refers to the 2008 economic problems, when financial speculation crashed in the physical world. Afterwards, SL rallied, and by 2013 it had approximately one million regular users. According to Ebbe Altberg, the recently-deceased CEO of Linden Lab, in 2015, "users redeemed $60 million (USD) from their *Second Life* businesses, and the virtual world's GDP is about $500 million, which is the size of some small countries."[2]

Much of this online business is buying and selling 'virtual real estate' (the combination of the language of 'virtual' and 'real' is fascinating—and revealing) to build places within SL; another major use is obvious from the female avatars who approached within minutes of my 'teleporting in', and locations graded as G(eneral), M(oderate), and A(dult). "If you let users make whatever they want, they'll make a lot of sex stuff. Dirty, kinky sex stuff to float any boat. . . . [T]he variety of virtual porn sites in *Second Life* are a strong draw for many regular users, especially because many of these sites feature extreme sexual kinks and fetishes that aren't readily available online elsewhere."[3]

While active users have now declined below a million (compared with the billions on Facebook and other social media), the combination of gaming, money-making, and sex will probably ensure its continuation, despite awkward, clunky, outdated graphics. When Facebook bought the virtual reality headset maker Oculus VR, in 2014, the Games correspondent of investment advisers Forbes headlined, "Mark Zuckerberg Wants to Build the Metaverse, and That's OK."[4] While SL will not take over the physical world

2. https://www.vice.com/en_us/article/z43mwj/why-is-second-life-still-a-thing-gaming-virtual-reality

3. https://www.vice.com/en_us/article/z43mwj/why-is-second-life-still-a-thing-gaming-virtual-reality

4. https://www.forbes.com/sites/davidewalt/2014/03/26/mark-zuckerberg-wants-to-build-the-metaverse-and-thats-ok/ It is significant that while this book was in its final stages of production, Mark Zuckerberg changed the name of his company, Facebook Inc., to Meta Platforms Inc., in a nod to the 'Meta Universe' - see https://

of First Life, let alone eternal life, it does provide an online environment to consider the next proposal for holy communion in "contagious times", the Anglican Cathedral on SL.

THE ANGLICAN CATHEDRAL OF SECOND LIFE

'Anglicans of Second Life' (AoSL) was founded in November 2006 by Rocky Vallejo, an American Episcopalian. The CEO of the New Zealand Bible Society, Mark Brown, offered to lead it in February 2007,[5] so they purchased a site on 'Epiphany Island' in SL and built a Cathedral.[6]

Daily Morning Prayer in the Meditation Chapel

Mark Brown was then ordained deacon in 2007 and priest in 2008, bringing AoSL under the authority of an Anglican diocese, Wellington, New Zealand. He and others met with Christopher Hill, then bishop of Guildford, in September 2007, followed by a conference at Willow Grange, the bishop's home, in May 2008, and a subsequent fringe presentation at the

qz.com/2081663/why-facebook-changed-its-name-to-meta/. The implicit claim, as with 'meta-physics' and 'meta-narrative' is to go 'above and beyond' (the meaning of *meta* in Greek) the physical universe.

5. See the very helpful and informative paper written in April 2009 by Ailsa Wright of (then) Wakefield Diocese (now the Diocese of Leeds), England, "Anglicans of Second Life—Some Reflections on Lived Experience," which can be downloaded from https://www.academia.edu/2068697/Anglicans_of_Second_Life-some_reflections_on_lived_experience; I am extremely grateful to Mrs Wright (aka 'Helene Milena' in SL) for all her help with and comments about this chapter.

6. A rather clunky and out-dated fly-by tour can still be found on their website history page, https://slangcath.wordpress.com/about/history/ or on YouTube at https://www.youtube.com/watch?v=AI98HIGHzX4

Lambeth Conference (July 2008). Mark Brown retired from active ministry in 2009, when AoSL's membership was nearly six hundred. Today a smaller community continues to run the Cathedral, with a full website detailing its services, activities, vision, values and core beliefs, and its leadership, worship, pastoral care, and Bible study teams.

The Cathedral's mission statement calls it "a distinctively Anglican church within SL for those who are Anglicans or who share the Anglican heritage, and for those of other denominations who value what we provide. We also welcome those who are exploring the Christian faith", while its doctrinal statement upholds the 'Chicago-Lambeth Quadrilateral 1888' regarding the scriptures, the Apostles' and Nicene Creeds, and the sacraments of baptism and communion.[7] Daily services of Morning Prayer (following Anglican liturgy and the Revised Common Lectionary) are held at 8am UK time (midnight SL/San Francisco time), with Bible studies, and the main Sunday service at 8pm UK/12 noon SL-PCT time.[8] All worshippers appear as avatars, who communicate by typing in text, although voice speech is also possible in worship. Finances are managed by 'Tithe Sixpence', the Treasurer: the largest expense is US$1,770 renting the space on Epiphany Island within SL, 83 percent of the annual budget of $2,343.[9]

Using my avatar, "Hezekiah", I 'teleported in' from a link on their website, and looked around a traditional stone-built, cruciform building, with nave, transepts, and chancel. I collected a candle and a liturgy for walking the Twelve Stations of the Cross around the walls. The four avatars pictured on a prayer ministry board were offline, but I sent a prayer request. My avatar, Hezekiah, then sat on the back pew to pray, while, back in First Life, I wrote this paragraph.

On my next visit, I discovered the Meditation Chapel, where daily Morning Prayers are held, so Hezekiah settled down to pray there, while I went back to writing. This was soon interrupted by the arrival of a leader's avatar, who had received my prayer request, and came to 'meet' me, and enable us to converse audibly. Another leader showed me round the Cathedral and its buildings, and kindly gave me $1,000 Linden dollars to help me get 'kitted up'; fortunately, I later discovered that this was worth less than US$20—but I did buy a silver cross and chain for Hezekiah to wear!

It quickly became clear that the Anglican community on SL may be thousands of miles apart and in different physical time zones, but they meet daily to pray (even if it is 8am only in the UK, but midnight in SL time

7. https://slangcath.wordpress.com/the-vision/

8. https://slangcath.wordpress.com/schedule/

9. https://slangcath.wordpress.com/financial-support/

(PCT) or late morning in Qatar and teatime across Australia!), to share their concerns and needs and to be prayed for by one another. Some bring those who live with them physically, but others live alone—and deeply value the sense of community in SL with dear friends around the world whom they have known for a decade. I (or my avatar, Hezekiah—see the discussion below) was quickly welcomed into the community, joining in the services, and getting frequent messages asking me about how this book was progressing, and praying for me. In fact, without the prayers and encouragement of this SL group, I may never have finished writing this book!

A CHRONOLOGICAL SURVEY OF THE DEBATE
ABOUT SACRAMENTS ON SECOND LIFE

Visiting the SL Cathedral is central to our concern about celebrating holy communion in the online digital world. Discussion at Willow Grange with Bishop Christopher Hill in May 2008 noted that "currently worship in the Cathedral is restricted to non-Eucharistic services but the issue of communion will need to be addressed at some point."[10] This is the exact question that we are exploring, which makes the SL Cathedral an excellent place to examine. It is also interesting and significant that, despite many papers over the intervening years, the question has *still* not been resolved. A brief account in chronological order may help before turning to the main issues.

The May 2008 conference at Willow Grange prepared the way for a presentation at the 2008 Lambeth Conference. Bishop Christopher noted that "it was decided—and both my ecclesiastical lawyer colleague and I endorsed this as important—that there are no sacramental services. Sacraments are personal, even physical, encounters. 'Virtual' is not (quite) real." He reiterated making a 'spiritual communion' at a 'virtual eucharist', and concluded that this "will be a refreshing change from other subjects at Lambeth".[11] Ailsa Wright/Helene Milena's paper notes "A leaflet was created for distribution at the Lambeth Conference and a presentation given there in one of the fringe sessions." Unfortunately, "Attendance was poor but those who did attend showed great interest in the potential of this ministry."[12] This was followed up by another meeting in November 2008, where Bishop Christopher presided over a physical service of holy communion in Willow

---

10. Ailsa Wright, "Anglicans of Second Life," April 2009.

11. Christopher Hill, "One Way of Growing a Global Mission," *Church Times* July 25, 2008, 13

12. Ailsa Wright, "Anglicans of Second Life," April 2009, 14.

Grange, while attending SL avatars made a 'spiritual communion'; various hopes for the future were discussed, but it is not clear how these progressed.

The following year, 'Cady Enoch', an AoSL leader, posted "one of the key challenges with online worship is how to incorporate the Eucharist. The Eucharist is a physical experience from witnessing the act to receiving bread and wine. But it is also a spiritual experience in that the key action is invisible, caused by God who acts within the liturgy. So would it be possible to have a virtual communion, a virtual sacrament?"[13]

Mark Brown, just retiring, asked Paul Fiddes (professor of systematic theology at Oxford, as well as the Baptist representative on the Church of England's General Synod) to write a short paper "Sacraments in a Virtual World?" An online discussion includes this summary:

> An avatar can receive the bread and wine of the Eucharist within the logic of the virtual world and it will still be a means of grace, since God is present in a virtual world in a way that is suitable for its inhabitants. We may expect that the grace received by the avatar will be shared in some way by the person behind the avatar, because the person in our everyday world has a complex relationship with his or her persona.[14]

Unknown to Fiddes, at Brown's request, the New Zealand liturgist Bosco Peters responded in his characteristically forthright manner: "Nor would I celebrate Eucharist and other sacraments in the virtual world. Sacraments are outward and visible signs—the virtual world is still very much at the inner and invisible level."[15]

A few years later, in July 2012, Bishop Christopher Hill explained his "solid theological underpinning, guidelines, or even ideas" in his paper "Second Life and Sacraments: Anglican Observations and Guidelines." This remains on the SL Anglican Cathedral website even today as its official statement about sacraments.[16] Employing a distinction between 'sacraments' and 'sacramentals', Hill discusses the history and theology of all practices considered to be sacraments, but while he supports the renewal of

13. Cady Enoch, June 23, 2009; this gathered three comments at the time, and three more in 2012, but nothing since; it remains still today as the main website statement, https://slangcath.wordpress.com/2009/06/23/virtual-holy-communion/

14. See the discussion at https://www.frsimon.uk/paul-fiddes-sacraments-in-a-virtual-world/

15. Rev'd Bosco Peters, "Can Sacraments Work in the Virtual World?" June 28, 2009, https://liturgy.co.nz/virtual-eucharist

16. Christopher Hill, "Second Life and Sacraments: Anglican Observations and Guidelines," available for download from and summarized at https://slangcath.wordpress.com/the-vision/sacraments-on-epiphany-island/

baptismal, ordination, or marriage vows online, conducting the sacraments themselves is not possible, but only 'spiritual communion'.

A few months later, the Rev'd Kate Lord submitted her Master's thesis, "Can Eucharist Be Administered in a Virtual World? Further Points for Consideration by the Anglican Cathedral on Epiphany Island in Second Life."[17] After a brief explanation of the history and activity of the Cathedral, she stresses the regular daily worship and pastoral care within the community, but notes that "the sacraments are not currently offered at the Anglican Cathedral of Second Life. Conventional wisdom demands the physical presence in the same geographic location of the priest, the congregation, the bread and the wine for the Eucharist to take place."[18] As well as Fiddes, Hill, and Peters, she considers other theses by Lara White (London 2009),[19] Anneke Klein (Amsterdam 2008), Heidi Campbell (Edinburgh 2004),[20] and Matthew Broaddus (Tennessee 2011),[21] before culminating with Tim Hutching's PhD thesis (Durham 2010), which identifies four dimensions of the relationship between online church and everyday life: "copying the everyday, becoming part of the everyday, remaining distinct from the everyday, and becoming distinctively 'online.'"[22] She includes a detailed discussion of Gregory Dix's famous fourfold shape of the actions in communion,[23] before considering some pastoral issues raised by the online world's ability to cross thousands of miles and all possible time zones. She concludes by arguing that this is a direct opportunity for the whole mission of the church.

17. Lord's dissertation was supervised by the Rev. Dr Ross Fishburn, for Yarra Theological Union (part of Melbourne College of Divinity, now the University of Divinity), submitted 8 Nov 2012; it can be downloaded from https://slangcath.wordpress.com/2013/02/11/online-sacraments-the-conversation-continues/; this page also contains Christopher Hill's paper—see previous note.

18. Lord, "Can Eucharist Be Administered in a Virtual World?" 7.

19. Lara White "The Body of Christ on the Internet: Personal Identity and the Sacramental in the Virtual World," https://lauraewhite.blogspot.com/2009/11/

20. Heidi Campbell, "Internet as Social-Spiritual Space," in *Netting Citizens* (Edinburgh: Saint Andrew Press, 2004), 208–31; https://www.academia.edu/697920/The_Internet_as_Social-Spiritual_Space

21. Matthew Broaddus, *Exploring the Lived Experiences of Online Worshipers* (Knoxville: Tennessee Research and Creative Exchange, The University of Tennessee, 2011), 5. http://trace.tennessee.edu/cgi/viewcontent.cgi?article=1010&context=ccisymposium

22. Tim Hutchings, "Creating Church Online: An Ethnographic Study of Five Internet-Based Christian Communities" (PhD diss., Durham University, 2010), 273.

23. Lord, "Can Eucharist Be Administered in a Virtual World?" 21–28; Dom Gregory Dix, *The Shape of the Liturgy* (Westminster, UK: Dacre, 1945), 103.

In September 2019, Simon Rundel[24] submitted a dissertation for an MA in digital theology with CODEC at Cranmer Hall, St John's College, Durham, entitled "Sacraments in Digital Space—A Theological Reflection of Three Church's Position Statements."[25] The Roman Catholic position statement was "The Church and Internet," from the Pontifical Council for Social Communications in 2002;[26] Christopher Hill's 2012 paper "Second Life and Sacraments: Anglican Observations and Guidelines" was the Anglican statement, while the Methodist statement was Paper 37, "Holy Communion Mediated through Social Media" from the Faith and Order Committee (2018).[27] Rundel remarks that "the conclusions of each were cautious and essentially prohibitive", so he set out to answer three objections:

- whether the presence of Christ can be located within digital space;
- whether the body of Christ as the church can be formed within digital space;
- the relationship between 'virtual' and 'reality' and whether digital space is merely a substandard substitute for physical 'analogue' reality.

After detailed argument on each point in separate chapters, he helpfully sums up his clear answers that:

- there is nowhere where Christ cannot be proclaimed as Lord (Phil 2:10–11). The Word of God caused light, (Gen 1:3), which is what powers all digital space, thus marking digital space as a creation of God and therefore subject to him. Christ is therefore able to be present in digital space.
- the gathering of the people of God within digital space creates community and therefore ekklesia; . . . the church can therefore meet legitimately within digital space.

24. Vicar of the Roborough Team Ministry, Parishes of Bickleigh & Shaugh Prior, Plymouth, Devon, he describes himself as "Politically radical, Unashamedly Anglo-catholic, Deeply Sacramental and wildly, rabidly Inclusive"; see his website, https://www.frsimon.uk/about-2/

25. Available on his website at https://www.frsimon.uk/ma-dissertation-sacraments-in-digital-space-a-theological-reflection-of-three-churchs-position-statements/, with no page numbers; all quotations taken from this source.

26. Published in the Vatican City, 22 February 2002, with John P. Foley as president and Pierfranco Pastore as secretary.

27. 2018 Methodist Conference Report Para 5.6 pp. 363–65; a formal response to Memorial 13 to the 2011 Conference from the South-East District Synod requesting the Conference "to instruct the Faith and Order Committee to form a policy regarding the practice of celebrating Holy Communion with dispersed communities via live, interactive media such as the Internet or video-conferencing . . . no later than 2018."

- the blending of the digital and analogue showed that through changes in perspective, the avatar moves from puppet to embodiment of the individual: an extension of ontological self into the digital space.

However, he ends with a disappointing conclusion, that "the *devotion of spiritual communion* is an authentic mode of understanding sacramental encounter both within digital space and as observed from without." Having made it clear that both Christ and the church exist in the digital world, and that the avatar is an "extension of ontological self", his distinction of spiritual communion from the physical receiving of bread and wine perpetuates the divide between the digital and the physical, online or offline, 'Second' or 'First' Life, and reinforces the implication that the 'virtual' world is less real than the 'real', material existence with the five senses.

The impact of Fiddes' 2009 paper has been obvious on subsequent writing and discussion. Fiddes himself returned to this topic at a symposium on "The Virtual Body of Christ? Sacrament and Liturgy in Digital Spaces" in April 2018,[28] subsequently written up for publication in 2020.[29] This begins with "A Cautionary Tale" because Fiddes was ignorant of both Peters' attack and Hill's 2012 paper, and all the subsequent debate until this 2018 conference. Fiddes was "astonished" that the debate had "largely ignored a key point" of his paper, his "suggestion about virtual sacraments thus falls somewhere into the spectrum between church sacraments of bread and wine and other sacramental media in the world". Hill understood this distinction, even if he preferred the word 'sacramentals' to contrast them with physical 'sacraments'. This problem of language, contrasting 'virtual' and 'real', suggests that the virtual is somehow *not* real—so Fiddes prefers to use the term 'local-church sacraments' to distinguish them from what happens online.

He expands his treatment, especially from the perspective of the Baptist tradition. In response to Hill's terminology, he wants "to assert a definite *continuity* with what I am calling a 'local-church sacrament'. . . . I prefer then to call these wider means of grace 'various *kinds* of sacrament' rather than 'sacramentals'" (85). Fiddes illustrates this from the experiences of Teilhard de Chardin, "who does not hesitate to use the word 'mass' in considering

28. Paul Fiddes, paper given at a symposium on "The Virtual Body of Christ? Sacrament and Liturgy in Digital Spaces", organized by the CODEC Research Centre for Digital Theology, Durham University, 19–20 April 2018; see the report of this symposium at https://bigbible.uk/sacrament-liturgy-in-digital-spaces/

29. Paul Fiddes, "Sacraments in a Virtual World: A Baptist Approach." In *Baptist Sacramentalism 3*, edited by Anthony R. Cross and Philip E. Thompson (Eugene, OR: Pickwick, 2020), 81–100; I am extremely grateful to Prof Fiddes for sharing an advance copy with me for inclusion here.

the sacramental consecration of the whole world", with two particular experiences, a mass on "a geological field trip in the bitter-cold mountains of Northern China in 1923" when he had neither bread nor wine, and another day "in the trenches of the First World War" (85). Fiddes compares these experiences with "poets such as Gerard Manley Hopkins [who] have testified to the same rapture of finding Christ present in a eucharistic form in the world—that is, present in the mode of sacrifice" (86), instancing Hopkins' poem about a hawk, "*The Windhover.*" Fiddes argues that the online or digital "world of cyberspace can be also part of this sacramental universe"; the key question for Fiddes is about

> *which* sacramental actions in this world can be means of grace.
> . . . [T]aking seriously our two factors of the presence of God in a virtual world and intimate involvement of the person with an avatar, it ought to be possible to have the same kind of eucharistic celebration as Teilhard found with his mass on the world, and Hopkins found in the watching of a bird in flight. It seems impossible to separate a sacramental world from a eucharistic world, if we take the sacrifice of Christ as basic to creation and redemption. (89)[30]

He suggests "a distinctively Baptist approach to the eucharist . . . a discernment of the body of Christ in the action of the meal and in the disciples who gather" (90). This is not confined to, or even 'distinctively', Baptist; even Fiddes himself acknowledges that the "modern ecumenical consensus on the eucharist has moved in this direction, away from a restriction of presence within the substance of the elements to encounter with Christ through the whole action of the rite" (90–91).[31] In arguing that the "essential conditions of eucharistic communion can be met in the virtual reality of the web", Fiddes is using not only the same approach as our set of 'criteria' or 'requirements' for a valid and effective communion, but indeed also some of the same conditions themselves.

Fiddes argues that Douglas Estes' four possible forms for sacraments in cyberspace are attempts "at *equivalence* with a local-church eucharist",[32]

---

30. Here he footnotes Hans Urs von Balthasar, *The Glory of the Lord: A Theological Aesthetics. Volume III, Studies in Theological Style: Lay Styles.* Translated by Andrew Louth, John Saward, Martin Simon and Rowan Williams. Edited by John Riches (Edinburgh: T. & T. Clark, 1986), 381–83.

31. He references the *Agreed Statement on the Eucharist,* 7 from the Anglican-Roman Catholic International Commission, Windsor 1971 (London: SPCK/Catholic Truth Society, 1972).

32. Douglas Estes, *SimChurch* (Grand Rapids: Zondervan, 2009), 118–23.

respectively: symbolic virtual communion (Hill),[33] avatar-administered virtual communion (easily trivialized and over-spiritualized), extensional virtual communion (Lord),[34] and outsourced virtual communion (using a physical church for an online eucharist). In response, Fiddes abandons any attempt at 'equivalence' between the online/local, virtual/real, digital/physical, Second/First Life by an analogy with what happens in Local Ecumenical Partnerships when a service of holy communion presided over by a Baptist minister takes place. He accepts that it is indeed "not an Anglican communion", but as a "Baptist Lord's Supper", it is "still a eucharistic form" and an occasion for grace.

Something similar also happened in my curacy in Bromley Ecumenical Parish in the 1980s with our regular team communion services: if they took place in our parish church, the vicar or myself presided according to Anglican liturgy, whereas in the Methodist or URC churches, their minister would preside, using their own liturgy and customs. As a result, I received communion regularly from the female Methodist minister a decade before the Church of England ordained women priests!

Fiddes concludes: "Is there an analogy here? Might mainstream Christian confessions simply say of a virtual eucharist, using virtual sacraments, that 'this is not an Anglican eucharist' or it is 'not a Baptist Lord's Supper' but that it is 'a eucharistic celebration in a virtual world'?" (95). Such a distinction avoids the problems caused by trying to assert 'equivalence' between the online/local, virtual/real, digital/physical, second/first life, but without retreating to the general sacramentalism of God's presence in the whole world.

We will return to this in our following discussion of *broadc*ast livestreams (Facebook and YouTube) and *narrowc*ast webinars (Zoom and Microsoft Teams). But for now, Fiddes' final conclusion provides a summary of this chronological survey, bringing us back to the basic challenge of holy communion "in contagious times".

> This paper has largely been a thought-experiment, rather than reflection on practices taking place on the web. But it is essential in our age to do this kind of digital theology. On the one hand it clarifies the very nature of sacraments by asking what qualifies as 'material' or created 'stuff' that can be the media for God's presence, and how God uses it as an instrument of grace. On the other hand, it takes seriously our situation today, in which 'virtual reality' needs to be understood theologically, rather than leaving it

33. Hill, "Second Life and Sacraments," 11.
34. Lord, "Can Eucharist Be Administered in a Virtual World?" 22.

simply to the realms of technology and sociology. Moreover, by practising the two sacraments—or sacramentals—of eucharist and baptismal renewal in a virtual world, we may come to experience more profoundly the created universe itself as not only eucharistic but baptismal, where created beings, by immersion into the waters of death, come to a new creation. (98).

Service in the Cathedral for Pentecost, complete with the descent of tongues of fire during reading of Acts 2, even upon the mermaid churchwarden in her pool!

ANALYSIS OF THE KEY ISSUES

This survey of various papers over more than a decade shows a lively debate about sacraments in the digital online world about which many remain ignorant. Interestingly, all of them discuss six or seven similar issues, which we will now consider individually.

1. The Reality of Virtual Reality

All our authors struggle with terminology to distinguish the two worlds, contrasting real/virtual, first/second life, analogue/digital, offline/online, etc. I have increasingly realized that these contrasts are more than just playing with words—but convey value judgements around the crucial question of whether the 'virtual' is actually 'real'. Christopher Hill's 2008

Church Times article makes this explicit: "'Virtual' is not (quite) real."[35] He uses similar distinctions consistently throughout his 2012 paper, as these extracts demonstrate:

- "Behind this reticence [about virtual sacraments] lies what is considered to be the necessity for a *real*, personal, as *opposed to virtual*, relationship in sacraments" (1);

- "The Salvation Army is described as being a para church on the absence of these [the Dominical sacraments]; does this distinction therefore apply to an 'expression of church' in Second Life, i.e., *not* church, but *virtual* church?" (5)

- "respect would need to be paid to Fiddes' careful use of the term 'virtual sacraments', implying . . . a proper distinction between a *virtual* sacrament and the '*real*' (i.e., non-virtual) world where physical, human presence is necessary"; (6)

- "No Christian church . . . from Baptist to Roman Catholic, could countenance a *virtual* baptism as a *real* baptism. . . . A *real* baptism could subsequently be celebrated with a *virtual* service of thanksgiving in the Epiphany Cathedral"; (7–8)

- "Some mechanism for any who wanted to be given more specific guidance through the *virtual* pastor as to how to obtain this personally from a '*real*' local church." (10)[36] (my italics throughout)

After reading an earlier draft of my manuscript, Christopher Hill emailed me to note, among other comments, that "I do now agree with Paul Fiddes that the distinction between virtual and real is not right. I usually put 'real' between commas even a decade ago, partially because I was not entirely happy with the word."[37]

---

35. Christopher Hill, "One Way of Growing a Global Mission," *Church Times* 25 July 2008, 13.

36. Christopher Hill, 'Second Life and Sacraments: Anglican Observations and Guidelines', pp. 1, 5, 6, 7, 8, 10; https://slangcath.wordpress.com/the-vision/sacraments-on-epiphany-island/ My italic emphases added.

37. Personal email from Bishop Christopher, August 16, 2021, which continues: "In any case it has bedevilled discussion about the presence of Christ in the eucharist for years. The virtual also has a God-given reality. Yet I think there must be a distinction, e.g., between a virtual meal and eating and drinking physically. But I also note your point about advancing technology in relation to virtual sensory perception. Happy for you to add my unease about the virtual/real language now."

Rundel's MA thesis,[38] similarly criticizes Hill's Anglican 'position state-ment' for making "a clear separation of life online and life offline, and the per-ception of *Second Life* is coloured by the insistence that the *Second Life* avatar is a fictional construct rather than an extension to the individual's reality"; similarly, the Methodist 'position statement' is "primarily focused upon the request to use digital space as a *means of communication* rather than a *means of existence*." For Rundel, "the final barrier needs to be overcome: the anxiety that the virtual reality of digital space is but a poor substitute for the reality of the everyday."[39] In response, he quotes Christopher Helland:

> As Internet technology has developed, people's level of engage-ment with the online environment has changed significantly. Over the past 30 years there have been revolutionary changes in the way we go online and the things we can do with this new form of media. Many people using the Internet no longer distin-guish between life-online and life-offline—rather, 'being online' has become a part of their life and social existence.[40]

Neither Hill's Anglican statement, nor that of the Methodists, have grappled with the implications of continuing technological innovation. While com-munication in St Pixels or even on SL began with users typing comments, and liturgy scrolling laboriously up the screen, recent innovation has seen the widespread use of sound, using built-in microphones to be able to speak directly with others, and to listen to music and other sounds.

When I/Hezekiah bend down to pet Demas, a beauti-ful diamond-coloured cat, who lies at my feet when I am pray-ing, he reacts by sitting up and glowing, and I can hear him purr; when I resume praying, he lies down again, his stom-ach visibly rising and falling as he goes back to sleep. Similarly, when I lean across the font in

---

38. Available on his website at https://www.frsimon.uk/ma-dissertation-sacra-ments-in-digital-space-a-theological-reflection-of-three-churchs-position-statements /, with no page numbers; all quotations taken from this source.

39. Chapter 5 of his thesis.

40. Christopher Helland, "*Ritual*," in *Digital Religion: Understanding Religious Practices in New Media Worlds*, edited by Heidi Campbell (Abingdon, UK: Routledge, 2013), 25.

the Cathedral to touch the dove of peace, perched with an olive branch in her beak, I usually discover from an audible splash and visible blue sprays that I have disturbed the water—or even fallen in!

In addition to these two physical senses of sight and sound, technology has advanced rapidly, especially through computer gaming, developing 'haptic' gloves, shirts, and even whole body suits, to provide 'touch' (from *haptō* = 'I touch' in Greek), allowing users to feel all that happens to the avatar, physical contact in a hug, or a punch, kick, or even being shot in the back.[41] Tesla, which began as the electric car company, but which is now internationally famous, not least for the exploits of its chairman, Elon Musk, and Space-X,[42] has developed the 'TeslaSuit', available for government and public safety services, business enterprise, athletics, and rehabilitation.

"Teslasuit's full body haptic feedback system" enables full sensation, "increasing immersion, fostering 360-degree awareness, and engaging muscle memory."[43] Athletes, soldiers, and security personnel can train actively in such suits, and perfect certain moves with 'muscle memory', thus avoiding entering into dangerous environments. Such suits will also doubtless prove popular in more 'adult' locations, if they are not already being used for virtual sex.

41. See various examples at https://www.amazon.com/s?k=virtual+reality+ha ptic+suit&crid=1AW244I6KAV4R&sprefix=haptic+virtua%2Caps%2C225&ref= nb_sb_ss_i_2_13

42. Elon Musk, born in South Africa in 1971, co-founded web software company Zip2 together with his brother Kimbal in 1995, followed by X.com, one of the first federally insured online banks and email-payment companies in 1999, and then by founding SpaceX in 2002, where he is CEO and CTO. In 2004, he became chairman of Tesla, becoming its CEO in 2008; see https://www.spacex.com/ and https://www.tesla.com/en_gb , and https://en.wikipedia.org/wiki/Elon_Musk

43. See their website at https://teslasuit.io/the-suit/

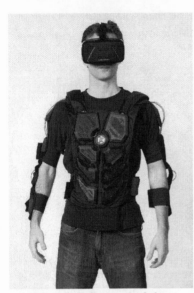

NullSpace's "full upper-body haptic feedback suit and gloves with standalone tracking for virtual reality"[44]

As well as the two clear senses in the digital world, the ability to *hear* and see, now avatars can *touch* things online—and users actually 'feel' that touch. If I wore a haptic glove, I could 'feel' Demas' fur, or the wetness of the water in the font. I expect olfactory devices to be developed (if they are not already) enabling 'smell-o-vision', and similar ways of transmitting the fifth, and final, sense of *taste*. The online world has now become the *immersive digital environment*, especially when combined with a full VR headset.

In fact, this technology helps those living without one of the physical senses. The 'SoundShirt', developed in 2016, enables deaf users to experience music physically through haptic sensations across the body, winning the 2019 UNESCO NETEXPLO innovation award.[45] With regard to sacraments and those deprived of one or more senses, Rundel observes:

> Pastorally, the Church does not exclude people with disabilities or head injuries, whose smell, taste, vision or hearing are impaired from sacramental engagement because they are not entirely sensate. It would be deeply troubling and pastorally insensitive to deny the sacramental effectiveness of the administration of healing at the end of someone's life ('the last rites') to an unconscious dying person, even when we have no idea whether that individual is aware of the sacramental act being administered.

On this basis, if I can 'hear', 'see', and 'touch' digital objects, why can they *not* be 'outward and visible' signs of the 'inward and spiritual' grace of a sacrament? As we begin to smell or even taste what avatars encounter in the digital world in future, the separation of digital and analogue, online or offline, or the contrast of the physical, *real* world with the digital, *virtual*

44. "A total of 32 haptic feedback pads are placed around the body with 117 built-in haptic effects" https://en.wikipedia.org/wiki/Haptic_suit; photo by Minswho - Own work, CC BY-SA 4.0, https://commons.wikimedia.org/w/index.php?curid=50348141

45. See further, https://en.wikipedia.org/wiki/Haptic_suit

environment as somehow *unreal* becomes difficult to sustain. Therefore, I have decided to stop contrasting the 'virtual' with the 'real' world. Both the digital and the physical, the online and the offline, are *equally real*—in the same way that the intellectual, or spiritual, or emotional worlds are not less real, despite not being physically material.

2. Puppet Strings? The Relationship of Avatar to User/Owner

Having argued that the online digital world is no less real than the physical, the next question concerns the relationship between the avatar and the human person. Thus, Peters directs his attack on Paul Fiddes:

> Professor Fiddes contends that God is present in a virtual world providing grace for its inhabitants. In Fiddes' theology God gives grace to the avatar. . . . The concept of an avatar being the receiver of God's grace is astonishing from an Oxford Professor of Systematic Theology. . . . Following Fiddes' approach one would logically hold that God gives grace to a cartoon character like Mickey Mouse with whom an observer (or cartoonist) identifies—and that Mickey Mouse passes this grace on to the observer or cartoonist.[46]

The unfortunate *ad hominem* attack on Fiddes reads more like one of Peters' April Fool articles, for which he is justifiably famous (or notorious?).[47] In contrast, Hill argues that "sacraments are 'graceful' inter-personal encounters between real people through the sacraments. At first instance the adoption of an avatar seems to add a barrier to direct personal encounter, almost like a mask, . . . a disguising of the person." Admittedly, I found it odd initially in the prayers and services in the SL Cathedral, where their strict Anglican liturgy contrasted with worshippers having fox or rabbit heads and tails, not to mention the churchwarden mermaid, complete with fish tail and strategically placed shells!!

While an avatar may seem like a mask, Hill responds: "On the other hand, all human communication, including direct face-to-face encounter,

46. Rev'd Bosco Peters, "Can Sacraments Work in the Virtual World?" June 28, 2009, https://liturgy.co.nz/virtual-eucharist

47. On April 1, 2012, Peters announced that "Pope Benedict XVI and Archbishop of Canterbury Rowan Williams today signed an agreement on sacraments in cyberspace"; the document, *In recognitionem sacramenta in virtualis mundi* (IRSIVM), resulted from years of work by a secret commission of Vatican and Anglican Communion representatives called "**S**acraments for **A**nglicans and **C**atholics **R**eal **A**lternative **M**eanings **E**volving because of **N**ew **T**echnologies (or 'SACRAMENT' for short); https://liturgy.co.nz/pope-archbishop-of-canterbury-recognise-virtual-sacraments

involves a projection through facial and bodily gestures; posture; clothes; make-up; jewellery; regalia; uniforms; vesture"—and this is especially true of a bishop's mitre and crozier, a priest's vesture, and monastic habits. As for hiding one's 'real' name and identity, "in a 'real' Cathedral, the personal identity of each member of the congregation or clergy is not always known."[48]

Spencer-Hall's study of the relationship between people worshipping in SL and their avatars, noted that:

> Explaining their understanding of the relationship between online avatar and offline body, several respondents in my study referred to the status of the avatar as a projection, and representation, of their offline selves. . . . The virtual body of the SL (Second Life) avatar, then, is a means of communicating the internal mysterious actions of the spirit that are taking place in the Christian's offline body, or the spirit's otherwise invisible presence travelling across wide geographical divides via the internet.[49]

Lord continues similarly:

> Residents of Second Life are able to customise their avatars to appear as anything they choose. While this might seem to be an avenue for deception, most users see it as an opportunity to express a deeper sense of who they really are than they feel might be seen with their physical body. . . . Research shows that many people feel that their avatars are a more authentic representation of who they feel themselves to be than their own bodies are. When a person is given the ability to create their own visual representation, one that enhances rather than impairs their ability to be accepted and therefore heard, they may be empowered to explore and express in new ways what they believe to be their true selves.[50]

Spencer-Hall observes, of a middle-aged man whose avatar is a small child, that his

> avatar is an authentic representation of his personhood as it reflects his spiritual self, and functions as a symbol of his spiritual intent, to follow the Lord's guidance and become as a little child

48. Hill, "Second Life and Sacrament: Anglican Observations and Guidelines," 5–6.

49. Alicia Spencer-Hall, "Pixelated Prayers—Christian Worship in Second Life," paper at the Annual Meeting of the American Studies Association, "Imagination, Reparation, Transformation," October 20–23, 2011, Baltimore, Maryland, p. 2; quoted from Lord, "Can Eucharist be Administered in a Virtual World?"

50. Lord, "Can Eucharist Be Administered in a Virtual World?" 8–9.

in his embrace. This avatar is a (virtually) physicalized rendition
of the Christian's interior (spiritual) condition.[51]

Certainly, while many regular AoSL members are clearly physically older
(judging from their voices), and retired, and their prayers are focussed upon
ailments like high blood pressure or heart issues, their avatars tend to be
young, fit, and healthy—and the ladies are very attractively garbed, if not
to say, in some cases, sexy! This demonstrates Lord's point about avatars revealing "a deeper sense of who they really are"—or perhaps how they would
like to see themselves.

We noted that early participants on the Ship of Fools and its Ark, as
well as St Pixels, discovered a sense of identity between their avatars and
their own selves, as a kind of 'extension' or even 'incarnation' within digital
space; they were surprised at the depth of connection that they felt with
their avatars. Indeed, there is increasing concern about children or teenag-
ers playing a lot of computer games whose avatar keeps getting killed digitally; it cannot but affect them in the physical world also.[52]

Peters counters, "This relationship is, in my opinion, akin to identifying with a character in a novel, play, or movie, or with a string puppet one is
controlling in a puppet theatre." However, even from my own brief connection with my avatar, Hezekiah, I am not surprised when those using their
avatar for years discover a real identification as a persona of the self, way
beyond identifying with a fictional character or puppet. Hezekiah quickly
became the *persona* that I not only presented to others on SL, but also with
which I interacted, prayed with them and for them, and received prayed by
them; I rejoiced over the birth of one's grandchild in RL, and they shared my
pain and difficulties, not least in writing this book.[53]

---

51. Spencer-Hall, "Pixelated Prayers" 3, quoted in Lord, "Can Eucharist be Administered in a Virtual World?" 9.

52. One Chinese father became so concerned about the amount of time his son
spent playing computer games and not getting a real job that he hired very high-level
game players as 'hit-men' to target and kill his son's avatars in an attempt to stop him
gaming; however, it appears not to have worked. See https://www.dailymail.co.uk/news
/article-2258877/Chinese-father-hires-virtual-hitman-kill-son-online-games--job.
html

53. After reading an earlier draft of my manuscript, Bishop Christopher Hill re-
marked that my choice of a biblical name like Hezekiah was similar to how members
of religious orders "take the name of a saint at their profession . . . and of course popes
taking a name indicating something of themselves and their future ministry, e.g. Pope
Francis'; personal email to me of August 16, 2021, quoted with permission.

Hezekiah lighting votive candles in the Cathedral (which burn down) before praying

After guiding my avatar around the Cathedral, I can testify to learning how to use three senses all over again, the *touch* of pushing different keys to make Hezekiah go this way or that, preferably without banging into pews or walls; the *sight* of changing the camera's viewpoint, let alone the gloomy darkness of SL's time zone in San Francisco (until I discovered that, like Joshua, I could make the sun go back and prolong the daylight!); and the *sound* of my own voice and others', the splashing of the water when I fell in the font, the tinkling as I played the piano, and the deep ringing from striking the COVID-19 bell as a sign of prayers for the pandemic's victims. While taste and smell cannot yet be communicated between the physical and digital worlds with current technology, presumably this will become possible in future.

The fusion of *persona* and my own *person* became clear when I found myself using the self-referential pronoun 'I' interchangeably between Hezekiah and 'me'—the very difficulty proves the point. Similarly, we accept such a fusion on a golf course of 'I' and 'my ball' every time we ask, "where am I?", "can you see me?", or "you are in the water—or a bunker"! Fiddes argues that such a fusion is certainly true not just of ourselves but also of God:

> Integrating our two reasons for thinking a virtual world can be sacramental—the presence of God and relation to an avatar, we should observe that avatars in a virtual church are not worshipping merely an avatar-God. There *is* only one God, for whom person and persona are identical and in whom "all things live and move and have their being" (Acts 17:28), including the beings of virtual worlds. . . .

> [C]yberspace is [not] a disembodied world. The net is composed of a form of energy, just as is the familiar 'physical' world in which we operate every day. Moreover, the persons behind the avatars are in physical connection with the virtual world—through many of the senses (sight, hearing, touch—i.e. keyboard, mouse). . . . There is a mysterious and complex interaction between the person and the persona projected (avatar), just as there is between the person and his/her personae (self-presentations to others) in everyday life. . . . The second reason for thinking that the world of cyberspace is part of a sacramental and eucharistic universe is the unique relation between the person entering this world and his or her avatar, or the *persona* that is being adopted. Within the logic of the virtual world, a virtual church such as the Anglican Cathedral in *Second Life* is a place where avatars worship God and avatars minister to avatars.[54] (89, 92, 88, 87)

3. Can God or Christ be Present in the Digital World—and How?

Peters' attack on Fiddes as an Oxford professor and Baptist minister is as confusing as it is unwarranted. Fiddes picks up his summary point that "God is present in a virtual world in a way that is suitable for its inhabitants" at the start of his 2009 paper, thus:

> The key theological question is whether the triune God is present, and whether Christ is incarnate (in some form, including the church) within the virtual world. If the answer is yes, then one can conceive of the mediation of grace through the materials of that world, i.e. through digital representations. Grace is, of course, not a substance but the gracious presence of God, coming to transform personality and society. In sacrament, God takes the occasion of bodies in creation to be present in an intense or 'focused' way to renew life.[55]

If the triune God is *not* present in the digital world, then this means that his human creatures with whom God has shared his creative powers in his continuing creation, have created something off-limits to God, where the omnipresent Creator of All cannot be present—which is surely

54. Paul Fiddes, paper given at the 2018 symposium on "The Virtual Body of Christ? Sacrament and Liturgy in Digital Spaces", see note 28 above; I am extremely grateful to Prof Fiddes for sharing an advance copy with me for inclusion here.

55. See https://www.frsimon.uk/paul-fiddes-sacraments-in-a-virtual-world/.

as unacceptable as it is illogical. Fiddes clarifies, "Avatars do not, however, worship merely an avatar God because there is only one God." Furthermore, since "he remembers that we are but dust" (Ps 103:14), the Creator does not overpower us, but respects our fragile human form in the physical world; it follows, therefore, that God will be similarly gracious in being "present in a virtual world in a way that is suitable for its inhabitants". Such a conclusion *is* worthy of both an Oxford professor and a Baptist minister.

From a theological perspective, Peters counters that "Christianity is an incarnational spirituality. If God were becoming incarnate today, this would not be in the form of an avatar on screens, who died and rose again solely online. We do not feed the hungry by sending them virtual bread. A sacrament is 'outward and visible.'" Peters does not complete the statement about a sacrament being 'an outward and visible sign of an inward and spiritual grace', and therefore *in*visible. Christian faith is indeed 'incarnational'—but Peters' use of the 'impossible condition', "*if* God *were* becoming incarnate today" (my emphasis), suggests that God is *not* "incarnate today". The orthodox tradition of *theosis* (or deification) teaches that the goal of salvation is that, through purification and illumination, we are to become like God—and this is only possible because Christ took humanity into the Godhead.

As St Gregory of Nazianzus the Theologian (AD 329–90) put it: "for where is the body now, if not with the one who assumed it?"[56] This of course leads to his famous dictum in only four Greek words, "for the unassumed, [is] unhealed", or as more generally quoted, "for that which is not assumed, is not healed". He continues, "but if it is united with God, then this is also saved".[57] Furthermore, St. Athanasius is clear that there cannot be 'no-go areas' for God: "if, even so, the Word of God is in the universe, which is itself a body, and has entered into all and every part by part, what is there surprising or out of place, if we say that he has entered also into a human being?"[58]

Fiddes' argument that "God is present in a virtual world in a way that is suitable for its inhabitants" must be true if "the Word of God . . . has entered into it in its every part."[59] "The key theological question is whether the

56. Ποῦ γὰρ τὸ σῶμα νῦν, εἰ μὴ μετὰ τοῦ προσλαβόντος; the Latin version is fuller, *ubi enim nunc corpus fuerit, nisi cum ea natura, a qua assumptum est*, "if not with that nature, by which it was assumed" Gregory Nazianzus, *Letter to Cledonius the Priest Against Apollinarius* (Epistle 101) https://archive.org/details/patrologiae_cursus_completus_gr_vol_037/page/n94/mode/1up pp. 181–82.

57. Τὸ γὰρ ἀπρόσληπτον, ἀθεράπευτον· again the Latin version is longer, *nam quod assumptum non est, curationis est expers* https://archive.org/details/patrologiae_cursus_completus_gr_vol_037/page/n95/mode/1up pp. 183–84

58. Athanasius, *On the Incarnation*, chapter 7, §41. https://archive.org/details/patrologiae_cursus_completus_gr_vol_025/page/n381/mode/2up, pp. 168–70.

59. It follows similarly that, if Christ needs to be incarnated on a planet of 'little green creatures', he will become a 'little green creature'!

triune God is present, and whether Christ is incarnate (in some form, including the church) within the virtual world. If the answer is yes, then one can conceive of the mediation of grace through the materials of that world, i.e. through digital representations." And if the answer is 'no', then we are back to my conundrum above where God the Creator gives his creatures (pro-)creativity to create a (digital) world where the Creator cannot be creatively present—which is surely impossible.

Rundel also considers *the presence of Christ within digital space*, the first objection in all three denominational statements as a "barrier to the representation of sacraments in digital space".[60] From the universal presence of Christ in all things (citing Ps 139:7–10; John 1:2; Col 1:15–17; 1 Tim 2:5–6), Rundel argues that this includes the "digital experience of Christ". "The argument of this project is that digital space is not a *separate* reality but a *transformed* reality and so if Christ is held to be present in the analogue world, so he must be present in digital also: it is not an option of either/or. If Christ is to be present, then he is present everywhere. Sacraments are the liminal mechanism where that presence is *most* keenly experienced."[61] Here too, we are back to Gregory Nazianzus and Athanasius, that the Creator of all cannot create creatures with the pro-/co-creativity to create an environment where the Creator cannot be present.

After his consideration of the "sacramental consecration of the whole world", as per Teilhard de Chardin and Gerard Manley Hopkins, Fiddes argues that the online

> world of cyberspace can be also part of this sacramental universe for at least two reasons. . . . First, the combination of the doctrines of the incarnation and the resurrection of Jesus encourages us to think that God is present in a virtual world in a way that is suitable for its inhabitants. In Christ, God becomes flesh. Then the risen Christ continues to inhabit the world in a universal lordship, unhindered by any one space and time, though taking special opportunities to be visible through a particular form of his body, the church. (87)

Fiddes' argument that "the world of cyberspace cannot be excluded from this mutual habitation" agrees with my own experience in SL:

---

60. Chapter 3 of his MA thesis, available on his website at https://www.frsimon.uk/ma-dissertation-sacraments-in-digital-space-a-theological-reflection-of-three-churchs-position-statements/, with no page numbers; all quotations taken from this source.

61. Italics added.

If a eucharist were offered, the 'person' could thus only receive a virtual sacrament *indirectly* through relation to the avatar. My argument is that the grace of God received by an avatar through a virtual means of grace, can be shared with the person whose avatar it is. This is because there is a mysterious and complex interaction between the person and the *persona* projected (avatar), and this is also the case between a person and his/her *personae* (self-presentations to others) in everyday life.

4. Nature of a Church Online

Rundel's thesis (chapter 4) explores "the manifestation of the Church, *the body of Christ within digital space*", starting with the experience of the Triune God: "All sense of Christian community begins with God, and the Trinity: a perfect model of living in mutual love and equality. The human struggle has been to try to emulate this." The Roman Catholic 2002 position contrasts the virtual and the physical with the church's need "to lead people from cyberspace to true community".[62] This dismissive statement ignores the true community reflected in digital groups, as we have discovered in the Ship of Fools' Ark, the Church of Fools, St Pixels, and supremely the SL Anglican Cathedral.

After only a few visits for daily Morning Prayers, it was clear that the SL Anglicans have formed over more than a decade a "true community" of prayer, expressing deep concern and love for one another—and quickly manifested in their welcome and their prayers for me and this book. Sixteen years after the Catholic statement, the Methodist 2018 document takes it "for granted that the use of electronic means of communication in Christian worship, education and mission will create 'online' or 'virtual' communities, though the precise nature and ecclesial status of such communities must await future treatment".[63] After over two decades of online communities, what "future treatment" is still needed is not obvious. The early Christians discovered the truth of Jesus' promise "where two or three are gathered together in my name, I am there among them" (Matt 18:20), and certainly that has been my experience in SL and online. Rundel concludes,

> For some, church expressions in digital space will be the Church people belong to because they do not have the access (perhaps

62. "The Church and Internet," the Pontifical Council For Social Communications, 2002, paragraph II.9.

63. "Holy Communion Mediated through Social Media," 2018 Methodist Conference Report, paragraph 2.

through geography, mental state or disability) to meet with others in a physical location. For them, this is what they need. For others, it is an adjunct to a regular Christian community: perhaps like visiting the Cathedral every-so-often for a change of style, community and teaching. For them, this is what they need.

While all three denominations express concern that digital space may be a distraction from 'real world' physical church, Rundel responds that "it should perhaps be viewed more constructively as part of a mixed economy of faith expression." According to Rundel, Fiddes' argument about "the 'internal logic of a virtual world' means that regardless of the response to it by external sources of authority, a gathering in digital space may choose to describe itself as a Church. If it functions as a Church within the logic of digital space, then it must be so."[64]

Lord also considers the pastoral possibilities in the online world's crossing thousands of miles and all time zones. She quotes Taylor:

> While we are online . . . we enter a world where time and space mean something else. In the on-line universe, there is no need for traditional senses of time and space because we are, in a sense, in a new dimension of both. It matters not whether it is day or night, because for other users it may be the inverse of our context. This discontinuous time . . . is also compressed time, where past, present, and future come together in continually new possibilities and configurations, allowing us to play with history, ideology, and information and create entirely new conceptions of life and living.[65]

When I was ill long-term recently, I formed an online group of my friends in all time zones, so that when I was awake at night (as I often was), there was always someone to talk with and to listen. Lord notes similarly:

> It is often in the middle of the night when people are beset with fear about real-life situations. The ability to go online and talk to people, who are, by virtue of the fact that they live in another time zone, awake and actively socialising, raises many opportunities for deep sharing and caring. . . . I have personally spoken with people who have been experiencing sleeplessness

64. At the end of Rundel's chapter 4, see: https://www.frsimon.uk/ma-dissertation-sacraments-in-digital-space-a-theological-reflection-of-three-churchs-position-statements/

65. Barry Taylor, *Entertainment Theology: New-Edge Spirituality in a Digital Democracy* (Grand Rapids: Baker Academic, 2008), 36

due to medical conditions, mental health issues, relationships concerns, and loneliness. Without exception, those who come to Second Life in search of someone to talk to express gratitude that someone is awake and willing to listen to and come alongside them.

But it is not just loneliness or sickness: in SL, "one can reveal oneself more easily, given the 'distance' between users on the Net. In other words, technology enables intimate discussion."[66] The ability to project what one wishes, or to hide behind an avatar can be helpful, as Lord quotes form Broaddus:

> Loneliness, the desire to connect with others, yet stay anonymous and avoid judgment, was one of the more interesting comments made. One individual experienced encountering feelings of judgment and pity when she attended traditional churches with her children and no husband. The anonymity of online church protects her from those perceived judgments. . . . You can be honest and not feel judged. That is one of the hugest plusses of church online. It is such a judgment-free zone.[67]

Lord continues our previous discussion about avatars:

> The avatar representing a person may be a more accurate expression of who they feel themselves to be than their physical body is. Indeed, for those who are disabled or disfigured, for those whose physical appearance, age, gender or ethnicity are a cause for judgment in physical society, the ability to create a different visual representation of the self can be greatly liberating.[68]

She concludes with a hard-hitting challenge to the mission of the church with regard to SL:

> If we revisit the reasons why people value Second Life and the community at the Anglican Cathedral of Second Life, it could be suggested that to offer the Eucharist is a pastoral imperative. People come seeking connection, and participation in the sacrament of the body and blood of Christ is the ultimate connection to God and to neighbour. People come seeking nurture, pastoral care, and healing; the Lord's Supper is broken bread representing the Body of Christ given for the healing and life of the world.

---

66. Tom Beaudoin, *Virtual Faith: The Irreverent Spiritual Quest of Generation X* (San Francisco: Jossey-Bass, 1998), 88.

67. Broaddus, *Exploring the Lived Experience of Online Worshipers*, 11.

68. Lord, "Can Eucharist Be Administered in a Virtual World?" 29–30.

> People come seeking mystery and spirituality, and central to the
> Eucharist is the mystery that is bread and wine transformed into
> the sacrament that provides for our spiritual sustenance. There
> seems, to me, to be no better way to meet the needs of seekers
> who find their way to Epiphany Island than to explore a way to
> help them participate in the sacrament of communion.

However, she does recognize that "it may stretch our current understanding of all aspects of the Body of Christ. It will likely take much thought, preparation and prayer on the part of the staff of the Cathedral." However, she argues, "if the parables of the New Testament show us anything, it is that it is in the nature of God to be generous."

I have quoted Lord's conclusions at some length since she delivered a clear theological, liturgical, and pastoral challenge to the church back in 2012, when she noted that "the Anglican Communion currently has no guidelines for the celebration of the Eucharist in virtual worlds. It is a frontier ministry. There is scope here for creativity and generosity." Nearly a decade later, still no one has responded, but in these "contagious times" of the coronavirus pandemic, her challenge still faces us—hence the explorations of this book.

5. Understanding Sacraments, Communion, and the Real Presence

All our writers discuss the meaning and validity of sacraments, especially within the range of beliefs and ideas held within Anglicanism, as befits the SL Anglican Cathedral. As the bishop providing initial guidance, Hill commended the AoSL leadership as "consistently reticent . . . to minister *virtual* sacraments" because of "the necessity for a *real*, personal, as opposed to virtual relationship in sacraments" (my italics),[69] although we have argued above that this understanding of virtual as somehow not 'real' has become increasingly untenable since 2012, as Bishop Christopher himself now admits.[70]

His paper provides a quick tour from sacraments in the New Testament, through the early church fathers, to Reformation debates about the two 'dominical' sacraments (baptism and the eucharist, both 'commanded by the Lord himself') , and the other five, often considered as sacraments: confirmation, marriage, ordination, penance, and the anointing of the sick, and how the later Anglican tradition treats this distinction. This raises the central question explored throughout this book, of "sacramental efficacy:

69. Christopher Hill, "Second Life and Sacraments."

70. See his recently emailed comment quoted in note 37 above.

can the sacraments 'work', that is to say bring us into a closer encounter with the risen Lord Jesus?"

As we argued above, a proper celebration of communion requires a duly ordained and authorized minister with the traditional narrative of the institution and the words of consecration; yet, sacraments are never just "machines, automatically dispensing grace understood in quantitative, almost physical terms. . . . But to be effective sacraments need to be *received* with a living faith." This coheres with our equal emphasis on the role of the laity, noted throughout. Hill considers each sacrament in turn: thus, while "No Christian Church that I am aware of from Baptist to Roman Catholic could countenance a *virtual* baptism as a *real* baptism", he does encourage online renewal of baptismal promises. The same goes for confirmation, marriage, and ordination, where although the actual sacrament cannot take place online, the appropriate vows can be renewed in digital services. While the sacrament of confession, absolution, and reconciliation cannot happen online (because of privacy, confidentiality, and assurance of identity—though these are equally difficult to ensure in a traditional, anonymously screened 'confession box'), "a general service of penitence, with corresponding general confession and general absolution as found in Anglican liturgical rites would be possible." Unction, both the anointing of the sick with holy oil and the laying on of hands, require physical actions as the 'outward and visible sign', which cannot happen digitally, but "an avatar could make a virtual gesture of healing by similarly stretching out hands" in a "general service of healing and intercession".

Thus, Hill cannot countenance theologically any *sacraments* in SL, but his helpful suggestions about *sacramental* renewals of vows mean that it is no surprise that he concludes, "what could be envisaged, if it is done clearly and explicitly, is for the persons behind their avatars to make a 'spiritual communion.'"

Although Rundel concludes his 2019 thesis by commending "a phenomenological understanding of the sacraments to overcome the metaphysical objections which place *undue emphasis on the physical embodiment of sacramental expression*", nonetheless he also encourages "the *devotion of spiritual communion* [as] an authentic mode of understanding sacramental encounter both within digital space and as observed from without." His "project has demonstrated that participants within a digital space may be able to use the senses made available to them within that digital space to make sense of a digitally mediated sacrament. If they are able to do this, within both a relationship with Christ and the context of a digitally mediated ecclesial community, then that *sacrament can be demonstrably valid and efficacious*" (my italics).

Peters is not convinced: "does all of the grace received by the avatar automatically get transferred to the person behind the avatar in a sort of *ex opere operato* mechanism? Or in some (many, most) cases is only some of the grace transferred, with the avatar retaining grace that was originally given by God to the avatar?" He suggests that in this approach, "God gives grace to a cartoon character like Mickey Mouse with whom an observer (or cartoonist) identifies—and that Mickey Mouse passes this grace on to the observer or cartoonist." However, grace is not some kind of substance like a cake, such that the avatar consumes a piece and then passes another slice to the user. It is perhaps more like the way that an honour received by my representative in my physical absence is simultaneously received by me.[71] It is not divided between us. As Fiddes reminds us, "Grace is, of course, not a substance but the gracious presence of God, coming to transform personality and society."[72]

The fusion of identity that we have demonstrated between the avatar and its user/owner, the *persona* with the *person*, means that they are increasingly one and the same. When SL Anglicans as far away as Australia, San Francisco, and the US deep South, pray "for Hezekiah and his writing", I believe that God hears those prayers as being for *me* and he is present with me in my physical environment in England (not to mention the intellectual, emotional, and spiritual worlds) to give me his grace and strength as I struggled to complete this book.

71. The same is true the other way round; speaking personally as someone who has been asked to be the representative of two archbishops of Canterbury at various events around the world over my time as dean of King's College London, I am well aware both of the honour I felt personally both to be so asked and so received at the time, as well as the honour those to whom I was conveying the archepiscopal greetings appeared to enjoy, as well as being instructed to take back their good wishes and greetings to Lambeth Palace, as well as special messages on some occasions.

72. Fiddes, "Sacraments in a Virtual World," 87.

**I keep the live feed of Hezekiah praying in the Meditation Chapel
to the side of my screen while writing; Demas, the companion,
seems asleep, waiting for butterflies or to be petted . . .**

We noted above how Fiddes concludes "the sacramental consecration of the whole world" from consideration of Teilhard de Chardin and Gerald Manley Hopkins that "the world of cyberspace can be also part of this sacramental universe for at least two reasons. The first is the willingness of God to enter and inhabit all worlds, and the second is the complex relation between the person and his or her avatar."[73] Having considered Fiddes' second reason (regarding the person and the avatar), we return to the idea of "the sacramental consecration of the whole world". This reflects the sacramental approach of the Fourth Gospel. John narrates neither Jesus' actual baptism by John the Baptist (see John 1:29–34; 3:25–30) nor the institution of the eucharist, focussing on the footwashing and the Farewell Discourses instead (see John 13–17). Yet, despite the curious absence of these narratives of the two dominical sacraments, no other gospel's theology is so sacramental, with references to being born of water and the Spirit, and streams of living water (1:26–33; 2:1–11; 3:5; 4:10–15; 5:1–9; 7:38; 9:7; 13:1–11) while bread and wine abound, supremely of course in the discourses about the True Vine (15:1–6) and the Bread of Life: "those who eat my flesh and drink my blood have eternal life, and I will raise them up on the last day; for my flesh

---

73. Fiddes, "Sacraments in a Virtual World," 87.

is true food and my blood is true drink. Those who eat my flesh and drink my blood abide in me, and I in them" (see 6:50–58).[74]

Whatever the reason for John's approach, we are back to the same conundrum with Athanasius and Gregory of Nazianzus, that it is impossible for God the Creator to give his creatures pro-creativity to create a (digital) world where the Creator cannot be creatively present. Similarly, as human pro/co-creators with God, we cannot create a world where the grace of the loving Creator cannot be sacramentally present, even if, as in our world, that needs to be in a manner appropriate to and consonant with how any particular world is created and exists. To quote Fiddes yet again, "In sacrament, God takes the occasion of bodies in creation to be present in an intense or 'focused'[75] way to renew life."[76]

Therefore, if a sacrament is an outward and visible sign of an inward and spiritual grace, to use the traditional definition, then digital bread and wine upon a digital altar in SL can be just as "outward and visible" as in the material, physical world. The "inward and spiritual grace" can only be appreciated within a person by their own faith in accordance with their theological understanding of sacraments. We have stressed throughout the need to recognize the range of understandings of the sacraments, especially holy communion, among various Christian churches, and especially within the accepted diversity of Anglican tradition, (as in Dyer's diagram in chapter 6).

For those at the 'lower' end of the candle with a more Zwinglian understanding in 'remembering' the sacrifice of Christ, observing a digital celebration of communion can be just as effective as a physical eucharist in effecting that memorial. Those from the 'higher', more Catholic tradition, which needs a canonically ordained priest who has been ontologically changed to effect a similar ontological change from proper (wheat) bread and wine (fermented from grapes) to the body and blood of our Lord Jesus Christ, will consider a celebration by an avatar over digital bread and wine clearly insufficient and unacceptable—but no more so than that celebrated by any Protestant minister, especially if using improperly baked bread and non-alcoholic grape juice. A Roman Catholic may attend a digital eucharist in the same way that they would any other non-Catholic physical church service—but in each case, they cannot receive the grace of the sacrament,

74. See my section, "Church and Sacraments," in Richard A. Burridge, *John*, The People's Bible Commentary (Oxford: Bible Reading Fellowship, 1998/2008/2010), 25–26.

75. Fiddes is using John Macquarrie's term from *Principles of Christian Theology* (rev. ed.; London: SCM, 1966), 449, quoted in Fiddes, "Sacraments in a Virtual World," 8 n. 27.

76. Fiddes, "Sacraments in a Virtual World," 8.

according to the teaching of the magisterium. Within the accepted diversity of Anglican tradition, those who find themselves at one or other end of this spectrum, Zwinglian or Catholic, will react to such digital celebrations as they do to physical eucharists.

We saw above how Fiddes cuts this Gordian knot by an analogy with when a service of Holy Communion in a Local Ecumenical Partnership is presided over by a Baptist minister:

> The Church of England does not, at present, recognize Baptist ministerial orders, and so, in its official theology, Baptist ministers cannot have a eucharistic ministry. Yet, by sponsoring the LEP, it encourages the Anglican worshippers present to regard the sacrament they receive as a means of grace. Rather than making the negative judgement that such a communion is 'not' a eucharist, the general Anglican approach is simply to make clear that it is 'not an *Anglican* communion' but it is (say) a 'Baptist Lord's Supper'. . . . [S]uch services still take a eucharistic form, and are presumably occasions for Christ to presence himself and give grace in a special way that nourishes the Anglican faithful. (94–95)

Fiddes concludes: "Is there an analogy here? Might mainstream Christian confessions simply say of a virtual eucharist, using virtual sacraments, that 'this is not an Anglican eucharist' or it is 'not a Baptist Lord's Supper' but that it is 'a eucharistic celebration in a virtual world'?"[77]

This distinction avoids the problems caused by trying to assert 'equivalence' between the online/local, virtual/real, digital/physical, second/first life, but without just retreating to the general sacramentalism of God's presence in the whole world. This is a brave attempt, but for anyone who believes in the need for physical bread and wine, especially with the wheat and alcohol required by canon law, such a digital celebration may be "eucharistic" in its literal sense of "thanksgiving", but can never replace physical sacraments. An 'online' digital eucharist is 'different' from celebrations in the physical, material universe, and may perhaps be considered 'equal but different' in terms of conveying a 'spiritual' effect in the grace of God, but it cannot provide the full sacramental benefit.

77. Fiddes, "Sacraments in a Virtual World," 95.

CONCLUSION: ONLINE COMMUNION IN SECOND LIFE— SOME POSSIBLE OPTIONS

In searching for options for holy communion in "contagious times," I set out "to boldly go" into cyber-space to visit Second Life—and frankly, I did not expect it to take long or find anything for our quest. But I discovered a small Christian, even Anglican, community in the Cathedral on Epiphany Island who made me very welcome indeed, some of whom have become 'real' friends, supporting me in prayer—even if they have no idea who or where I am, or what I am doing, in the physical, material world. They have been praying together for over a decade—but what possibilities might exist for them to have holy communion?

Option 1: Spiritual Communion, but No Sacraments in SL

In his initial meetings (both online and in person at his home, 2008/9), Bishop Christopher Hill was clear that they could not be a eucharistic community; he even commended their leadership for being "consistently reticent . . . to minister *virtual* sacraments" because of "the necessity for a *real*, personal, as opposed to virtual relationship in sacraments" (my italics).[78] It is a tribute to both their faithfulness and their Anglican identity that they have kept that line, quoting Hill's dubious distinction between the 'virtual' and the 'real' on their website, a distinction that, as we have seen, Bishop Christopher himself no longer maintains:[79]

> Following extensive consultation with one of the bishops who helped us in the early days . . . [whose] paper forms the foundation for our position on virtual sacraments at the Anglican Cathedral of Second Life. In essence, our position at this point is that we do not believe it is possible to practice the Sacraments of Holy Communion or Baptism in a virtual context because of what is considered to be the necessity for a real, physical and personal interaction and relationship expressed in and through the sacraments.[80]

This online community have, therefore, kept for over a decade a 'eucharistic fast', the first option that we explored in this book, so that all their services are ministry of the word, with liturgy, scripture, and prayers. Hill also

78. Christopher Hill, "Second Life and Sacraments."

79. See his recently emailed comment quoted in footnote 37 above.

80. https://slangcath.wordpress.com/the-vision/sacraments-on-epiphany-island/

commended the practice of 'spiritual communion' for those present online
at the initial eucharist in 2008, and he reiterated this in his 2012 paper:

> Whether or not the persons behind the avatar actually take bread
> and wine is not that determinative, for the reality of spiritual
> communion is by definition a reality without actual reception
> of the physical sacrament. A 'spiritual communion' can be made
> with nothing, or with an 'agape' style token of bread and wine.

In fact, such 'spiritual communion' SL services are extremely rare, and I am
not aware of 'spiritual communion' happening with virtual bread and wine.

Option 2: Blending First and Second Life in a Remote Eucharist

After her detailed study of Dix' four-fold actions of taking, blessing, breaking, and giving, Lord suggested that participants place 'real' physical bread
and wine before their device's screen to be consecrated through the SL service, and then consumed it at home. Lord uses a 'check-list' of criteria or
requirements for a valid and effective communion, as we have also been
developing, and suggests that such an online celebration of the eucharist
with real bread and wine may indeed fulfil them all:

> The suggested method for celebrating the Eucharist online is
> Anglican in both its structure and its generosity. The entirety of
> the Eucharistic practice will still be in place. Ordained ministers
> will still pray the words of the Great Thanksgiving. The people
> who make up the Body of Christ will still be gathered, albeit
> it throughout space and connected through the technology of
> virtual worlds. Bread and wine will still be consumed. People
> will still be nurtured. God will still be glorified. "Even though
> virtual Communion will seem strange to many today . . . virtual
> churches should not fear people's opinions or church traditions
> but should fear dishonoring Jesus' request: 'Do this to remem-
> ber me' (Luke 22.19)."[81]

Since we shall explore such remote consecrations later, I will not comment
here for now.

---

81. Douglas Estes, *SimChurch: Being the Church in the Virtual World* (Grand Rapids: Zondervan, 2009), 123.

Option 3: Virtual Reality Holy Communion in SL

Rundel's concluding suggestion was for a full-blown holy communion service involving digital elements representing bread and wine:

> participants within a digital space *may* be able to use the senses made available to them within that digital space to make sense of a digitally mediated sacrament. If they are able to do this, within both a relationship with Christ and the context of a digitally mediated ecclesial community, then that *sacrament can be demonstrably valid and efficacious.*

There appear to be two separate ways to understand a SL eucharistic celebration with digital bread and wine.[82]

(a) It could seen as a form of the 'spiritual communion' as commended by Hill, in which Christ is remembered and celebrated. However, the BCP rubric for this still assumes a real consecration of physical bread and wine, which does not happen here. At best, this service may be 'sacramental'—and could convey real blessing—but it cannot be a sacrament.

(b) On the other hand, Rundel argues that it *"can be demonstrably valid and efficacious,"* considering it to be an actual sacrament, a real eucharist—but without physical bread and wine. This is the most controversial proposal for celebrating SL holy communion.

Fiddes' final suggestion cut the Gordian knot of 'equivalence' between the worlds of online/local, virtual/real, digital/physical, second/first life, thus stopping the debate about whether a digital communion service could be considered 'an Anglican eucharist'. Instead, he argued that it was a different thing altogether, comparable to when a non-Anglican minister presides over their own liturgy in a Local Ecumenical Project. It would depend on one's theology of the eucharist and the real presence, whether one could view such a service as valid and effective, or 'different but equal'.

However, a more recent statement from the Church of England's House of Bishops recognizes services as "an agape meal" or allowing participants who have watched "a live-streamed celebration of Holy Communion" to "eat and drink as if sharing a meal" but only "*after*" it has ended—and just so long as everyone understands that it is "*not* a sacrament" (my emphases).

---

82. I understand that one member of AoSL Cathedral who has been physically ordained in so-called 'real life' has attempted to provide digital elements on the altar during some 'spiritual communion' services online, although I have not been able to follow this up personally.

The bishops "*commend the questions raised by this practice for further theological reflection.*"[83] This will take us from SL into other online services through platforms like YouTube and Zoom, to which we will shortly turn, but first in order to explore such issues with "*further theological reflection*", we need next to examine the central issue of the celebrant's *intention*.

However, it would be remiss not to conclude this chapter without recognizing that this rather longer stage in our quest discovered a faithful, worshipping Anglican community who are still obeying a (now retired) bishop's instructions given to them over a decade ago, meeting to care and pray for one another on a daily basis (thereby putting many 'real' churches in the physical world to shame), yet they are still unable to share the grace of the sacrament. I am quite convinced that God nonetheless pours his abundant grace upon each and every one of them each day, regardless of our human rules and regulations. Their situation may be 'irregular', but it appears that their desire for God and God's grace is as pure and equally real as any physical congregation in the material world—and so their situation remains a challenge as part of our overall quest about how to celebrate holy communion online, when material circumstances, such as pandemics or just separation by large distances and time zones, do not allow celebrating the eucharist together in the physical world.

83. "COVID-19 Advice on the Administration of Holy Communion," version 1, issued on June 9, 2020.

13

Background 3
The Celebrant's Intention and Large Eucharists

THIS ENTIRE PROJECT STARTED with a question posted on Facebook by a friend who lives in South Africa: "So I have been wondering who to ask, . . . what is the range of consecration? If I have the elements in front of me and you are consecrating in the knowledge that that is the case, why would it not work?? Just so you know, I am genuinely asking this." In order even to begin to put together an answer to her question, we need to consider several issues about our understanding of 'consecration', including who actually manages to effect it, what their intention is, and how the different roles of the priest, the people, and all three persons of the Triune God combine to 'consecrate' bread and wine into "the body and blood of our Lord Jesus Christ".

LEARNING HOW TO PRESIDE OVER COMMUNION AND CELEBRATE THE EUCHARIST

First, let us return once again to the young, inexperienced curate serving in Bromley Parish Church in the mid-1980s. During twelve months of ordained ministry as a deacon, complete with a plastic clerical collar and getting used to being called 'the Reverend', under the guidance of the vicar, who, as a wise older priest, had been tasked with the tough assignment of being my 'training incumbent' (someone had to do it!), I had learned much about the ministry of the word, the daily and weekly services of Morning and Evening Prayer, reading the scriptures publicly, and preaching and expounding them. Of course, I had also already had eight years' experience as a reader, a lay minister, with the bishop's licence to do all of these things— so the main new elements in the first year of my curacy had been learning to do funerals and baptisms.

Preparing for the bishop's hands looming up to ordain me a priest meant learning how to preside over the holy communion, or how to celebrate the eucharist. What had been an interesting academic exercise at theological college, studying the great work by Dom Gregory Dix on the 'fourfold' action—that the priest follows Jesus' example in taking, blessing, breaking, and giving the bread and wine—suddenly turned into an obstacle course: how *do* you reach across a large, wide altar to 'take' bread and wine without knocking over the chalices, or allowing the voluminous sleeves of your robes to catch fire from the candles? What about receiving the elements from a server? What did you whisper to them—'thank you'? When did you have to put your hands out for them to sprinkle purifying water over them, making sure that they were over the '*lavabo*' (Latin for 'I will wash'), the bowl to avoid spilling everything and making the floor dangerously slippery—and trying to remember the right words to say quietly in prayer for cleansing from your own sin as your hands were washed (traditionally extracts from Psalm 51)?

How on earth would I get the right musical note to sing the *sursum corda*, the invitation to "Lift up your hearts," and could I keep a straight face when the choirboys were in hysterics about how off-key I was, deliberately pulling faces to try to make me laugh? Could I remember the 'manual actions', when to touch which of the many silver patens, chalices, and ciboria, the plates and cups, and to try to do so in the *right* order; when to lift which ones up, and how to genuflect at the right moment as a sign of humility before the coming presence of the Lord? And that was before you thought about what you had to say! I spent much of the silent retreat before my priesting desperately reciting the words of the (quite long) Eucharistic Prayer, trying to memorize it, or at least begin to feel its rhythm and cadences. Plus, I was mugging up my essay of reflections on the diaconate year for my personal examination by the bishop to see if I was fit to be made priest by him on Sunday morning. If I survived that huge ordination ceremony in the Cathedral, and the celebratory lunch back at the parish, then there loomed up the ritual of my first mass that evening, when I had to get all the words and actions right with everyone who had played any part in my spiritual journey coming to witness it, and praying desperately for me not to mess it all up, slip on the floor, or set the place on fire . . . ! Strange to relate, I don't remember many extended periods of blissful silent prayer, or just enjoying the presence of God, on that retreat—can't think why not!

In the midst of this whirlwind of words and deeds with all the possibilities for water to overflow and fire to break out, I was learning the importance of discerning the 'still, small voice', the 'sound of silence', in which, like Elijah, I was to seek the very presence of God, praying that somehow, however he chose, Jesus would make his presence in the bread and wine real enough so that I could feed his faithful worshippers with his body and blood, to 'build up their common life', and to give them the spiritual strength to carry on with whatever challenges they were facing or burdens they carried—the 'intention' of my eucharistic prayer and actions.

CONSECRATION AND THE INTENTION
OF THE PRIESTLY CELEBRANT

We saw in the last chapter that, as Bishop Christopher Hill put it:

> In considering the sacraments *the doctrine of intention is very important*. A contrast with 'magic' is instructive. In a magic spell it is held that the correct words and actions are absolutely necessary. Because sacraments are acts of prayer and not magic our inner intentions (including that of the celebrant . . .) are sufficient, even if there is some deficiency or mistake in the outward form, or even lack of fervour or devotion.[1]

Bishop Christopher's "contrast with 'magic'" is important; it is usually thought that the 'magical' words *hocus pocus*, so beloved of children's tales and stage magicians, are probably a corruption of the eucharistic words said by mediaeval priests in Latin, *hoc est corpus meum* (= *hocus pocus*), "This is my body."[2] The origins of the catholic (big and little 'c's!) practice of 'elevating the host', lifting up the paten or chalice, usually accompanied ringing bells, were not only designed to get the attention of the congregation, who had been sitting around chatting while the priest burbled on in Latin, but also to denote the 'holy moment' of transubstantiation, exactly *when* Jesus entered into the bread and wine, changing the substance of its 'breadness' and 'wineness' into his body and blood. So when the people heard *hoc est corpus meum*, "This is my body", the 'magic' had happened, *hocus pocus*!

---

1. Bishop Christopher Hill paper, "Second Life and Sacraments," section 5a, p. 8; my italics for emphasis.

2. Wikipedia notes that "This explanation goes back to speculations by the Anglican prelate John Tillotson, who wrote in 1694: In all probability those common juggling words of *hocus pocus* are nothing else but a corruption of *hoc est corpus*, by way of ridiculous imitation of the priests of the Church of Rome in their trick of Transubstantiation." See https://en.wikipedia.org/wiki/Hocus-pocus#Dog_Latin

This mechanistic, almost magical sense of the efficacy of a priest merely saying the right words of the institution of the Lord's Supper is best illustrated by the story of a mad (or drunken?) priest who supposedly went into a bakery, waved his hands about, saying "*Hoc est corpus meum.*" As a result of this 'hocus pocus', they had to burn everything in the place because it had all become the body of Jesus by the miracle of transubstantiation! Such a mechanistic, or almost magical, understanding of 'intention' suggests that human beings, even priests, can somehow control God by compelling Jesus to enter everything in a place, merely because of the ramblings of someone like this apocryphal priest.

Similarly, one of my fellow curates down the hill at the next-door parish got a bit carried away at his first early Sunday morning 8am Book of Communion Prayer Holy Communion Service, upending all the flagon of fortified communion wine on the altar into the large silver chalice—only to find that a mere four of the six or seven elderly faithful worshippers present actually wanted to receive communion. Since that church did not practice the reservation of the sacrament, he had to consume it all by himself afterwards; I think he slept through the main 11am service that day!

Therefore, we need to consider the president's intention in celebrating the Eucharist if only to discover how we avoid consecrating everything in the church—let alone the bakery or off licence next door. As my South African friend's question put it, what is the *range* of consecration? How far does it extend? My training vicar taught me that consecration was primarily a result of the priest's intention: thus traditionally, one places enough wafers or breaks off enough bread (you soon learn to snatch a quick head count just before, to avoid my friend's enthusiasm) onto the paten(s) and fills the communion cup(s), and places them on the 'corporal', a "*fair white linen cloth*" upon the table, the square of linen required by the rubrics of the 1662 Book of Common Prayer to be placed on the altar. The priest then has a 'sacramental intention', to consecrate everything on the corporal, but nothing more; it acts therefore as a kind of 'zone of intention'.[3]

This means that even if the flagon of wine or the box of wafers or the rest of the loaf is still left on the altar, it does not all get consecrated automatically. According to the 1662 Book of Common Prayer's rubrics (instructions originally printed in red), when the priest "hath so ordered the Bread and Wine, that he may with the more readiness and decency break the bread before the people and take the cup into his hands, he shall say the Prayer of Consecration." The BCP also makes provision for consecrating more elements if "the

---

3. I am grateful to the archdeacon of London, Fr Luke Miller, for our conversation in which this helpful phrase emerged—though neither of us is sure who invented it.

consecrated Bread or Wine be all spent before all have communicated." In other words, one does not just pour more wine out of the flagon or take extra *un*consecrated wafers from the box, or more bread from the loaf, without repeating part of the Prayer of Consecration over the new elements.

Afterwards, the rubric is clear that "if any of the Bread and Wine remain unconsecrated, the Curate shall have it to his own use": thus, what was not put on the corporal, and therefore that which was *not* consecrated by the president's intention, that they can take home and eat there for their lunch afterwards. In contrast, "if any remain of that which was consecrated, it shall not be carried out of the church, but the Priest and such other of the Communicants as he shall then call unto him, shall, immediately after the Blessing, reverently eat and drink the same." There is therefore a clear distinction between the general items or containers of bread and wine, and those elements chosen and set aside to be consecrated by the celebrant's deliberate intention.

For those of a more formal, 'high' or Catholic tradition, consecration should include not only the particular intention of the celebrant, but also the manual acts of the priest placing their hands upon the bread and wine at the 'moment' of the eucharistic words of the institution narrative, and even elevating the paten and chalice, probably accompanied by ringing bells and/or genuflecting in humble worship at this most holy 'moment' of the sacred words, when the real presence of Jesus transforms the bread and wine into his body and blood. The rubrics of the 1662 Book of Common Prayer provide specific instructions for the manual acts for the priest, of taking "the Paten into his hands" at the words that Jesus "took bread"; that, at the words "he brake it", the rubric says "and here to break the bread", and during the eucharistic command to "take, eat . . . in remembrance of me", the priest must "lay his hands upon *all* the bread" (my emphasis); similarly at the mention of "likewise after supper he took the cup", the priest "is to take the Cup into his hand", and once more during the words of institution, he is "to lay his hand upon *every* vessel (be it Chalice or Flagon) in which there is any Wine to be consecrated" (again, my emphasis). I gather that there is even an old catholic tradition that the president should insert his fingers into the ciborium and stir round the wafers, so that they are all physically 'touched' by him (and it is likely that it would have to be a 'him'!).[4]

However, it may also be argued that the Church of England has moved away from a precise *moment* of consecration, that of saying the words of

4. Again, I am grateful to the archdeacon of London, Fr Luke Miller, for describing this practice in a personal email; however, he was also keen to point out that "I think that putting your fingers in the ciborium is mad, and not something I would encourage!! Indeed to the contrary."

institution complete with the manual acts over the elements (with or without elevating the host, genuflecting, or ringing bells), towards seeing consecration as happening through the eucharistic prayer *as a whole*. Thus the rubrics of the *Alternative Service Book* 1980 include Note 3 that while "local custom may be established and followed", nevertheless "the Eucharistic Prayer (sections 38, 39, 40, and 41) is a single prayer, the unity of which may be obscured by changes of posture in the course of it" (ASB, Rite A, page 115).[5] This was a clearly designed attempt to change the longstanding habit of congregations standing for the first part of the Eucharistic Prayer, and then 'flopping to their knees' after the *Sanctus*, to be ready for the more holy, central narrative of the institution! Judging by the stubborn continuance of that change of posture after the *Sanctus* in many churches today, the attempt has not been entirely, or even mostly, successful.

THE IMPORTANCE OF 'INTENTION' IN LAW AND ETHICS

I recognize that this stress on that which the priest does intend, or does not intend, to consecrate can seem like so much 'logic-chopping' or 'hair-splitting' to some readers, especially perhaps to those of a more evangelical or low-church tradition. Therefore, please allow me to demonstrate briefly why it is actually very important to split these hairs: in many areas of our lives intention is crucial. Thus, it is a critical distinction between 'murder', where it has to be demonstrated in court that the accused *deliberately intended* to kill the victim, and 'manslaughter', where a death occurs that was *not* intended, such as drunk driving. In certain American states that still have capital punishment, 'intention' can literally make a difference of life or death for the accused. The importance of this became evident while I was writing this book, through the killing of George Floyd, whose death on May 25, 2020 in Minneapolis, Minnesota, sparked many Black Lives Matter protests around the world. Initially, the police officer was charged only with 'third-degree murder' and 'second-degree manslaughter', neither of which requires the 'intention' to kill. However, as more facts emerged, including video-recordings, the charge was upgraded to second-degree murder, and

5. Fr Luke Miller's email notes, "Cranmer thought the consecration was completed in the body of the communicant—hence the splitting of the EP [Eucharistic Prayer] so that the prayer of oblation happens after the communion of the people; an odd mixture of receptionism and Catholicism. That's why so many catholics make the prayer of oblation either silently or out loud after the end of the BCP consecration prayer despite the Amen at the end of it! In the days of the ASB my training incumbent would not allow me to make the elevations on the grounds that the whole EP consecrated and we were only to elevate at the end."

the three other officers were all charged with aiding and abetting second-degree murder, all of which *do* require intention to kill—and are therefore much more serious charges, with potentially lethal consequences.[6]

Similarly, intention is crucial in medical ethics, where the 'principle of double effect' (PDE) is routinely used, especially in the final stages of terminal illnesses in which a patient is in excruciating pain, and everyone, including both the family and the doctors, agrees that the best thing is to end the loved-one's suffering. However, if one was to smother the patient with a pillow to put them out of their misery, as some relatives have attempted in their awful desperation, that is still considered to be murder, causing death with a deliberate intention to kill—no matter how good the motives may have been, and they have to go to court. PDE, however, allows a doctor deliberately to inject a large dose of a painkiller, like morphine, which has *two* effects: the *first*—which the doctor understands, foresees, and intends—is to alleviate the patient's pain and suffering; however, the *second* potential effect may be to hasten the person's death, something that the doctor certainly *does not intend*, even if they foresee that possibility. It is on this basis, and only on this basis of intention, that such doctors are *not* prosecuted for murder or even manslaughter. In both cases, the effect and the consequences are the same: the patient's suffering is ended, but at the cost of their death. However, one requires the deliberate intention to kill, while the other only intends to relieve the suffering.

As we just noted, this may seem like 'logic-chopping', but it is crucial. We must also note that not everything can be justified by such 'hair-splitting' using PDE. For example, some excuse the use of nuclear weapons on Hiroshima or Nagasaki by arguing that the 'real intention' of the Americans was to bring about the end of the war, and thus save the thousands of (American) lives that would be lost in a land assault on the Japanese home islands. But one cannot really argue that the instant horrifying death of between 60,000 and 80,000 civilians, and the final death toll of 135,000 at Hiroshima was only an "unintended consequence" of dropping the atomic bomb to bring about peace! It is an integral part of bombs that they are intended to kill, and nuclear weapons kill indiscriminately.

---

6. See "George Floyd Death: All Four Ex-Officers Involved Now Charged, in Custody", *CBS Minnesota*. June 3, 2020; Minnesota has the additional category of 'third-degree murder', defined by their statutes as "Whoever, *without intent* to effect the death of any person, causes the death of another by perpetrating an act eminently dangerous to others and evincing a depraved mind, without regard for human life, is guilty of murder in the third degree and may be sentenced to imprisonment for not more than 25 years" (my italics for emphasis); however, second-degree murder carries the death penalty. Statutes of Minnesota, 2019, 609.195.

EXPANDING AND EXTENDING THE INTENTION OF AUTHORS

Such life or death uses of ideas of 'intention' may seem a long way from our discussion of a priest's intention in celebrating the eucharist. However, the vexed debate about how much an author's intention can delineate the meaning of a text illustrates how the consequences of an action can go beyond the person's original intention. My doctoral work about how an author's intention guides a reader's interpretation demonstrated that the Gospels share all the literary and generic features common to ancient biography—and that therefore they should be interpreted in this way, in comparison to other ancient Lives, but not be expected to conform to the canons of modern biography.[7]

More problematic are the debates about readings of ancient texts that increasingly reflect modern concerns—such as feminist, post-colonialist, or gay and liberationist readings. Are such interpretations 'valid' or 'effective', to compare to a priest's intentions in celebrating the eucharist? The literary theorist, E. D. Hirsch, stressed the importance of the authorial intention for determining textual meaning. Professor Mark Brett, a renowned Australian Old Testament expert (particularly on 'post-colonial' readings as they affect the (Ab)original inhabitants) kindly wrote in response to my first draft:

> I was provoked by your essay to consider an analogy between *authorial* intention and *priestly* intention in the Eucharist, not least because the later Hirsch was engaged with the question of how a 'zone of intention' may be legitimately expanded beyond the face-to-face model of communication. . . . Hirsch came to see a limited 'indeterminacy' that applies especially to particular kinds of literary, legal, and religious texts. In such texts, he finds that "while it is true that later aspects of verbal meaning *are* fixed by its originating moment in time, that moment has fixed only the *principles* of further extrapolation," a point that is almost self-evident when it comes to the legal interpretation of constitutions.[8]

Similarly, lawyers and judges continue to debate the meaning of laws passed by parliaments and governments, and to what extent new interpretations are still coherent with the original intentions of the lawmakers.

The Greek historian, Thucydides, wrote an extensive history of the great Peloponnesian War between Athens and Sparta during 431–404 BC, totalling 153,260 words. In a famous part of his introduction, he makes

---

7. Richard A. Burridge, *What Are the Gospels? A Comparison with Graeco-Roman Biography,* Third (25th Anniversary) Edition, Baylor University Press, 2018.

8. Hirsch, "Meaning and Significance Reinterpreted," 204, discussed in Mark Brett, *Biblical Criticism in Crisis?* 23–25; Cf. Huscroft and Miller, eds., *The Challenge of Originalism.*

clear his intention in writing to be 'useful', because something 'similar' is bound to happen again and again in the future, human nature being what it is; his explicit intention is to write a "possession for all time" (*ktēma eis aei*), rather than showing off his brilliance just for his contemporary audience (I.22). Later, during the revolt of Corcyra (modern Corfu), he shows how "war is a harsh teacher" (*bebaios didaskalos*) (III.82). He depicts how Athens' proud democratic beliefs and previous merciful leniency towards defeated enemies eventually broke down under the 'harsh' pressures of war and made them behave just as violently and brutally as their autocratic Spartan enemies, for instance when the Athenians executed all the men and enslaved all the women and children of the island of Melos, to provide a lesson to others tempted to revolt (V.84–116). Thucydides' *History* is still taught two-and-a-half thousand years later as a basic set text in departments of war studies, such as at King's College London, something that the author could never have foreseen—and yet which is entirely consistent with his intention to extend his account "for all time".

EXPANDING AND EXTENDING
THE CELEBRANT'S INTENTION IN LARGE EUCHARISTS

Often at very large events, such as ordination services, there is simply not enough room for all the patens and chalices to be physically placed on the altar, let alone upon a single piece of linen or corporal. This is even more true in the case of very large celebrations—such as when I participated in the 2008 Lambeth conference with thousands of bishops and their spouses. In such cases, those lay and ordained ministers assisting with distribution of the eucharist are given their patens and chalices *already* containing (so far *un*consecrated) bread and wine as they gather around the altar, often in a circle; all that remains is for them to hold up these patens and chalices before the celebrant or president at the relevant points during the eucharistic prayer, before then taking them (now consecrated) off to the far-flung corners of the Lambeth marquee or the cathedral's transepts or the lower nave to distribute to the faithful congregants.

When this practice was first used at a National Liturgical Commission Conference in Cambridge many years ago, it did provoke significant debate.[9] However, it has now been followed by cathedrals for many years at large eucharists. What is significant for our purposes here is that, if one believes that the celebrant must physically touch the elements, or at least, cover them with

9. I am grateful to the Rev'd Canon Gilly Myers, a liturgist and canon emeritus of Southwark Cathedral, for this account.

their hands while saying the special words of the institution (even if not accepting a magical *hocus pocus*), then one cannot accept as a valid and effective communion a practice like this where the elements to be consecrated are not only not on the linen corporal nor the altar, but actually out of the celebrant's reach, many yards away. All the president can do is to hold up their hands, and—significantly—broaden out their 'zone of intention' to include all the bread and wine in the patens and chalices that they can at least see before them in their sacramental desire to consecrate, even if they cannot see the actual bread and wine within them, much less touch it.

However, given the move away from a 'moment' of consecration and from mechanistic, or even magical, understandings of any eucharistic change in the elements and the real presence (however understood), together with the complementary stress upon the intention of those wishing to receive the body and blood of our Lord Jesus Christ (as discussed in chapter 5 above, and to which we will shall return below shortly), this wider consecration of a circle of chalices and patens has become not only common at large events, but even regular practice in places like Southwark Cathedral.[10] In Anglo-Catholic circles, such as at large eucharists at the shrine of Mary at Walsingham, this practice also provides an opportunity for priests among the distributing eucharistic ministers to perform whatever manual acts they wish over their elements and to say the actual words of the institution, thus literally '*con*-celebrating', celebrating *with* the president.[11]

Similarly, but at the 'opposite end of the candle' from Walsingham perhaps, the UK's Greenbelt music and arts festival has always included a massive communion service on the Sunday of the August Bank Holiday for some five decades now. With numbers attending often in excess of 20,000, not only is there no table large enough for sufficient chalices and patens to be within range of the celebrant's 'consecrating touch', but also any attempt to distribute communion by a small group of eucharistic ministers would take all day! The usual pattern that has evolved over the years is thus similar, in that festival goers are encouraged to sit on the grass in small groups (a bit like the Feeding of the 5,000 in John 6!), with each group given a bag containing some bread and a small bottle of wine. During the eucharistic prayer, someone in each group is encouraged to hold up their bread or wine at the appropriate point, in a manner similar to the large services mentioned above, while the celebrant on the main stage stretches out their hands towards the field with

10. I am grateful to Bishop Christopher Chessun, bishop of Southwark, for explaining this regular practice in his Cathedral in a private email and his permission to quote him on this.

11. Once again, I am grateful to the archdeacon of London, Fr Luke Miller, for pointing this practice out.

the intention to consecrate all the various breads and wines stretching out into the distance before them. The small group then share this (now consecrated) bread and wine among themselves—and consume any remaining elements, and perform any ablutions they consider necessary.

This takes us back to the practical, if somewhat trite-seeming, question from my South African friend: how far *can* the 'zone of intention' be extended? If it can be confined to a small area like the corporal without unintentionally consecrating nearby elements remaining in the flagon or wafer-box, yet also it can extended to a group of eucharistic ministers standing in a circle around the altar some ten or twenty yards away, why can it not equally extend hundreds of yards across a muddy field at Greenbelt? When I have mentioned this practice to some of my more Anglo-Catholic colleagues, they sometimes have a visceral feeling of opposition or rejection of the idea—even though they are honest enough not to seem able to come up with any reasonable theological justification for confining the 'zone of intention' to a few yards around an altar, but not hundreds of yards across a field. We are back to the basic doctrine of the creation and incarnation: either Jesus is Lord of *all* time and *all* space, or he is Lord of none of it; he cannot be confined to a "piece of fair white linen" like a corporal, or a single altar—any more than he can be confined by a stone rolled over his tomb, as the Risen Christ's victory is depicted by so many great painters.[12]

12. Piero della Francesca, *The Resurrection* (1463). https://en.wikipedia.org/wiki/The_Resurrection_(Piero_della_Francesca)

So this leads us, at last, back to our key question: why can the 'zone of intention' not be extended through virtual space to physical spaces on the other side of the planet? After all, even if 10,000 miles might seem a long way to us, mere grasshoppers on the surface of the globe, it is as nothing to the One who can traverse the entire universe in the blink of an eye.

WHO IS ACTUALLY PRESIDING OVER THE CELEBRATION OF THE EUCHARIST—PRIEST OR PEOPLE?

Such reasoning can also be reinforced by combining with some of our reflections about presidency. In chapter 6 above, we discussed the question of Bishop Andy Doyle, bishop of Texas, who is praying the eucharist?[13] In his pastoral letter, Doyle argues that "the Eucharistic prayer, prayed by priest and people, is a reunion from being apart [to now being] gathered to pray, hear the word of God, and to say the words over the bread and wine. The priest may say the prayer aloud, but it is the solemn assembly reunited and praying in one voice the liturgy of Eucharist—the Great Thanksgiving." His argument, like that of Cranmer and the Anglican mainstream tradition, is that if the people need the priest to celebrate the eucharist for them, then equally the priest needs the people in order to be able to do so, which is why solitary communion (as discussed in chapter 3 above) is essentially 'un-Anglican'. He goes so far as to say that

> when the celebrant says, "Let us give thanks to the Lord our God," the celebrant is asking for "permission to offer thanks in the name of those present".[14] . . . This is not an act the priest makes, and the people then receive. We are singing, praying, administering, and acting as one—physically together. Our agreed-upon Eucharistic Theology found in our tradition and exemplified in the 1979 Book of Common Prayer is that the Eucharistic act is not about the priest doing something for others.[15]

If this is true, then we need to ask about the sacramental intention of not just the priest, but also of the lay people themselves. As my South

---

13. I am very grateful to the Rt Rev'd C. Andrew Doyle, bishop of Texas, for sharing with me his pastoral letter "A Reflection on the Eucharist during the time of COVID -19." Both this question and much of what follows in this section is taken from this letter, which can be downloaded from this page: https://www.epicenter.org/resources/covid-19-hub/virtual-liturgies/#holy-eucharist; see pp. 4–7.

14. Hatchett, *Commentary on the American Prayer Book*, 361 and 373.

15. Bishop Doyle, https://www.epicenter.org/resources/covid-19-hub/virtual-liturgies/#holy-eucharist, p. 7.

African friend's question put it, "if I have the elements in front of me and *you are consecrating in the knowledge that that is the case*, why would it not work??" (my italics). Not only do I know that she has the elements in front of her, but she is also telling me that *her sacramental intention as a lay person is that she wants me to consecrate them for her* so that she can receive the body and blood of our Lord Jesus Christ—especially in the lockdown when she cannot go to church to receive the sacrament.

As already noted, Cranmer and the Reformers moved away from the mediaeval Catholic concept that the consecration of the elements was some-thing effected automatically—or even 'magically'—by the 'right' person (an episcopally ordained—and therefore ontologically changed—priest) saying the 'right' words accompanied by the 'right' manual actions. One example of Cranmer's shift in emphasis from consecration being effected not just by the words of the priest to including worthy reception by the people is seen in the 1662 Book of Common Prayer's first Exhortation: ". . . our spiritual food and sustenance in that holy Sacrament. Which being so divine and comfortable a thing to them who receive it worthily, and so dangerous to them that will presume to receive it unworthily; my duty is to warn you . . . ." The same point is made in the second Exhortation: "For as the benefit is great, if with a true penitent heart and lively faith we receive that holy Sacrament; . . . so is the danger great, if we receive the same unworthily." Clearly, in both cases, the communion elements have been consecrated by the priest saying the right words with the right manual actions, but their spiritual and actual physical effect depends upon the attitude of the person receiving them.

Similarly, immediately before the words of institution with the manual acts the Prayer of Consecration says, "grant that we receiving these thy crea-tures of bread and wine, according to thy Son our Saviour Jesus Christ's holy institution, in remembrance of his death and passion, may be partakers of his most blessed Body and Blood." Thus, the object of the eucharistic prayer is not so much a change to the elements in themselves, but to "we receiving these thy creatures."[16] Fr Luke Miller notes:

> Cranmer thought the consecration was completed in the body of the communicant—hence the splitting of the EP [Eucharistic Prayer] so that the prayer of oblation happens after the commu-nion of the people; an odd mixture of receptionism and Catholi-cism. That's why so many catholics make the prayer of oblation either silently or out loud after the end of the BCP consecration prayer despite the Amen at the end of it![17]

16. I am grateful to Bishop Graham Tomlin, bishop of Kensington, for the points made in this paragraph.

17. Here also, I am grateful to the archdeacon of London, Fr Luke Miller, for this point in his personal emails to me; see above footnotes.

Therefore, there needs to be a sacramental intention on the part of *both the priest and the laity present* in order to consecrate bread and wine as the body and blood of our Lord Jesus Christ, whatever one's view of the real presence, and whether there is any change in the elements, and if so, what and how.[18]

THE EUCHARISTIC PRESIDENCY OF GOD THE HOLY TRINITY

However, we also noted above that eucharistic presidency belongs supremely to Jesus Christ himself, according to the Lima document on *Baptism, Eucharist and Ministry*:

> It is *Christ who invites to the meal and who presides at it.* He is the shepherd who leads the people of God, the prophet who announces the Word of God, the priest who celebrates the mystery of God. . . . The one who presides at the eucharistic celebration in the name of Christ makes clear that the rite is not the assemblies' own creation or possession; the eucharist is received as a gift from the living Christ in his Church.[19]

18. In his response my earlier paper, the Rev'd Dr Paul Roberts noted, "There are also a few questions about differing interpretations of how Christ is present in communion. Although Cranmer had, by 1552, developed, and in it, articulated, his own distinct understanding of how communion 'worked', this is not the official teaching of the Church of England, which is contained in the text of 1662. Cranmer is interesting, because, like Calvin, he knew what Zwingli was trying to get at, but did not like the way he got there—Zwingli was simply playing with the terms of signification linguistically, rather than thinking more biblically and theologically. Cranmer's theology has some similarities to Calvin's but diverges, largely because they were both tackling the weaknesses of Zwingli's approach in their own ways and arriving at slightly different solution. *However*, it is clear that Cranmer's theology was not universally acceptable to the Church which reconstructed itself under Elizabeth, and the result was the tension between Puritans and the others which rumbled on for eighty more years. Key to this period is the development of the Caroline divines, together with the Elizabethan influence of Hooker and Jewel in taking a more ambiguous view of the presence of Christ, somehow localised, within the elements of the bread and wine. As we all know, the result was a 1662 rite with a clear doctrine of consecration and localised presence in the elements, which the later Cranmer would have hated. But this is the definitive model, and both Catholics and Evangelicals have bits they like and bits they like less. 1662 essentially was a victory for Caroline Anglicanism, but with enough limitations to allow moderate Evangelicals to accept it—the rest left, and the result is Anglicanism. This means that somehow, any Anglican rite of communion must have scope for some sense of 'consecration' in the presence of an episcopally ordained priest or bishop. Your paper seeks to maintain this." I am grateful to Dr Roberts for permission to quote his email.

19. World Council of Churches, 1984; *Baptism, Eucharist and Ministry—Faith and*

In the light of this clear expression of Christ's presidency, Kate Lord concluded, "Given the Christian understanding of God in all places and all times, it is not outside the realms of possibility that the bread and wine that is in front of each person, wherever they be on the face of the earth, will be transformed into the sacrament of the body and blood of Christ."

Furthermore, we have to recognize that alongside the *human* sacramental intention of both priest and people, as well as the eucharistic presidency of Jesus Christ himself, that all three *divine* persons of the Triune God are personally active in the act of consecration. The 'inward and invisible' grace that we seek in all 'outward and visible' sacraments cannot be any other than the grace and love which ever flows throughout the cosmos from the heart of the God and Father of us all. If God the Father longs to pour upon us and all his children the gift of his grace, and Jesus Christ the Son not only provides his own example of taking, blessing, breaking, and sharing bread and wine, but himself presides over every consecration, then it is the activity of God the Holy Spirit that makes that consecration effective in both bread and wine, and also within each of us who desire the sincere intention to be fed with the body and blood of our Lord Jesus Christ.

This aspect of the eucharistic prayer is known as the *epiclēsis*, which means in Greek the 'calling down onto' (from *epi-kaleō*, giving us *epi-klēsis*) of the Holy Spirit, the Paraclete, the one 'called alongside' (*para-kaleō*) us (John 14:16, 26; 15:26; 16:7). The priest 'calls' upon the Holy Spirit to descend down upon not only the bread and wine but also upon the people present. Thus, in the Orthodox Liturgy of St James, the celebrant prays "Thy same all-holy Spirit, Lord, send down on us and on these gifts here set forth", while the Liturgy of St Basil the Great has "through the favour of Thy goodness send Thy Holy Spirit down upon us, and upon these Gifts presented here, and bless them, sanctify, and manifest them."

To return briefly that green, young curate in Bromley, I was instructed not merely in the manual acts over the bread and wine, but also how to call down the Spirit onto all the people gathered together in the church, as well as upon the elements of bread and wine. So today, when I celebrate communion, I take the paten or chalice and cover them with my hands while I say the words of the Last Supper narrative ("This is my body," "This is my blood") making the sign of the cross over them as I say one of these sets of words:

Order Paper No. 111, Article E29, p. 14; https://www.oikoumene.org/en/resources/documents/commissions/faith-and-order/i-unity-the-church-and-its-mission/baptism-eucharist-and-ministry-faith-and-order-paper-no-111-the-lima-text. My italics here for emphasis.

... grant that by the power of your Holy Spirit and according to your holy will, these gifts of bread and wine may be to us his body and his blood (Prayers A & B)

... send your Holy Spirit, that broken bread and wine outpoured may be for us the body and blood of your dear Son (E)

... by your Holy Spirit let these gifts of your creation be to us the body and blood of our Lord Jesus Christ; form us into the likeness of Christ and make us a perfect offering in your sight (F)

... pour out your Holy Spirit as we bring before you these gifts of your creation; may they be for us the body and blood of your dear Son (G)

Then shortly afterwards, I like to stretch out my hands over the congregation as I pray for the Holy Spirit to come upon them all:

Send the Holy Spirit on your people and gather into one in your kingdom all who share this one bread and one cup, so that we, in the company of all the saints, may praise and glorify you for ever, through Jesus Christ our Lord; (Prayer B)

Send your Spirit on us now that by these gifts we may feed on Christ with opened eyes and hearts on fire. (Prayer D)

Look with favour on your people, gather us in your loving arms and bring us with all the saints to feast at your table in heaven. (E)

Look with favour on your people and in your mercy hear the cry of our hearts. Bless the earth, heal the sick, let the oppressed go free, and fill your Church with power from on high. (F)

As we eat and drink these holy things in your presence, form us in the likeness of Christ, and build us into a living temple to your glory. (G)

In many ways, this second *epiclēsis*, calling the Spirit down upon the people, is almost more important than the first one upon the elements, since I am praying for the people to be fed and strengthened by the consecrated elements upon which I have also called down the Spirit; then, having been fed "with the body and blood of your Son Jesus Christ" they are able to pray "through him we offer you our souls and bodies to be a living sacrifice" to be empowered to be sent "out in the power of your Spirit to live and work to your praise and glory", in the words of the post-communion prayer.

To conclude this discussion, let us note several important points which will govern our consideration of online communions in the next two chapters:

- Most Christian traditions consider that the bread and wine at the eucharist or communion is 'consecrated' *through the words and actions of a properly ordained priest or authorised minister,* even allowing for different theological understandings and interpretations of both the ontological status of the priest or minister, and of the nature of the 'presence' of Christ in the duly consecrated bread and wine.

- While previous tradition seems to have focussed upon the actual 'moment' of consecration, identified by certain key words or manual actions (leading to ideas of *'hocus pocus'*), more recent liturgical and theological approaches emphasise *the importance of the whole eucharistic prayer as the 'act' of consecration.*

- Therefore, *the intention of the priest or minister to enable this to happen is crucial,* and traditional liturgical actions allow for that intention to be 'limited' to certain elements, such as those on the corporal (but not in the containers to one side), or 'extended' to other elements, which may be in vessels held up by others while the celebrant recites the eucharistic prayer.

- Anglican understandings since the time of Cranmer also stress the importance *of the intention of those about to receive the bread and wine,* including especially the laity, and their desire to receive the body and blood of Christ—even allowing for differing understandings of what that means.

- None of this, however, should be understood as 'automatic' or 'magical' or even *ex opere operato,* to use the Latin phrase, nor does it depend upon the holiness or worthiness of the minister or the recipients, because of *the primacy of the grace of God and the activity of the Holy Spirit,* which the celebrant 'calls down' in the *epiclesis* both upon the physical elements of bread and wine to effect whatever understanding is held about them becoming the body and blood of Christ, but also upon themselves and all the people of God to be able to receive Christ in the communion.

With these points in mind, we can now finally turn to consider the attempts to conduct digital communion services online through both 'broad-' and 'narrow-' casting, using various available platforms and technologies.

14

Proposal 9
Broadcasts and Livestreaming

IN EARLY CHAPTERS, WE noticed both the sense of the 'alone-ness' in the first days of the lockdown under the coronavirus pandemic, and also, that 'solo' communions are profoundly un-Anglican and against the rubrics of the Book of Common Prayer, which prohibit celebrating communion alone. Thus it was not surprising that, instead of solitary communions, the archbishops stated that "Live streaming of services is more important than ever and is still permissible from homes. We encourage us all to consider how we can be as creative as possible with streaming services and other resources."[1] Of course, such "livestreaming of services," which are often pre-recorded, is actually no different from other forms of broadcasting, so we will consider these first before turning to so-called livestreaming on platforms such as YouTube and Facebook.

HOLY COMMUNION IN TV BROADCASTS— LIVE AND PRE-RECORDED

As Christopher Hill noted, "When TV became popular for the first time in the mid-twentieth century there were regular Sunday/Festival broadcasts of the Christian eucharist. Was it 'real' if (say) a housebound couple ate bread and drank wine accompanying a televised eucharist? No Church denied this was a good thing. But no Church acknowledged that this was the

---

1. Second Letter from_Archbishops_and_bishops, March 24, 20200324.pdf

same as participating personally in the sacrament."[2] Such issues provoked lively debates in the UK during the 1960s–80s, but the definitive text, Colin Morris' *God in a Box*, was published during my final year of ordination training in 1984, which shows how much things have changed.

Morris begins chapter 6, "Sacred Conundrum", noting that the great pioneer of the BBC "John [Lord] Reith was anxious to broadcast worship because it was, for him, the most significant thing Christians did together. He wanted the airwaves to carry the Gospel into every home. So the linch-pin of religious broadcasting was the church service in one form or another." There are, of course, other formats—discussions, drama, music—"but worship was the paradigm of religious radio". Morris noted debates about "whether it was possible to broadcast worship without changing its nature", even on radio, but "television has added several layers of complexity[;] . . . television creates a sense of an alternative reality."[3] The internet has added even more complexity, not to mention other versions of 'alternative reality'.

Morris describes the debate as between "two sharply contrasting groups", 'conservatives' and 'radicals', although "at root, this argument is not only about worship but also about the nature of television. The conservative is a one-cosmos person—there is a real world (where true worship takes place). . . . The radical believes there are two cosmoses—the so-called real world, and then its mirror-image, television, which is an alternative form of reality. It offers a universally accessible experience which competes with the rest of our experience."[4]

Conservatives argue that worship is "a team activity" (watching foot-ball is different from playing it), "about commitment", and a "sacramental activity" that is "corporeal", involving all the senses, not just eyes and ears; furthermore, worship also needs silence and stillness, which television can-not do. Radicals respond that these distinctions are "based on outmoded presuppositions about science, theology and liturgy. It is Stonehenge reli-gion to believe that individual people watching TV screens are separated because they are not simultaneously in one stone building."[5] Those watch-ing TV are not isolated, but may enjoy "a more intimate experience" than being at the back of a vast cathedral, or a large football stadium, where it is hard to see what is happening.

2. The Rt Rev'd Christopher Hill, "Second Life and Sacraments: Anglican Observa-tions and Guidelines," available for download from and summarized at https://slang-cath.wordpress.com/the-vision/sacraments-on-epiphany-island/, p. 11.

3. Colin Morris, *God-in-a-Box: Christian strategy in the Television Age*, Hodder & Stoughton, 1984, 101.

4. Morris, *God-in-a-Box*, 102–3.

5. Morris, *God-in-a-Box*, 104.

Meanwhile, conservatives are worried about "doctrinal confusion", since TV offers a whole range of traditions, requiring "considerable sophistication and spiritual maturity", while radicals suggest abandoning broadcasting church services in favour of more inclusive programming better suited to a studio. "The key problem of televised church services is exquisitely simple and insoluble. Television is a visual medium, but the object of worship, God, is, by definition, invisible. He is not accessible to cameras and microphones. Nowhere else in television does it happen that the star of the show is off-camera altogether."[6] We do not watch audiences watching a drama or comedy show or spectators watching a football match—but here we make "the worshippers the focus of attention rather than the one who is being worshipped".

However, "one of the most articulate and expert of television producers", Ian MacKenzie, BBC head of religious programmes for Scotland, argued that: "God is in the editing channel, in the studio, and in the room at home. The editing material being used—airwaves, machinery, electronic patter, film—these are, in God's hands, and in caring human hands, the bread and wine, broken, shared, for the world. That is liturgy."[7] Morris describes one series, *This Is the Day*, transmitted from a family home, rather than a church, to viewers gathered similarly in their homes:

> At the beginning of the programme, viewers at home are invited
> to light a candle and put it on the television set together with a
> hunk of bread. At the climax of the service, the preacher breaks
> bread and hands it to the members of the family from whose
> home the service is coming; the viewer is invited to break bread
> and eat bread at the same time. It is spelt out that the breaking of
> bread is in no way intended to be some form of televisual mass
> or eucharist; no words of consecration are spoken over it.

Morris suggests two reasons for doing this: in engaging touch, smell, and taste besides sight and sound, "it becomes more nearly a fully corporeal act", and also it "overleaps some of the inevitable isolation of the television experience". Morris, himself a Methodist, links this, not to communion, but to the "old Primitive Methodist love feast, . . . the symbolic meal". He also quotes a "most welcome theological commentary" from Professor J. G. Davies in the journal *Theology*, who compares the idea to Eastern Orthodox *antidoron*, bread which is blessed, but not consecrated, and then given to non-communicants. Davies suggests that a local minister could deliver to the homes of the housebound before transmission either the

6. Morris, *God-in-a-Box*, 110.

7. Morris, *God-in-a-Box*, 112.

reserved sacrament for communicants, or blessed *antidoron* bread for non-communicants who wished to participate, to be eaten at the climax of the *This is the Day* broadcast, or indeed at the end of a televised eucharist.[8]

Many aspects of this discussion from four decades ago anticipate current debate, not least the discussion about two different 'cosmoses', which resonates with the relationship of the 'virtual', online, digital world with the physical, offline, analogue cosmos—and which is more 'real'? Ian Mac-Kenzie's argument about the presence of God in all the technical aspects is similar to ours about God's ability to be present in the so-called 'virtual', or digital, world. And, as we shall see later, the comparison to the Methodist love feast has also been made during the pandemic by the bishops of the Church of England.

One aspect of TV that has changed very significantly since those debates is the ability to watch it at a time of one's own choosing. This came about by the arrival first of video, then DVD recorders, then of streaming services such as BBC iPlayer and other on-demand systems, such as Netflix, Amazon Prime, and the like. Colin Morris takes it for granted that TV broadcasts were watched by families and communities *at the same time*, in a major corporate act. The highest spike in demand for electricity from the National Grid in the UK was caused at half-time in the 1966 World Cup Final between England and Germany as everyone across the country dashed to the kitchen to put the kettle on! Equally, the whole fun of growing up as a fan of shows like *Monty Python's Flying Circus* was the shared experience of going into school the next day with other devotees wearing knotted handkerchiefs on our heads, or rolled up trouser legs, or talking in a Yorkshire accent about "lookshuray" (luxury!)—and our teachers not having the faintest idea about it all.

In these days, when TV is 'consumed' on demand by individuals *when*, *where*, and *how* they wish, and boxsets of entire series can be 'binge-watched' in a weekend, that *community* experience as the essential requirement for a broadcast *communion* service has gone. Even so, while recognizing a wide range of understandings of eucharistic theology among Anglicans, those who cherish any concept of the 'real presence' (however defined), or the importance of priestly consecration of the actual elements of bread and wine for the eucharist to be 'valid' or 'efficacious' (in popular language, 'does it work?'), find suggestions of putting bread before TV broadcasts unacceptable for *communion*, no matter how they might maintain a sense of the church *community* during a crisis.

8. Morris, *God-in-a-Box*, 113–15.

Pre-recording makes this even more pertinent. Discussions about whether TV communions could consecrate bread and wine placed nearby were based upon the assumption of a 'live' broadcast, so that at least the celebrant on TV and the person at home were worshipping God together *at the same time*. Even radicals who wanted to allow bread and wine on or by the TV accepted that the service must be 'live' for it to 'work'; a rescreening of something recorded days, months, or even years previously could not effect a consecration in the here and now. On the other hand, it is interesting that under today's budgetary pressures, it is not uncommon to record more than one service in an outside visit of the evergreen BBC series *Songs of Praise* once the cameras and lights are all set up, even it means the minister and congregation, not to mention the church, have to be redressed to be suitable for both a Harvest Festival and a Christmas Mass! Colin Morris' opening words in his preface are prophetic: "Some books are written to be superseded. This is one." Therefore, bearing these previous debates in mind, we shall consider how broadcasting happens today.

HOLY COMMUNION ON TWITTER

As we saw above, on August 20, 2010, the *Church Times* reported that Tim Ross, a Methodist minister, had been 'urged' or pressurized by Methodist Church authorities to cancel plans for the first service of Holy Communion on Twitter (where he had over 1,200 followers). In the *Methodist Recorder*, Ross said that the Methodist Church Faith and Order Committee objected that "it was 'not a valid communion'. The idea of 'remote communion', where participants receive the bread and wine at the same time, but in different places, 'conflicts with the ethos of the [Methodist] Conference report, *His Presence Makes the Feast* (2003)'." For Ross, "the issue boils down to two questions: Is remote communion a valid communion? Is the Christian community on the internet a valid, gathered Christian community? If the answer to both these questions is 'Yes', then a communion service performed by such a community of believers must be valid and may be performed."[9] However, he refrained from doing it so the Methodist Church authorities could "reflect and pray deeply" about such developments; in 2012 Kate Lord noted laconically, "two years later, no response had been received from said officials"[10]—and I am not aware of any response even ten years later.

9. "Methodists halt Twitter Service" https://www.ukpressonline.co.uk/ukpresson-line/database/search/preview.jsp?fileName=ChTm_2010_08_20_001, p. 9.

10. Lord, "Can Eucharist Be Administered in a Virtual World?" 10.

Unsurprisingly, Simon Jenkins from *Ship of Fools* joined in the following week, addressing the key question: Can online communion be real? He set the Methodist ban in the context of the above debates about religious TV broadcasting; the Oxford i-Church, St Pixels, as well as the Anglican Cathedral on Second Life were all refraining from it, following the bishop of Guildford's advice for 'spiritual communion', even though Fiddes had given "theological support for the idea", as we have seen above.[11] Jenkins did, however, quote Tim Ross himself: "What I love about Twitter is the instantaneous contact it gives you with your followers. It gave me the idea that we could do a live communion service for believers around the world, sharing together the bread and wine as the one Body of Christ." Later, Jenkins concluded an expanded version of this article with the prophetic comment:

> Only a few years ago, the Internet was a strange place you entered and exited via a dial-up connection. But now, as it becomes increasingly integrated into our daily lives, with Facebook friends, BBC iPlayer, supermarkets online and 1001 apps for your mobile phone, the virtual world is getting less virtual and more real by the day. In fact, the virtual was never unreal; it's just taken us half a generation to get used to it. And with that change, a growing number of people who can't or won't go to churches made of bricks—through illness or old age, or because of past bad experience of church, are choosing to worship online instead. Whether the historic denominations are going to allow these places of worship to break bread and drink wine together is not a small matter. At heart, it's a question of whether they are recognised as genuine churches at all.[12]

The extraordinary, and ironic, thing is that ten years and a global pandemic later a "growing number of people who can't or won't go to churches made of bricks . . . are choosing to worship online instead"—but the churches have *still* not decided whether they can break bread and drink wine together!

We also saw above that the liturgist Bosco Peters was happy to parade his own credentials: "with over 74,000 followers on twitter, and my profile devoted to liturgy, I come with a positive, not negative attitude to what can be done with social media." Nonetheless, his polemic is again dismissive:

---

11. Simon Jenkins, 'Can Online Communion Be Real?' https://www.churchtimes. co.uk/articles/2010/27-august/comment/can-online-communion-be-real, p. 9.

12. See http://www.ship-of-fools.com/features/2010/holy_communion_in_six_ tweets.html

> Encouraging 'experiments' in twitter sacraments and the like does nothing to enhance ministry and mission online, but reinforces the appearance that the church online is for wacky, nutter, extremists. . . . Holding bread and wine in front of a screen, where a YouTube video is playing of a priest reciting the Last Supper story, may, at its most generous, be a pious exercise resulting in spiritual communion—at its worst it becomes a mockery of the Christian mystery. . . . Nothing has altered my position: don't take up *Ship of Fools'* challenge to mock Christ's sacraments by experimenting with having a communion service on twitter.[13]

Since those debates, Twitter increased to a peak of around 336 million monthly active users in 2018, although it has dropped back since then to around 150–200 million 'monetizable daily users'.[14] Barack Obama is the most-followed person, with 130 million followers; the next popular are various musicians, ranging from 114m to 84m, and one footballer, Ronaldo (95m). While he was US president, Donald Trump accounted for about half the world's daily tweets, but his actual followers were only equal to Lady Gaga's (82m).[15] Despite 'government by Twitter', there have been no further attempts to celebrate communion there. Presumably the limit of 140 characters makes it difficult (even if 'crammed' to 280)—but a large number of Twitter accounts do include the word 'communion', often about specific services, or groups for 'first communion'.

However, Twitter may still play a role in online communions alongside more conducive—and much larger—platforms. Its total daily users of around 200 million compare poorly with Facebook's inexorable rise to around 2.9 billion daily users and YouTube's 2.1 billion users at the time of writing.[16] Therefore, we should turn to consider these giants as possible platforms for celebrating holy communion in "contagious times."

13. https://liturgy.co.nz/twitter-communion

14. https://www.statista.com/statistics/282087/number-of-monthly-active-twitter-users/#:~:text=How%20many%20people%20use%20Twitter,daily%20active%20users%20(mDAU); https://www.statista.com/statistics/242606/number-of-active-twitter-users-in-selected-countries/

15. Figures from October 15, 2021 according to https://en.wikipedia.org/wiki/List_of_most-followed_Twitter_accounts; see also https://www.businessofapps.com/data/twitter-statistics/

16. https://www.statista.com/statistics/264810/number-of-monthly-active-facebook-users-worldwide/; https://www.statista.com/topics/2019/youtube/

LIVESTREAMED EASTER COMMUNION
FROM THE ARCHBISHOP'S KITCHEN

The archbishops stated that "*Live streaming of services is more important than ever and is still permissible from homes.* We encourage us all to consider how we can be as creative as possible with streaming services and other resources. There are many, many fantastic examples of churches and clergy using technology to reach and engage communities."[17] Their third letter a few days later makes *not* livestreaming from church even clearer: "Therefore, for a season, *the centre for the liturgical life of the church must be the home, not the church building.* We recognise that this has its challenges. But many clergy and lay people have already started streaming and *live streaming daily worship from their homes.*"[18] And to reinforce the point, the archbishop of Canterbury livestreamed his Easter Sunday morning service on BBC1 from his kitchen in Lambeth Palace, even though in fact it had been totally pre-recorded and edited days earlier, with him mostly looking down and reading the script off his table, rather than at those audience watching.

Interviewed afterwards on the BBC 1 *Andrew Marr Show*, Marr asked if this was the first time communion had been celebrated with "the archbishop's toaster in the background"; this became a joke in the discussion on air, and subsequently in the press, but even more on social media. Actually, closer inspection reveals that what is displayed on the worktop (to the archbishop's left, viewer's right) is actually a digital radio. Many noted that this Easter Day broadcast was from the archbishop's private kitchen, despite having two internal chapels in Lambeth Palace, normally used for regular worship of the household, staff, and young religious community based there, The Community of St Anselm. In fact, the first 'official' Church of England broadcast had come two weeks earlier, on Passion Sunday, from the archbishop of York in his chapel at Bishopthorpe; however, this use of an ecclesiastical setting denied to 'lesser mortals' by the archbishops' decree apparently provoked some negative reactions. In response, clearly, Archbishop Justin wanted to make a point, either about expressing solidarity with clergy who did not have two private chapels, and so had to use their kitchen, or in his determination to shift the emphasis away from 'the church as buildings' to 'the church as communities meeting in people's homes'. This latter point fits in with both his comments throughout the pandemic (see the various

17. Second Letter of March 24 from the archbishops and bishops, *my italics for emphasis*; it referred readers to https://www.churchofengland.org/more/church-resources/digital-labs/labs-learning-blog/beginners-guide-going-live-your-service-or

18. Third letter of March 27 from the archbishops and bishops; *my italics for emphasis*.

archepiscopal letters), as well as his expressed agenda for the Church of England, and was welcomed by those supporting his more informal and congregationalist approach. Others, from the Baptist or free church traditions, who had no option but to celebrate communion on kitchen tables because of persecution by the Church of England in past centuries, protested at the backlash; the Baptist theologian Steve Holmes from St Andrew's, wrote movingly about a Baptist Chapel cottage from 1709:

> The phrase 'kitchen table Eucharists' seems to have become, in the last few weeks, the chosen sneer of a number of Anglicans angry at their Bishops' guidance, revised yesterday, on clergy not entering their churches. . . . I am concerned, as others have been, about the denigration of domestic space implied by this sneer, and by the gendered implications of that. I am at least as much concerned by the implied criticism of the faith and practice of our persecuted sisters and brothers around the world right now, who find the kitchen table the only eucharistic site available to them.[19]

Similarly, Welby's detractors complained about a 'downgrading' or 'cheapening' of the eucharist; those from a more Catholic tradition, who see beauty reflecting the transcendence of God as a vital visual aid in worship, found being confronted with a close examination of the delicately painted Welby family china behind the celebrant at best a distraction, which perhaps even destroyed their attempt to receive the real presence of Christ 'spiritually', at the very moment when the archbishop said "Though we are many we are one body because we all eat of the one bread" in the captions. Traditionally, bishops' palace chapels are more likely to display graphic mediaeval frescoes of the wicked, damned souls being toasted on demons' pitchforks, than seeing an archepiscopal 'toaster'—even if it did turn out to be a digital radio!

19. Holmes, "On Kitchen Table Eucharists: A Plea to My Anglican Friends": http://steverholmes.org.uk/blog/?p=7725

This debate, especially on social media, quickly moved from being about simple aesthetics to, on the one hand, *ecclesiological* arguments about the national role of the Established Church ('the church as buildings') as opposed to the cozy, comfortable congregationalism of the gathered community of the faithful ('the church as communities meeting in people's homes') and, on the other, *theological* debate about the transcendence versus the immanence of God; it is hard to contemplate that it is "a terrible thing to fall into the hands of the Living God" if you are in his kitchen!

So we can learn from all the subsequent discussion that *the context and setting* of worship, not to mention something as obvious as *the visible background*, especially when broadcast or live streamed, can have huge ecclesiological consequences and theological implications for our understandings of the very life and being of God, of the nature of the church, of the mission of the church, of the eucharistic or ecclesial *community* that is gathered for the *communion*, way beyond what either the celebrant or the TV producer might have intended . . . . The cartoonist in the *Church Times*, David Walker, made the point by depicting various possible backgrounds for clergy to use in broadcasts, from the scholarly (books), artistic, spiritual, and 'realistic' (lots of piles to sort out).[20]

LIVESTREAMED COMMUNION FROM A LONDON CHURCH

Even before the outbreak of the COVID-19 pandemic, parishes and clergy aware of social media were already experimenting with livestreaming services on various platforms such as Facebook or YouTube. The Diocese of London published a list of these on March 12, 2020,[21] but on March 22 they restricted livestreaming to coming only from church buildings where "Clergy who live adjacent to their churches [otherwise known as 'within the curtilage']"[22] may still go into the building and pray and even celebrate the Eucharist."[23] Nonetheless, by the next day, March 23, they were still too many to list individually.[24]

---

20. For David Walker's cartoons during the pandemic, see, for instance, https://cartoonchurch.com/content/cc/category/2020-cartoons/

21. https://www.london.anglican.org/articles/accessing-christian-services-and-resources-digitally-for-those-who-cant-get-to-church/

22. That is, when there is direct access between the vicarage and the grounds of the church without needing to go through a public street or over public land.

23. https://www.london.anglican.org/articles/closure-of-church-buildings/

24. https://www.london.anglican.org/articles/live-streaming-worship/

A picture taken by the author of his own communion set in front of the livestream coming from the main altar in St Luke's Church with the familiar triptych behind the vicar as he celebrates communion.

With this closure of churches, St Luke's Church in West Holloway, London, which I had attended for the previous two decades, began livestreaming its usual weekly Sunday morning communion service from within the church, which could be accessed by the vicar, the Rev'd John MacKenzie, and his household through their garden (i.e., within the curtilage).

It also included pre-recorded contributions from its talented lay people, such as readings, prayers, video diaries, as well as music from the choir, including the music settings for the eucharist, pre-recorded individually and edited together, for those watching online, like me, to join in with at home.

I found watching, or even participating, very comforting and helpful personally, particularly since I had not yet settled into a local church following the earlier move from London to the North. I was in bereavement, missing this church, which had been so important to me, and even more, all its wonderful people. It was reassuring to see the much-loved triptych behind John presiding at the altar, below the marvellous East Window of the Risen

Christ astride the earth with the four evangelists. It felt very familiar and similar to the experience of being in this sacred space over nearly twenty years. Sadly, however, on Tuesday of Holy Week, April 7, 2020, the London College of Bishops issued a new statement instructing everyone, including those able to access church 'within the curtilage', "to stop all live streaming from your church buildings for the time being".[25] This instruction was not just sent round to all clergy, but was also followed up by an archdeacon to check that it was being observed, and that the churches really were closed up.

Thus, even St Luke's had to resort to the weekly eucharist being celebrated in the vicar's home. Certainly, I for one, missed the church backdrop, no matter how attractive any vicarage kitchen table might be. I was grateful that John MacKenzie took care to set things up properly, with part of the triptych and other items brought from the church to provide continuity. Instead of using the dining or kitchen table, he set things up in another room, using an altar tabletop, especially painted by an artist in the congregation. This room was kept as a 'sacred space', and not used for other purposes— certainly not eating or meals. Thus, there was no opportunity to inspect the vicarage crockery, or to wonder about toasters or radios! Also, the vicar, who had robed in church, considered dressing up in eucharistic vestments at home inappropriate, so presided in a clerical collar and ordinary clothes.

St Luke's, Holloway - Easter Sunday Service - 12/04/2020 | 11:00am

When churches reopened later in 2020 for both private prayer and for livestreaming services, the Sunday morning eucharist was filmed in a side prayer chapel, again accompanied by well-known and loved pictures or other items from the main church. This decision was driven by practical

25. https://www.london.anglican.org/articles/church-buildings-remain-closed-the-church-remains-open/

concerns: with the main nave now open for socially distanced individual prayers, there were concerns about infection control and regular cleaning, and also security issues regarding the cameras and lights. So for the next few months, the Sunday service was then streamed from the prayer chapel, which was set up and could be locked up from one week to the next, with the vicar or the assistant priest presiding.

A picture taken by the author of his own bread and wine in front of the livestream of the Assistant priest, the Rev'd Martin Wroe, celebrating communion in the side prayer chapel during vicar's summer holiday.

At the actual communion, John encourages all those who wish to bring bread and wine close to their device at the Offertory, to leave it there through the prayer of consecration, and then to receive communion all together at the appropriate time: before commencing the eucharistic prayer, he says words like, "so we come to the time for our communion this morning—please have your wine and have your bread prepared on your table. . . . Do eat and drink with us—we pray that God chooses to make of it what God will!" After the eucharistic prayer, the Lord's Prayer, and the fraction or breaking of the bread, then John and members of his household gave each other communion, while the audience or congregation who are watching or participating (the language one chooses to use is indicative of what one believes is happening) were encouraged to eat their own bread and drink their own wine.

There is no doubt that similar practices were quickly adopted by hundreds of churches livestreaming their services, and by thousands of individual worshippers locked down at home, whether the presiding celebrant encouraged this practice or not. Thus, at one of the early livestreamed services presided over by the bishop of Manchester, the Rt Rev'd Dr David Walker, someone posted on the bishop's newly set-up Facebook page this picture of their own bread and wine next to their smart phone showing the broadcast from the bishop's personal chapel, assisted by his wife (also a priest). Unlike the vicar of St Luke's, the bishop of Manchester could not give people permission or even encouragement to do this because of the Church of England's official position—but I am sure that he was well aware that many would be doing so.

As lockdown began to ease after Easter 2021, St Luke's moved into a 'blended' Sunday service, a mixture of livestreaming of the service taking place actually live in the church. At first, only fifty people were allowed to be present in the actual building, so that exact number of chairs would be spread around the main body (to allow for social distancing), and people had to 'book in' for a seat with the parish administrator by the previous Friday. Everyone else still attended online—either participating in it at the same time, joining in the live-chat, and going to the Zoom coffee groups afterwards, or catching up by watching later without those simultaneous possibilities. The main leading of the service, including a small socially distanced choir, and the celebration of the eucharist would be live, but readings, prayers, and sermons from guest preachers could be pre-recorded, so large TV screens were erected in the church for the small congregation to be able to see these parts of the service. As numbers have gradually been allowed to increase, more have been able to come to worship in church—but at the time of writing, it is expected that this 'blended' approach will be followed for the foreseeable future. Some stalwarts would doubtless like to go back to the 'old days' of just the physical congregation attending in due course—but this would disenfranchise all those who have joined the church for worship during the lockdown periods, which included people not just across the UK, but even as far afield as Australia! The total numbers in church, participating online at the same time, or catching up watching later, run into several hundreds—far more than could ever be accommodated in the physical building, and John, as incumbent, is understandably reluctant to lose them all.

Alongside Sunday morning services, St Luke's morning prayers, which used to take place in a side chapel in the church building, moved online into a daily Zoom service at 9.30am London time, which quickly attracted a faithful community of regular attendees. However, this includes someone who had worshipped at St Luke's regularly as a student in the 1990s, but who was now long settled and married back home in Melbourne, Australia, who reconnected with the church online. Now she and her husband tend to lead daily prayers on Mondays (the vicar's day off), while various of their friends also attend, even it if is early evening Down Under! Daily attendance is usually between twelve and twenty people, out of the thirty signed up as regulars to the inevitable WhatsApp group. Here also, if the vicar were to move the morning office back into a draughty side chapel this winter, this community, which have supported and prayed for each other over the last year, would be lost. Meanwhile, Bible study and Lent groups have also been taking place online, as well as PCC meetings and the long-delayed Annual Parochial Church Meeting, with its election of churchwardens and officers. So the whole pattern of the church with its services, meetings, events, and so forth has been changed by and during the pandemic—and it is unlikely to go back to its former ways in the future.

THE OFFICIAL CHURCH OF ENGLAND POSITION ON LIVESTREAMING

Like the proverbial elephant in the room, there was no mention of communion or eucharist in either of the early letters from the archbishops (both March 24 and 27). However, many churches, such as St Luke's, took the archbishops' instruction to "be as creative as possible with streaming services" as a 'green light' to encourage those watching locked down at home to have their own bread and wine by the side of their computer, tablet, or smartphone. It was therefore not surprising that the official statement regarding Holy Week and Easter 2020 services finally contained the direct instruction—or rather, what was essentially a ban:[26]

> Participants in a streamed service of Holy Communion should *not* be encouraged to place bread and wine before their screens. Joining together to share in the one bread and the one cup as those physically present to one another is integral to the service of Holy Communion; this is not possible under the current restrictions, and it is not helpful to suggest otherwise. *Any idea of the 'remote consecration' of the bread and wine should be avoided.* (My italics for emphasis)

This meant, of course, that St Luke's and all the other churches that had been offering 'remote consecration' were now doing so against the direct instructions of the Church of England bishops. However, there was no suggestion from its clergy or people that St Luke's should stop something that literally hundreds of people were finding so helpful and beneficial every week.

The Episcopal Reflection Group, which included consideration of my original paper, turned into the House of Bishops' Working Party, and drafted the next official statement after a couple of online meetings, which was then agreed and published by the House of Bishops.[27] This contained a couple of pages of practical guidance (about communion in one kind only, sanitizing hands, face masks, altar rails, reserving the sacrament, etc.), followed by a five-page statement of "Some Guidance on the Celebration of Holy Communion" detailing several important relevant points, which are worth quoting in detail:

> If such services of Holy Communion are recorded or live-streamed to others, it will be important that those watching can *see the president receive the bread and wine*, emphasising the Anglican principle that the sacramental meal is always to be consumed (§ 1.c). (My italics for emphasis)

Significantly, this had *not* happened in the archbishop's Easter Day celebration from his kitchen, since after the breaking of the bread, despite the subtitles on the screen "though we are many, we are one body because we

26. This had been drafted by the bishop of Lichfield, the Rt Rev'd Michael Ipgrave, who was chairing what was then the Episcopal Reflection Group (later the House of Bishops Working Group on Holy Communion), to which my original paper was submitted; as explained in a personal email to me on April 26, 2020 and quoted with his permission.

27. "COVID-19 Advice on the Administration of Holy Communion", June 9, 2020 which can be downloaded from https://www.churchofengland.org/more/media-centre/coronavirus-covid-19-guidance-churches#na

all eat one bread", and the liturgical invitation that "Christ our Passover is sacrificed for us", the camera cut away to the words of 'spiritual communion' and we never saw the archbishop himself receive.

On the other hand, we also noted earlier my own feelings of exclusion on Maundy Thursday, watching the bishops of Southwark and Salisbury receive communion by themselves, even suggesting that this was somehow being done on our behalf. If this instruction that "those watching can see the president receive the bread and wine" is to be observed, then the unfortunate impression of one person feeding themselves in the face of others watching but going hungry needs to be avoided. Jesus' words at the final judgement ("I was hungry and you gave me no food, I was thirsty and you gave me nothing to drink", Matt 25:42) come to mind. At least, the subsequent paragraphs attempt to recognize this disparity and bereavement, but only suggest 'spiritual communion' as the alternative:

> Many will *grieve the physical absence of the sacrament from their lives*. Yet this time may be an opportunity to re-discover and recognise some of the other ways in which we participate in the paschal mystery (§ 6).
>
> When services of Holy Communion are broadcast live (whether live-streamed or through videoconferencing), *those who tune in are participating in a real Eucharistic assembly*. Those who participate remotely in this way, but who are unable to be present physically, can practise a form of Spiritual Communion . . . available on the Church of England website (§ 7).
>
> The act of Spiritual Communion can take place at the point in the service when the participant would normally receive the bread and wine—perhaps after having seen the president consume them (§ 8). (My italics for emphasis)

It is crucial that these paragraphs do actually assert that "those who participate remotely . . . are participating in a real Eucharistic assembly" even if they "grieve the physical absence of the sacrament from their lives" and have to watch the president consume it alone. I therefore repeat that if the bishops' above points are true, serious attention must be given to preventing the unwelcome impression of exclusion. It is central to television and all mass communication that it is not what *you* say or intend that matters, but what the *audience* sees, feels, or thinks they hear. *Tele-vision* means 'seeing' from 'afar'—yet at the heart of the eucharist is "when we were still far off [*tele-*], you met us in your Son and brought us home", as the post-communion prayer puts it. It is important that words used in liturgy actually reflect what is happening—and we are not being "brought home" by this practice, any more than we can pray, "may we who share Christ's body live his risen life; we who drink his cup bring life to others" if we do *not* share his body or drink his cup. The bishops' statement is surely right, therefore, to try to find some more positive alternatives to the impression of being excluded and not fed:

> In some churches an *agape* meal (sometimes called a Lovefeast) is sometimes shared, to recall the meals shared by Jesus with his disciples and to express the fellowship afforded within the body of Christ. Such meals, whether conducted online or in the home, *are not a celebration of Holy Communion*, which must be presided over by a bishop or priest (§ 9, my italics for emphasis).

> After a live-streamed celebration of Holy Communion has ended, participants who wish may choose (in the time after the service which would often be devoted to fellowship and hospitality in a church context) to eat and drink as if sharing a meal together. As the Methodist Church puts it, "there is no question of action towards the food/drink that is shared, other than being thankful for it and consuming it [. . .] a Love Feast is *not a sacrament*." (§ 10, my italics for emphasis).

However, despite claiming to address the grief arising from the loss of the sacrament, the bishops' suggestions nonetheless remain *essentially negative*. They are more concerned to stress that this is "*not* a celebration of Holy Communion" and "*not* a sacrament" than to exercise pastoral care for people watching or participating. Sadly, the 'pastors of the pastors' seem more interested in communicating what things are *not* and what we are *not* allowed to do, than in trying to help 'Christ's flock' which they are called to shepherd to experience the grace of God and receive his nourishment in such difficult times. I am however grateful that they at least included a final paragraph, even though they marked it as an *Appendix* in italics, rather than being part of the official Statement:

> We recognise *a real desire of many for some physical engagement* during the online celebration of Holy Communion. In some cases, participants in online services have consumed bread and wine in their own homes during the service. Whilst we recognize that this practice may have spiritual value for some, *participants should not be encouraged to believe that any bread and wine brought before screens during online Holy Communion has been 'remotely consecrated'*. However, we commend the questions raised by this practice for further theological reflection (*Appendix*, § 11; again, my italics for emphasis).

At last, this finally names the elephant in the room, and "recognizes a real desire of many for some physical engagement" and admits that, despite the lack of episcopal encouragement, the negative official statements, and even prohibitions, "participants in online services have consumed bread and wine in their own homes during the service." Shock! Horror! God's people consume their own food and drink in their own homes! Summon the archdeacon—or archangel?

Nonetheless, the statement continues to insist that "participants should *not* be encouraged to believe that any bread and wine brought before screens during online Holy Communion has been 'remotely consecrated.'" The bishops' statement does not seem to be trying to "hear what the Spirit is saying to the churches", let alone grapple theologically with the question of *why* so many hundreds of churches and thousands of people are ignoring their instructions. Fortunately, it does at least "commend the questions raised by this practice for further theological reflection"—and it is in that spirit that my original paper was submitted to them and also that this subsequent book is offered.

Similarly, this encouragement for "further theological reflection" led to an online Zoom study and reflection days to which all the bishops of the Church of England were invited on October 26, 2020. A very helpful background note was produced by the Liturgical Commission/Faith and Order Commission Working Group chaired by the bishop of Lichfield, dated October 7, 2020. This contained substantial reflection around 'the Administration and Reception of Holy Communion' (especially with regard to communion in one kind only, the common cup, intinction, and so forth) and on 'the Eucharist in a digital medium', raising the issues covered within this book such as the eucharistic fast, spiritual communion, livestreaming, etc. It concluded, as in the above statement, that "In some cases, participants in online services have consumed bread and wine in their own homes during the service (and in some cases this practice has been encouraged by the presiding priest)." However, the background note remains quite clear: "It is recognised that this practice may have spiritual value for some, but to consider the possibility that such bread and wine brought before screens is 'remotely consecrated' would require a significant shift in the current understanding and practice of the Church of England." The note also posed some 'questions for discussion' which are very relevant to our concerns, including:

> c. What are the differences between live-streamed and recorded celebrations of the Eucharist, and what implications might there be for the constitution of the Eucharistic community?

d. Where participants at a service of Holy Communion are separated geographically but present in the same digital space and
at the same time, is it possible for them to receive Holy Communion by placing bread and wine before their screens? What
theological issues are at stake?

The morning session was devoted to these issues around 'the Eucharist
in a digital medium', with presentations from myself, the Rev'd Julie Gittoes
(whose paper on the eucharistic fast we considered in chapter 1 above), and
Dr Colin Podmore, while the afternoon concentrated on the other aspects
concerning 'the Administration and Reception of Holy Communion', also
with presentations from significant theologians. The presentations, papers,
and notes about the day were then circulated around the bishops to encourage this "further theological reflection"—but it has not yet led to any further
publications or other theological documents.

The official statement from the House of Bishops Recovery Group
on 'COVID-19 Advice on the Administration of Holy Communion' available on the CofE website has been updated many times with regard to the
practical questions about celebrating communion in church buildings, face
coverings, sharing the Peace, hygiene measures, communion in one or both
kinds, reserving the sacrament, etc. The latest statement on "Opening and
managing church buildings in step 4 of the Roadmap out of Lockdown"
deals very fully and helpfully with all these practical issues.[28]

However, it completely ignores the theological questions around 'the
Eucharist in a digital medium' and online communions. All the previous
statements, including the latest (version 5.3 from January 12, 2021, which
is still available on the same webpage at the time of writing August 2021,
though marked as "non-current or still awaiting review")[29] still repeated the
original five-page statement of "Some Guidance on the Celebration of Holy
Communion" from June 2020—unchanged—with all its negative rejection
of ideas about receiving bread and wine through online communion, and it
still concludes with the original commendation of "the questions raised by
this practice for further theological reflection"! I understand that the House
of Bishops' meeting in January 2021 decided not to vote upon any proposals, but sent this task back to the working group for more reflection.

28. Version 1.0, dated July 19, 2021; see https://www.churchofengland.org/resourc-
es/coronavirus-covid-19-guidance

29. Version 5.3, dated January 12, 2021, which was "Updated from version 5.2: the
document has been reviewed following the announcement of a new national lockdown
on the 4th January, but has not been changed", see https://www.churchofengland.org/
resources/coronavirus-covid-19-guidance

Similarly, although I was honoured to be asked to share a paper about my work for consideration by the American Episcopal bishops at their "Table in the Wilderness" in the late summer of 2020, nothing concrete or further has emerged.

One wonders when such "theological reflection" might be published or acted upon, especially given the recognition that livestreamed communions have nonetheless continued and become the norm in many churches for nearly two years under the pandemic, despite the beginnings of a welcome return to communion services in church buildings more recently, even if in one kind only. We therefore still need to consider the possible problems in such services that might lead to, or justify, the bishops' negative assertions, declarations, or even prohibitive statements, and what, if anything, might be able to offset, ameliorate, or at least mitigate them.

DIFFICULTY ONE:
TIME, AND THE USE OF PRE-RECORDING

The first crucial aspect that needs consideration is that of *time*. Since most 'live'streamed services are still essentially a 'broadcast', they raise all the questions previously discussed at the start of this chapter about whether one could put bread and wine in front of a TV broadcast and expect it to be consecrated. As we saw, any possible arguments for the validity of doing this required that it was, at least, a *live* broadcast, with those watching at home worshipping and consuming bread and wine *at the same time* as the president and others were celebrating communion. No arguments were advanced for how a pre-recorded service might bring about a valid and effective celebration a different time, weeks, months, or years ahead.

The bishops' statement makes this clear. They wish to reassure people that "when services of Holy Communion are broadcast live (whether live-streamed or through video-conferencing), those who tune in are participating in a real Eucharistic assembly" (§7). However, footnote 8 states that "whilst services may be pre-recorded for practical reasons, we see the practice of making recordings of services of Holy Communion as distinct from live broadcasts, and as affording different opportunities for participation." This suggests that archbishop of Canterbury's Easter service on March 12, 2020 was *not* in fact "a real Eucharistic assembly"; not only did we not see him (or anyone) actually receive communion, the entire programme had been pre-recorded, and all nicely edited together. The BBC might just as well have dug out an old recording of an Easter service in, say Canterbury Cathedral, from a previous year, and broadcast that instead.

To be totally honest, we must recognize that many so-called 'live'-streamed services are not in fact 'live'—any more than the various 'live'-streams of concerts and theatre shows broadcast throughout the pandemic were actually happening 'live'. They were all old recordings—and the only 'live' element was that people were encouraged to watch them together *at the same time*, even if by necessity all locked-down *in different places*. Even in livestreamed broadcasts of communion services, certain aspects had to be pre-recorded. For instance, choir items or other musical contributions required the musical director to record a backing track to provide both the right time and key. The singers then all recorded themselves individually, singing their part in key and time (as the essential headphone earpieces made clear). All these individual contributions then needed to be spliced together with the music track to form the choral, musical pieces with which we have become familiar, with lots of separate little windows of each person singing or playing along.

Similarly, other contributions, reading lessons, leading prayers, or even preaching, also needed to be recorded elsewhere in advance and sent in to be edited together for the overall service. The printed orders of service for St Luke's were quite clear:

> We're grateful to [the vicar and household] for hosting and film-ing the parts of our service previously coming from St Luke's itself. And grateful to a wider technical and creative team for pulling each Lockdown Liturgy together. To ensure the live event doesn't go down, leaving everyone with unfinished prayers or half sung songs, we now record services beforehand, broadcasting as live at 11 on Sundays.

However, the very word, 'livestreaming', suggests that at least the over-all service itself ought be 'live', that is, happening at the same time as those watching. Equally, the bishops argue that such services must be "broadcast live (whether live-streamed or through video-conferencing)" for us to be able to participate in "a real Eucharistic assembly" (§7). Thus, the priest should be leading the service *in real time*, welcoming people at the start, with music, readings, and even perhaps the sermon, pre-recorded and 'dropped in' at the relevant moments; being 'live' is especially necessary for presiding over the eucharistic elements, which the celebrant should have before them *at the same time* as the 'audience' watching, if they are to become instead a 'congregation' participating. If we are truly to be "one body because we all eat of the same bread", then the celebrant and those participating online should be eating and drinking at the same time, even if it is not the 'same bread' or wine. And yet, this faces the technical possibility mentioned by St

Luke's that the live event might "go down, leaving everyone with unfinished prayers or half sung songs"—or even receiving the real presence of Jesus in the bread, but breaking down before the wine! We will, therefore, have to return to this issue shortly.

DIFFICULTY TWO: SPACE, AND THE GATHERED EUCHARISTIC COMMUNITY

But secondly, we also discussed the importance of *place* above, noting the concerns raised by the Easter Day broadcast from the archbishop's kitchen, and also how the vicar of St Luke's carefully created a 'sacred space' within his vicarage for streamed services. I am, therefore, glad that the bishops are clear that "those who participate remotely . . . are participating in a real Eucharistic assembly." One aspect that makes these services a corporate act of worship (rather than a pre-recorded broadcast) is that while they are being livestreamed or broadcast on YouTube, 'live chat' allows those participating to type in comments as it is happening. Alongside the (pre-recorded) video of the service not only the words of the liturgy are being screened in time with the service, but also there is a 'live feed' of these 'live-chat' comments. Thus, in the ten minutes or so before the service starts, music is playing as people log in, announce their presence, say hello or share news, just as when arriving physically at church. This 'live chat' continues throughout, with people noting appreciation for some music or pre-recorded item, or their reflections upon the sermon, or to offer or request prayers. Even the priest and his household would attend and participate from the vicarage!

This engendered the feeling of a 'live' act of worship within a real ecclesial and eucharistic community, with everyone still gathering together, just as previously, sharing the same time and space, even if the space is digital rather than physical. I even found that I like and appreciate the comments from friends, while, true to form, some comments from certain people annoyed me just as much as the people themselves used to in the past! But this is the *real* nature of any Christian church: it is never just a gathering of like-minded 'people like us', but one body formed from very differing members (1 Cor 12). As with my experiences on Second Life, the reality and continuity between the digital and physical worlds is clear.

If the livestream is on a platform without such a 'live-chat' facility, another option would be to use Twitter, which we did say might still have a role to play alongside another options. Using a Twitter #hashtag, like #communionAug2 for instance, would enable congregational members watching to become participants by tweeting comments before and after, as well as throughout the service.

The service ended, as in church, with notices or pre-recorded comments from individuals about an issue, or upcoming event—and then this 'live-chat' facility closed when the broadcast stopped. There is, therefore, a real difference between participating in the service 'live' along with the vicar and all the rest of the congregation—and merely 'catching up' later on one's own on YouTube. There was even 'church coffee time' on Zoom, where people made their own coffee, go online, and met up virtually to chat to the clergy ('lovely sermon, vicar!') or their friends; the host could put people into clusters in 'break-out' rooms for a short while, and then mix up the groups chatting, just as in church in pre-pandemic days! The video recording remains online for people to watch later, especially shift or key workers who miss the livestream. However, it is significant that St Luke's made a conscious decision that these broadcast services should only remain available for a couple of weeks before they are removed in a deliberate act to try to keep them as 'live' as possible.

THE INTENTION OF THE CELEBRANT

We spent a lot of attention on the importance of intention in the last chapter, so now it is time to see if that can help us with these two difficulties of *time* and *space*. I noted that the vicar of St Luke's prays over the elements of bread and wine not only before him and also those before people gathered in their homes that "God may choose to make of it what God will." Here, a churchmanship divide may quickly emerge. Those of an informal, 'low', more evangelical tradition will probably find this an acceptable form of consecration, and be perfectly happy to leave it to Jesus how he chooses to manifest his presence in or through the communion. But, as previously noted, for those of a more formal, 'high', Catholic tradition, consecration must include the particular sacramental intention of the celebrant, as well as the manual acts of taking bread and wine, placing their hands upon them at the 'moment' of the eucharistic words of the institution narrative, and even elevating the paten and chalice, probably accompanied by ringing bells and/or genuflecting, which is possible online for only the priest's bread and wine, but no one else's.

To return to the manual acts for the priest to take, bless, break, and share in the four-fold action, clearly in a livestream the celebrant cannot physically 'touch' *any* elements not directly in their presence, no matter how close they are placed to the laptop. Therefore, those who consider it essential for a properly authorized minister manually to touch the communion elements physically can never accept consecration via broadcasting or livestreaming, even when genuinely 'live', and much less when pre-recorded. On the other hand, we noted that in larger services in cathedrals or festivals, the celebrant equally cannot touch all the elements—but rather they extend their 'zone of intention' to include those elements being held up before them to enable their consecration also as the body and blood of our Lord Jesus Christ.

It follows, therefore, that the celebrant could similarly extend their 'zone of intention' to consecrate elements of bread and wine in different people's homes. I asked the vicar of St Luke's Church exactly what he thought he was doing in such livestreams and what his intention was in saying the eucharistic prayer and presiding over the elements. John replied that even in the days of celebrating communion in church, he believed that, as a priest presiding over a eucharistic celebration, he offered himself as "bridge or channel" for the grace of God to nourish his people. This is, of course, similar to traditional theological understandings of the priesthood as 'mediatorial', representing God to the people and the people to God. The pope's Latin title *'pontifex'* literally means 'bridge-maker' (*pons*, a bridge, and *fex*, from *facio* to make). John's sacramental intention, therefore, in celebrating a livestreamed service of holy communion and presiding over the elements is actually 'pontifical', as he intends to open himself up as a channel whereby God's grace can reach all those receiving bread and wine, to enable the divine presence to become 'real' in their homes, whenever and wherever they are able to participate. He described rather movingly that, as he looks into the camera recording it all, he tries—or *intends?*—to see *through* the lens to all the people on the other side, gathered in other places, that they might be enabled to know and receive God's grace and real presence.

Significantly, he observed at the time that even though it was recorded usually on a Thursday to give time for editing, for him it was *still* the main Sunday parish celebration, and that his intention was to celebrate for those who would gather and participate in it all together as an ecclesial eucharistic community the following Sunday. Also, his intention included those who have no choice but to watch it later, especially key workers and healthcare professionals not free on Sunday mornings. In fact, on those Sunday mornings, he and his family would sit down to watch the livestream, and participate in it, joining in, and responding to the live chat; like everyone else, he has bread and wine before the screen, which he takes, blesses, breaks, and shares with his household at the same time as all the rest of the congregation. John's response was that the Triune God is Lord of all time and space, and all moments are 'live' and real to him; if a thousand years are but as a day with the Lord (Ps 90:4; 2 Pet 3:8), then why cannot a service pre-recorded on Thursday be the same spiritual event when broadcast on Sunday?

THE INTENTION OF THE PEOPLE

We have also stressed throughout that the president's sacramental intention must be met with a similar intention from people who wish him or her to consecrate the elements for them to consume—and that without both the presence and invitation of the people, a priest or minister cannot celebrate selfishly to feed themselves alone. We demonstrated above the important sense of a 'live' act of worship within an ecclesial and eucharistic community engendered by people contributing 'live chat' with comments or prayers during the progress of the service. Therefore, the laity are, in fact, playing their part in preparing to be worthy recipients just as the priest prepares to be a worthy celebrant. John told me that within any congregation—perhaps especially among the variegated nature of St Luke's—he notes a wide range of understandings about communion; even in church, his intention is to provide for each and every one what they need and desire individually. St Luke's contains some people from more congregationalist traditions with a Zwinglian approach to remembering Christ's sacrifice on the cross through sharing in the Lord's Supper; others wish to offer all their work, talents, and lives to God in thanksgiving at the eucharist with a more catholic desire to receive the real presence of Jesus in the bread and wine to feed them with his body and blood—however that may be understood. It is part of the glory—and sometimes the confusion!—of the Anglican tradition that *all* these individual understandings are valid and acceptable in conscience. Therefore, in livestreamed services, as John looks *into* the camera but sees *through* its lens to all the people gathered together on the other side, his prayer is that God will minister grace to each and every one of them, and provide what they need and desire individually, just as much through the streaming, as in church itself. The priest's intention in celebrating must be met therefore by the intention of those gathered and participating online, and by their own prayer that God in Christ will come to them in love, grace, and healing, to meet their needs, and to feed them with his body and blood, regardless of—or perhaps in line with?—their own understanding of it.

This aspect of gathering as an ecclesial eucharistic community could be further strengthened by the opening rubric of the 1662 Book of Common Prayer Communion Service, which has fallen into disuse. Cranmer instructed that "so many as intend to be partakers of the holy Communion shall signify their names to the Curate." Thus, it would be possible for every member of the congregation who "intend to be partakers" by gathering in a livestreamed communion to "signify their names" to the celebrant either emailing in advance, or signing in on 'live chat' or Twitter at the start. Thus, they shift from being mere observers in an audience watching, to becoming active and willing congregational participants gathered together for the eucharist, which the priest will celebrate in response to their invitation (and which he or she cannot do if no one attends, even online, see chapter 3 on 'solitary communion' above).

I even suggested that John could read out all the names so signified before the Eucharistic Prayer, but with over 300 people attending or watching or participating (again, one's choice of vocabulary is instructive), he considered that idea impractical. It might be easier in a smaller congregation, but that still leaves those who forgot to 'sign up', or who arrive late, being excluded.[30] Nonetheless, a priest could make explicit their intention, desire, and willingness to consecrate *all* the various breads and wines being taken or lifted up at home, not only by those who have signified their intention in advance, but all those who wish to participate, so that everyone can pray separately in mere geography, but together in sacred space and time to receive the grace of God in bread and wine, whether they understand it to be the body and blood of our Lord Jesus Christ, or whatever. As in the parallel with larger services in cathedrals or festivals, the people at home could be asked simply to hold up their bread and wine at the appropriate moment with the celebrant in order to make clear their own sacramental desire that "these gifts of bread and wine may be to us his body and his blood", as the priest prays in the Eucharistic Prayer.[31] By thus extending

30. Bishop Michael Ipgrave, who chaired the Episcopal Reflection Group, later the House of Bishops Working Group on Holy Communion, responded very helpfully to an earlier draft of this section in his personal email of April 26, 2020, quoted with his permission: "I can also see how the invitation-only celebration of the Eucharist in a small group who all bring their own bread and wine as part of their participation could work, as the celebrating priest's intention would be clearly defined. In practical terms, though, I do not see how they would play out in the case of a larger group, or an online celebration that was public in the sense that no invitation was needed[;] . . . there is good reason why that practice [of the BCP rubric] has fallen into desuetude in a society much more mobile than Cranmer ever envisaged, and to try to introduce it online would surely introduce even more complexity[;] . . . the presiding priest would not be able to form any sense of his or her 'zone of intention' (great phrase!)"; my expansion above is an attempt to meet this objection.

31. This would also deal with the possible objection about people trying to get hold of consecrated elements for nefarious or sacrilegious purposes. Merely holding up elements at home while the prayer is said online without any intention to partake of Christ's body and blood is back to quasi-magical ideas of '*hocus pocus*', and will not make them consecrated; once again, I am very grateful to my editor, the Rev'd Dr Robin Parry, for this point also.

the mediatorial 'zone of intention', this active partnership between priest and people could thus form a 'bridge' or 'channel' for God's grace in a truly 'pontifical' manner.

THE INTENTION AND ACTION OF THE TRIUNE GOD

Finally, we saw in the previous chapter that the intentions of both priest and people are worthless without the grace and action of God the Holy Trinity, in which the Father longs to pour out his grace, the Son offers his body and blood to feed and nourish his people, and the Holy Spirit is waiting to be called down through the act of *epiclēsis*, the invocation of the Spirit upon both the elements and the people. It is not a magical *hocus pocus*, where the priest—through saying the 'right' words with or without the 'right' actions—causes some effect or change in the bread and wine (however understood), but the work of *the Holy Spirit*. As John MacKenzie argued, the priest is merely the 'channel' through which it happens—but he or she is also the one who 'calls down' the Spirit onto the bread and wine.[32] Might it not also be possible, therefore, for God the Holy Spirit to respond to the priest's intention in this 'calling' to fall upon not just the priest's own elements, but also onto all the other elements of bread and wine on the various tables before all those who are watching, or rather participating, whether they have "signified their names" or not. The crucial point is that both the priest's sacramental intention and the people's earnest desire to feed upon Christ "by faith with thanksgiving" is a plea to the heart of God for his nourishing grace that we may all, as the invitation to communion puts it:

> Draw near with faith.
> Receive the body of our Lord Jesus Christ
> which he gave for you,
> and his blood which he shed for you.
> Eat and drink in remembrance that he died for you,
> and feed on him in your hearts
> by faith with thanksgiving.

If the celebrant intends to make this possible for the people, who in turn wish the celebrant to do that because they desire to receive Christ, then who are we to limit the grace and love in the action of the Holy Trinity to fulfil those intentions and meet those desires with abundant grace as the Holy Spirit comes upon the bread and wine and Jesus makes his presence real

32. Again, I am also grateful to Graham Tomlin, bishop of Kensington, for reinforcing this point.

in whichever elements and whatever way he chooses? Surely, our doctrinal concerns or human prohibitions cannot be binding upon the freedom and grace of the Holy Trinity?

CONCLUSIONS—CHECKING THE CHECKLIST

We began this chapter by considering older debates about whether TV broadcasts, particularly when 'live', could actually effect a consecration of nearby bread and wine. The consensus, even at the time, was that such events were at best 'something else', akin to Methodist 'love-feasts' or Orthodox *antidoron*. Similarly, early attempts to celebrate communion on Twitter failed because of both official disapproval and the practical considerations of one-way communication in limited characters. However, the development of the hugely popular platforms of Facebook livestreams and YouTube recordings offer a real possibilty for celebrating communion online.

Our journey through all the possible options gradually produced a 'checklist' of criteria required for a valid and effective eucharistic celebration, so we need to 'check' such livestreamed or broadcast communions against it:

- Whether bishops and church authorities like it or not, it must be recognized that such online services of holy communion were widely adopted in such "contagious times" and continue to take place as an alternative to *fasting from communion* or *solitary eucharistic celebrations*. There can be no doubt that they have become important and precious to many living alone, those who still wish to live locked down at home, or who cannot physically attend church buildings, being prevented either by health concerns or simply geographical distance. They can provide real nourishment from physical elements of bread and wine which those from a 'lower' Zwinglian tradition appreciate as a true memorial of Christ's passion and death. Catholics and those from a 'higher' tradition of priesthood and the 'real presence' will have serious concerns about whether such bread and wine can really become the body and blood of our Lord Jesus Christ, not least because of the need for a priest's consecration for people gathered together in the same place and time. As with the old TV debates, this is made even worse by pre-recording such services for later broadcast.

- However, if everyone in an ecclesial community (a.k.a. 'church'!) gathers at the same *time*, it can be seen as a proper and valid gathering for *a full liturgical service*, including the ministry of the word, reading and expounding the scriptures, as well as confession, praise, and prayer. The additional use of things like 'live chat' allows for the sharing of hopes and fears, joys and sorrows, and opportunities for fellowship. It can therefore be argued that people are not mere observers watching but *active participants* gathering in the same (digital) *space*, even if mediated online through the wonders of technology. This is even more true in a 'blended' environment where a full communion service is being livestreamed and includes contributions from others who are not physically present in church.

- If the celebrant is a *canonically and episcopally ordained priest* (for Anglicans and Catholics, large and small 'c'), or a *duly recognized minister* (for other denominations), this satisfies those who require proper authorization; it will also be necessary that the service accords with the *liturgy and practice* of the particular church tradition.

- If the *celebrant's intention* to celebrate holy communion is met with a *similar intention or desire* from the people, this fulfils the requirement for *full participation by the laity*, thus enabling them to receive the grace of God in bread and wine, both in the church building or, if they prefer or their circumstances necessitate, online at home.

- Those from Catholic and Anglican traditions who wish to observe the instructions of canon law can ensure that their *bread is made from wheat and their wine* is "the fermented juice of the grape", again both in church and at home online.

- Because each individual or household supplies their own bread and wine, there is always the right amount, enough for everybody without any need for secondary consecration; furthermore, those for whom this is important can ensure that everything which has been consecrated is *properly and reverently consumed*, together with any required *ritual ablutions of the vessels used* at the end of the service.[33]

The above checklist will be sufficient for many to affirm that everything *humanly* possible is being done, but that ultimately it must be the *divine* responsibility of the Holy Trinity to make any such service a 'valid and effective celebration' in which God the Father pours out his grace and

33. I am grateful to the Rev'd Gilly Myers for making this point in a private email to me. In his emailed response, Bishop Michael Ipgrave also noted about a wider communion broadcast on a public platform like Facebook or YouTube: "As a corollary to that, if there were an undefined number of unknown individuals bringing bread and wine to an online celebration of the Eucharist, I think there would be a real concern about the reverent disposal of the consecrated (?) eucharistic elements."

the Lord Jesus Christ makes his presence real in bread and wine through the descent of the Holy Spirit upon both the eucharistic elements and also the people of God.

Others, who earnestly long to celebrate communion may still have anxieties about whether such Facebook livestreams or YouTube broadcasts can actually be a real ecclesial gathering and a sacramental community. Such concerns may increase through a hierarchy of possible scenarios, all of which are open to the necessary sacramental intention of the priest or minister and the corresponding desire of the people to be fed with God's grace:[34]

In the first place, a 'blended' consecration performed by an authorized minister in a church building with some congregation physically present but also broadcasting *live* to a (geographically) dispersed, but still gathered (online), group of people who participate fully with their own bread and wine at home or wherever can most easily be considered as a true ecclesial eucharistic community.

Secondly, while pre-recorded anonymous broadcasts with no sense of the 'audience' watching are not acceptable, a service including a consecration that is pre-recorded and edited for practical purposes, can still allow a group gathered online at the same time to become participants rather than observers, especially if simultaneous involvement is permitted by extra measures such as 'live chat', as we saw in the example of St Luke's Holloway under the lockdown.

Thirdly, such a pre-recorded broadcast being watched later by a lone individual raises more difficulties for any concept of a gathered community sharing the same experience in the same time and same space. However, it may be argued that the way that the *space* is still the same *digitally* can also allow the *time* to be the same *liturgically*; this could be considered especially so for those who were not able to be present at the same moment as the main congregation because they were actually working in health and other essential services at that point but who now desire to 'catch up' with their community and receive God's grace and strength to continue making life possible for everyone else in these difficult "contagious times." Further, anxieties about leaving pre-recorded broadcasts on individual platforms to be watched or downloaded whenever can be alleviated by restricting this 'catch-up' time for the service to a week or two, in the manner of TV iPlayer platforms, again following the example of St Luke's Holloway.

34. Once again, I am very grateful to my editor, the Rev'd Dr Robin Parry, for helping to clarify this approach.

This discussion beginning with older considerations about 'broad'-casting from earlier days of TV but continuing through to online platforms like Facebook and YouTube, based upon my experience of one north London church, has demonstrated that it is possible for such broadcasts not only to be considered true communions by those of a 'lower' Zwinglian understanding, but also—under certain conditions and provisions—as sacramentally valid, dealing with the concerns raised for those of a 'higher' more catholic tradition. Our quest for a way of celebrating holy communion in "contagious times" has therefore finally managed to produce at least some possible solutions. All that now remains to be seen is whether a more 'narrow'-casting approach through certain webinar applications such as Zoom or Microsoft Teams might provide even more satisfactory outcomes.

15

Proposal 10 (and Solution?)

Narrowcasts and Participatory Webinar Platforms

THE PANDEMIC PRODUCED A wide variety of online broadcasts of worship, using platforms like Facebook livestream and YouTube. Whether bishops or church authorities like it or not, this rapidly came to include celebrations of the eucharist through which many churches, individuals, and house-holds found great solace and comfort in bringing bread and wine before broadcasts from their local church, presided over by their own priest or minister. Such 'virtual celebrations' may even be welcomed by those of a 'lower' churchmanship. Those with a Zwinglian theology of remembrance, in which the bread and wine are symbols or 'aides-memoires' of Jesus' sav-ing passion and death, and those with a slightly 'higher' understanding of 'sharing' communion in Christ's self-giving sacrifice can respond positively to such online celebrations.

However, allowing those watching to participate with their own bread and wine often seems to appear unacceptable to those with any catholic understanding of priestly presidency and the 'real presence'. Despite the wide diversity of interpretation within Anglicanism, archbishops, presiding bishops and corporate episcopal meetings have all issued statements against such online communions—and the same is true with many authorities in other denominations and church traditions. As we just saw, several simple steps could be taken to make these communions more congruent with our criteria, such as insisting on a 'live', and not pre-recorded, broadcast, at least, of the Eucharistic Prayer, and also encouraging congregation members to participate together at the same time through 'live-chat' or Twitter. The priest could also use the Book of Common Prayer rubrics for lay people to 'signify their intention' to receive communion, reading out names if time permits, or at least stating explicitly that he 'intends' to consecrate all the elements produced by those who 'intend' and desire to 'feed on Christ in their hearts with thanksgiving'.

Nonetheless, the impenetrable barrier in such *broad*casts between celebrant and congregation, between priest and people, means that the person presiding over the elements cannot see—let alone touch—the bread and wine upon which the *epiclēsis* calls down the Holy Spirit to fill them with the real presence of Jesus Christ. During the pandemic, while some things like groceries and online shopping could be done easily on *broader* websites, the *narrower*, participative software of webinar platforms such as Microsoft Teams and Zoom rapidly became the 'go-to' solution for anything that required discussion, debate, and decision-making between people acting together in real time, such as in business, education, and government. Indeed, even the churches used it for binding decisions like House of Bishops' meetings (who, perhaps amusingly, used it to agree their very statements against online consecrations) or the General Synod. It remains to be seen whether such '*narrow*casts' on webinar platforms can also help us deal with this final difficulty preventing *broad*casts (whether live or pre-recorded) from being acceptable for holy communion in "contagious times."

PARTICIPATING IN A LIVE CELEBRATION
OF THE EUCHARIST ON ZOOM

As previously noted, I had recently moved from London to the rural Greater Manchester area just before the pandemic lockdown. I had not managed to find a church 'home' to help that sense of bereavement in missing St Luke's Church, Holloway. Thus, during the pandemic, like many other former members of its congregation now dispersed across the country and around the world, I found myself gravitating back to the YouTube livestream of its services—and especially joining in with old friends through the 'live chat' during service and the Zoom coffee afterwards, as we have just discussed.

However, I had begun a spiritual discipline of cycling to our nearest parish church for the quiet said Holy Communion on Wednesday mornings. Here up to about a dozen mostly elderly or retired folk gathered for what was not a brief service, but which included the full liturgy with all the lectionary readings and a proper sermon, lasting the best part of an hour. I was grateful to be welcomed, and even allowed myself to be enticed into the vicarage for coffee afterwards! However, as fears about COVID-19 began to rise, first the chalice was removed for 'communion in one kind', followed afterwards by the service ceasing altogether with the closure of the churches.

About this time, I received the Facebook query from my South African friend about how far priestly intention or eucharistic celebration might be 'extended'. Therefore, on the Feast of the Annunciation, March 25, 2020, we started experimenting with a small participatory mid-week Zoom communion to fill the void left by being unable to receive communion in church. The regular participants were initially a mixed group of ten to twenty lay and ordained individuals who live in four different continents (several parts of Europe, the USA, South Africa, and Australia) and from at least five different traditions and denominations: the majority are Anglicans of varying churchmanship, but it also includes a Roman Catholic, a couple of Lutherans (one from the USA and one in Estonia), a Baptist or two—all hosted on Zoom by a Quaker! The group is evenly split between men and women, with about a third being ordained, a couple of licensed lay ministers, and the other half lay people. There have been also another ten to twenty people on the email list each week, some of whom come as or when they can, and others who are interested in hearing how it is developing—including several bishops, who have come once or twice when duties have permitted.

Screenshot taken by the author showing the official Church of England liturgy with various participants and their bread and wine clearly visible.

A ZOOM LITURGY

We tend to follow Order 1 (contemporary) liturgy from the Church of England *Common Worship*,[1] with different people reading the scriptures (the daily *Revised Common Lectionary*), leading intercessions, giving a homily,

1. https://www.churchofengland.org/prayer-and-worship/worship-texts-and-resources/common-worship/holy-communion#na.

or, if ordained, presiding at the eucharist. I choose several pieces of music each week, often beginning with a quiet Taizé or Gregorian chant to set the theme, and ending with an appropriate classic hymn for communicants to be able to 'let rip' and blast it out at home, safely muted, of course. I also insert video musical clips for the liturgy, such as the Gloria, Sanctus, Agnus Dei, etc. Something much appreciated is the occasional inclusion of one choral piece, complete with the score, as a short anthem for the good singers to sing along with in their part as Soprano, Alto, Tenor, or Bass at home—though of course once again with their microphone muted! Given that singing together has not been allowed because it spreads contagion, this practice has been especially welcomed.

I produce an individual order of service each week, with the readings and details of the music or videos, and appropriate illustrations. Many scroll that order of service alongside the live video feed, or separately on their smartphone. I originally acted as host, in order to be able to control muting or unmuting everyone at appropriate moments, introducing recorded music, or playing a relevant video through screensharing. This has become an important role, which Jonathan Gebbie from St Mary's Stoke Newington, in London, called a "Zoom verger" in a fascinating *Church Times* article.[2] When I presided over communion myself, someone else would take on this task; increasingly, our Quaker host settled into performing this role for which we are all very grateful.

One practical problem is that Zoom has difficulty picking up more than one person speaking at a time, so we moved away from saying longer items (like the Gloria or the Creed) or prayers together at the same time, preferring to use either a recorded musical version, or moving to antiphonal confessions and creeds, with one-line responses, like the *Kyries*. We have found that there is something important in still saying these short responses together as one body, despite the problems. However, another widely used solution, especially for longer prayers, is to have one person unmuted as the congregational representative, speaking all the responses. The rest can also join in at home—but muted. The host usually mutes everyone (e.g., during music or the homily); during more open times, like prayers of intercession, individuals take it in turns to unmute themselves to pray or say something, and then re-mute afterwards.

Despite being a very mixed group, who only had in common knowing me or another member of the group through various connections, we 'gelled' surprisingly quickly into a real ecclesial community of praise and

2. https://www.churchtimes.co.uk/articles/2020/24-april/comment/opinion/how-to-be-a-zoom-verger

prayer, sharing our hopes and fears, joys and concerns for our loved ones (at least a couple of which are frontline essential workers in the health service and elsewhere). With a significant proportion of us in active ministry, we can pray for the sick, funerals being taken, or pastoral situations some were facing.

As essential in our list of criteria required for a valid and effective communion, we combine the ministry of the word with the sacrament, and we have been blessed with a range of thoughtful and challenging homilies or expositions of the day's readings (three or four of the participants are biblical scholars, so it can be a bit daunting!). The address is usually followed by a relevant piece of music, space for reflection and meditation, leading into a time of sharing prayer needs together.

CELEBRATING THE EUCHARISTIC PRAYER ONLINE

Because of our range of traditions, each week the celebrant to decides how they want to lead it, what they want to wear (clerical collar or robes), whether they wish to sit or stand, choose pottery vessels or traditional chalices and patens, use candles, icons, incense, or other accoutrements, or whatever. On one occasion, my former Baptist colleague led his online liturgy for Bloomsbury Baptist Church in central London.[3] This all reflects whatever we used to do in 'pre-virus days', and has stimulated interesting discussion and debate among us!

At the eucharist itself, those who wish lay out a clean white handkerchief as a 'corporal' for their own wine and bread in accordance with the 1662 Book of Common Prayer rubrics. Some participants have a special communion set, a silver or pottery chalice and paten, while others just use an ordinary plate and glass. A practice that developed almost naturally is to angle laptop lids or webcams *down* for the consecration, so that the president can actually *see* all the different plates, glasses, or communion sets on the screen before them. As discussed above, the celebrant's intention is to consecrate the contents of all these vessels visible to him or her, matched by each person's intention and desire to receive the body and blood of our Lord Jesus Christ. Again, as discussed above, since these various communion vessels appear much closer to me than the twenty yards or more of eucharistic assistants around an altar in a large communion in a cathedral or festival, I have no difficulty when presiding in intending to consecrate

3. See   https://baptistbookworm.blogspot.com/2020/03/scattered-yet-gathered.html

all I can see in my 'zone of intention' in accordance with the intentions and desire of each person present.

Indeed, when presiding, I sometimes found myself explicitly expanding the *epiclēsis* in the eucharistic prayer, thus:

> Lord, you are holy indeed, the source of all holiness;
> grant that, by the power of your Holy Spirit, and according to
>   your holy will,
> these gifts of bread and wine *here before me on this table and*
>   *visible on this screen*
> may be to us the body and blood of our Lord Jesus Christ;
>
> As we offer you this our sacrifice of praise and thanksgiving,
> we bring before you this bread and this cup
> *on our tables and seen on this screen*
> and we thank you for counting us worthy to stand in your pres-
>   ence and serve you.[4]

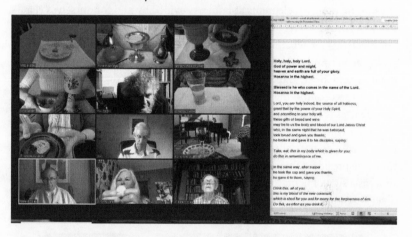

Screenshot taken by the author showing all the various breads and wines visible on the screen before him while presiding and praying for the Holy Spirit to fill them with the real presence of the risen Christ

At both points, I extend my hands over not just my own chalice and paten, but also out over the computer screen. Similarly, at the second *epiclēsis*, calling the Spirit down upon the people, when I previously stretched out my hands over the congregation before me in church, now I stretch my hands out not only over the bread and wine before me but also to encompass the screen with all the people I can see, upon whom I wish the Holy Spirit to

4. Eucharistic Prayer B, https://www.churchofengland.org/prayer-and-worship/worship-texts-and-resources/common-worship/holy-communion#mm7c10

fall in blessing as well as upon their breads and cups: "Send the Holy Spirit on your people, and gather into one in your kingdom all who share this one bread and one cup."

This is a not unreasonable extension of lay and ordained assistant eucharistic ministers in larger services holding up patens and chalices for the president to consecrate and bless, as discussed above. Thus, it allows an online eucharist to be fully inclusive through this interactive *narrow*cast in a participatory webinar software package like Zoom or Microsoft Teams.

After the eucharistic prayer and the Lord's Prayer, everyone breaks their bread together with the celebrant at the Fraction, leading to the climax of actually receiving bread and wine. Clearly, the celebrant cannot physically distribute the elements. At first, after the *Agnus Dei*, the president invited everyone to communicate themselves at the same time. Of course, this happened quickly, and some negative reactions were expressed that it did not 'feel' like receiving consecrated bread and wine from the president but merely consuming our own elements at home, provided by and for ourselves (Paul's strictures in 1 Cor 11:34 come to mind), as well as excluding those present but not receiving for whatever reason. Therefore, the president now addresses each person by name in turn, with the traditional words for the distribution of the Body of Christ, and each communicant waits until they have been so addressed to consume their bread individually; at the end of the 'round', the president asks someone else to invite them to receive the bread, as well as blessing anyone choosing not to receive, like our Quaker host and any bishops present who do not communicate in order to respect the current official position. The president then invites us all to drink our wine together are the same time, as a sign of being 'one body', sharing 'one cup'. This method has become a very powerful experience eliciting strongly positive reactions as the 'high point' of the service, as it should be.

After that, we pray the post-communion prayer of offering ourselves, who have been fed with the 'bread of heaven' and the 'cup of salvation', to the service of God in one another and his world, followed usually by belting out a classic hymn at full volume—with microphones muted of course! The criteria for a valid and effective eucharistic celebration also include an opportunity for fellowship with sisters and brothers in Christ—the inevitable post-service church tea and coffee. Indeed, in some traditions, people find greater fellowship in the coffee cup than in the wine! Our current participants are all busy people who, in the midst of a busy weekday, mostly choose to slip away fairly quickly—but there is opportunity for those who wish to stay and talk; we have had some fascinating discussions, and there is also the opportunity for people to go into a 'break-out room' for confidential conversation or private prayer.

Another innovation helping the sense of fellowship is linking all our mobile cell phones in a WhatsApp group. With short instant messages, this is ideal for anyone at whatever time of day or night to leave a brief message, providing a news item, or asking for prayer for something that has just come up or they are doing. Because the group spans all time zones, usually somebody is awake somewhere, and thus a quick response is often received.

THE 'CHECKLIST' OF THE CRITERIA FOR A VALID AND EFFECTIVE EUCHARISTIC CELEBRATION

It is time to check our Zoom communion against the 'checklist' of criteria required for a valid and effective eucharistic celebration, which emerged in our journey through the possible options:

- These services of holy communion remove the need to *fast from communion* in "contagious times" and provide real spiritual nourishment from physical elements of consecrated bread and wine for spiritual growth, in accordance with traditional Christian teaching and spirituality, even if the online method is innovative.

- The group celebrates (in all senses of the word) together, avoiding *solitary or 'solo' communions*; this has been particularly valued by many who live alone and locked down for months at home, never seeing another human being.

- Because everyone gathers at the same *time*, regardless of different time zones, it has become a proper ecclesial gathering and can function as a eucharistic community, which also gathers in the same *space*, even if that space is mediated online through the wonders of technology.

- The *celebrant's intention* to celebrate holy communion in accordance with the *similar intention or desire from the others,* including lay people, satisfies that requirement for *full participation by the laity.*

- *The celebrant has been a properly authorized minister.* In our case, this has been canonically and episcopally ordained Anglican priest, except when an authorized, recognized minister from another denomination has led the service according to their particular church's liturgy and practice.

- The eucharistic prayer and the receiving of holy communion take place as the *climax of a full liturgical service,* including the ministry of the word, confession, praise and prayer, and opportunities for fellowship, the sharing of hopes and fears, joys and sorrows.

- Those from Catholic and Anglican traditions who keep the *instructions of canon law* can ensure that their bread is made from wheat and that the wine is "the fermented juice of the grape."

- Each person supplies their own bread and wine, so there is always the right amount, without any need for a secondary consecration, and everyone can ensure that all consecrated elements are *properly and reverently consumed.*[5]

- Those from traditions requiring *proper and ritual ablutions of the communion vessels* can do so.

5. Again, I am grateful to the Rev'd Gilly Myers for this point in an email. In his email, Bishop Michael Ipgrave also noted about a wider communion broadcast on Facebook or YouTube: "if there were an undefined number of unknown individuals bringing bread and wine to an online celebration of the Eucharist, I think there would be a real concern about the reverent disposal of the consecrated (?) eucharistic elements." Given the limited numbers in a eucharist on a webinar-type platform like Zoom, this risk is significantly mitigated, if not eliminated.

Our search down 'the long and winding road' travelled together has finally brought us to a liturgical form and practice that satisfies all the 'criteria' and requirements for the celebration of the eucharist to provide the grace of God and the real presence of Jesus Christ in the elements of the bread and wine shared in holy communion together through the *epiclesis* for the Holy Spirit to fall upon both the people and the communion elements. One participant spontaneously wrote me a similar 'check-list' soon after they joined the group:

> Thank you for your response about Zoom communion and your invitation of welcome to continue. I absolutely considered it a 'valid' Eucharist—the people of God were gathered together, the gospel was read and proclaimed, there was an ordained person presiding, the liturgy was in accord with the catholic tradition, the physical elements were present, the intention of all was to have Eucharist, the biblical formula for consecration was used, the Holy Spirit was invoked. . . . And I was touched at the way the universal church was geographically represented in ways that we can't actually get in person but through prayer! . . . It was beautiful. Simply advocating a eucharistic fast during the present time, as many are doing, is too cautionary, in my opinion, and not theologically and liturgically imaginative enough to see God's creative and generative power at work to create and perpetuate the church in all seasons and places and circumstances.

Others have sent similar reactions in personal emails:

> Thank you for inviting me to these Zoom communion services, Richard. It feels like the 'real thing' to me. But I love [X]'s (and Ignatius') assertion that God is in all things, and so, for me, this service unequivocally is a sacrament that helps me to realise the 'inward and spiritual' truth that matter matters.
>
> Certainly, the whole thing had the form and the feel of a Eucharist for me. Once we had settled down it all flowed well. Overall, I have been blessed by this experience, so thank you.

A CONSIDERATION OF SOME POSSIBLE OBJECTIONS

While writing the above account of our Zoom communion services, I realized that there are several possible objections that are still made about them, concerning the extreme 'range of consecration', being one body through one bread and one cup, and the relationship of the digital and physical universes. We will take them each separately:

1. What is the range of consecration?—
just how far can intention be extended?

This is the original question that stimulated not just the Zoom experiment but also this very book. In discussing this with some Roman and Anglo-Catholic friends, there was an almost visceral reaction about 'physical distance'. Thus, while all agreed that it is *not* necessary for the celebrant actually to touch the elements physically, but just to see them and include them within their priestly intention to consecrate (hence they are happy with administrants around the altar in a large service, or even further away at their stations, holding up their chalices and patens at the appropriate moment in the eucharistic prayer), nonetheless, they had a deeply felt 'gut-reaction' to further distance. Thus, an Anglo-Catholic friend expressed deep unhappiness about Greenbelt groups 'holding up' bread and wine across a large field; however, to his credit, he admitted that it was 'just a feeling', and he could not give any theological reason why the large service in the cathedral was acceptable (or even larger at Walsingham) while the gathering in the Greenbelt field was not.

On the other hand, a Roman Catholic priest colleague described how pleased and excited he was as a eucharistic minister at the papal mass canonizing his order's founder, distributing the consecrated elements among a crowd of hundreds of thousands to a million, gathered not just in St Peter's Square, but jamming the roads down to the Tiber. He was 'on duty' half a kilometer down the Via della Conciliazone leading to the river, where in a little communion tent a priest was (con-?)celebrating over bread and wine at the same time as the pope was presiding over the main altar in the Square. My friend considered that he and the hordes around him were all participating in the same mass with the Holy Father, but somehow it was not enough just to 'hold up' a chalice and paten so far from the main celebration, where the pope could not know they were there, let alone see them. But like my Anglo-Catholic friend, he also could not give me any theological reason about how far the 'zone of intention' could be extended—20 meters? 50 meters? 100 meters? 500 meters?!

And how is this distance measured actually—by how far the celebrant can see or hear, or be seen and heard? We are back to my South African Roman Catholic friend's question—"what is the range of consecration?" In our Zoom eucharist, she may be nearly 10,000 miles away in physical distance as the crow (or South African Airways) flies, but her face, her voice, her mediated presence, and also her bread and wine appear less than a yard in front of me in her own Zoom square on my laptop screen—as visually close as any elements on the altar at church, or even closer. I can even touch their images on my screen, or hold the palms of my hand over them, just as over elements in front of me. We should not think of consecration or the 'zone of intention' in terms of 'physical distance'—after all, how far does Jesus travel to enter bread and wine with his 'real presence' in a church communion? Where is his starting place, or where he is coming from? How far away is his home in heaven—thousands of light years, or the merest breath away?

Therefore, because of my friend's innocent question, I cannot understand why her bread and wine, which I can see and touch and pray over on my laptop screen, cannot be open to the real presence of Christ just as much as my own bread and wine. Following our discussion of both the priest's and the people's eucharistic intentions above, clearly, as celebrant, I *intend* to be a channel whereby God can bless her with his grace in bread and wine; similarly, it is her intention and heartfelt desire as a lay person to 'feed on him with thanksgiving'. Are these not valid and effective sacramental intentions? And if not, why not?

Furthermore, we clearly rejected mechanistic or quasi-magical interpretations of the actual Words of Institution, to avoid any unfortunate implications of *hocus pocus*. If the *epiclēsis* is the prayer in which I, as celebrant, invoke the Holy Spirit to come upon "these gifts of bread and wine" [including hers, visible before me] that they "may be to us [including to her, also visible before me] the body and blood of our Lord Jesus Christ", then who am I to say that Jesus cannot fill her elements of bread and wine with his divine and real presence, just as much as I pray that he does mine—regardless of the geographical distance between us, however measured. Regarding the *hocus pocus* priest consecrating a bakery, or those concerned about real bread leaving "fragments of our Lord all over the carpet", we recalled Bishop Mark Santer's wise words, "if Jesus can get himself into these elements, he can also get himself out." The same must apply to elements equally present before me on the table and on my screen. Surely, I do not—or even cannot—compel or prevent Jesus being present in either set of elements? It is all his grace, after all.

2. Are we "all one body" because we all share in "one bread" and drink from "one cup"?

We have noted how saying at the breaking of the bread, "Though we are many, we are one body, because we all share in one bread" can cause a feeling of disjuncture in a broadcast or online communion. Although the archbishop of Canterbury used these words in his kitchen on Easter morning 2020, and the subtitles repeated them as he broke the bread and held the two separate sections aloft, in fact *nobody* was seen to share in any bread or drink from any cup, not even Archbishop Justin himself, as the camera cut away to the text for 'spiritual communion'. On the other hand, in other broadcast services celebrated online by various bishops, only they as presidents (or in one case, including his wife) got to eat and drink the elements, even 'on behalf' of those watching (a particularly unhelpful comment).

By contrast, even if people do eat bread and drink wine all at the same *time* and in the same virtual *space* through participative webinar technology, despite separated geographical locations, how can it be *one* bread, or *one* cup—or even *one* service? Thus, the Rev'd Dr Paul Roberts, the liturgist from Trinity College, Bristol, suggested that "what is being celebrated is not a single eucharistic liturgy, but simultaneous eucharists, with or without an ordained presidency."[6] Of course, such lay presidency is problematic, not only for Anglicans, but also for many other denominations also, as we saw in chapter 6 earlier.

In the *Baptist Times*, Simon Woodman, reflected upon the liturgy 'Scattered yet Gathered', which he wrote for 'virtual communion' and used when he presided for us on Zoom:

> when God's scattered people share bread and wine intentionally and in harmony, the sacramental moment is still to be found. . . . The key difference between Baptists and some other denominations, is that our doctrine of the priesthood of all believers allows in theory for anyone authorised by the congregation to preside at the Lord's Table, even if this is 'normally' done by the minister. The bread broken and wine poured at home can be for us as sacramentally valid as that which normally happens in our church buildings.[7]

6. Personal email to me of April 8, 2020, quoted with his permission.

7. I am grateful to my Baptist colleague, Simon Woodman, for his "Scattered Yet Gathered: A Reflection on the Sharing of Virtual Communion," *Baptist Times*, April 3, 2020, https://www.baptist.org.uk/Articles/571834/Scattered_yet_gathered.aspx

Similarly, the theologian from St Andrew's, Scotland, Steve Holmes, suggested that for Baptists,

> there are two possible ways of asserting that an online/scattered Eucharist is possible: . . . both are completely dependent on distinctives of Baptist ecclesiology. The first is the suggestion that we can have many household communions at the same time; the second the idea that we might celebrate one communion, even if we are in separate homes as we do.[8]

I recognize that both these theologians draw upon Baptist theology and ecclesiology whereby the priesthood of all believers allows a lay person to preside over communion in certain circumstances. Thus, even if the presiding authorized minister's intention does not quite get extended all the way to the participant's bread and wine in, say, Cape Town, this does not matter because it is met (half-way?) by that lay person's own intention to receive communion, so that there are "many household communions" all happening "at the same time".

Another free church and Baptist point may be useful here regarding the more catholic criticism of using individual little cups as vitiating the 'one cup'; this can be overcome by everyone waiting for everyone else to receive their cup and then all drinking simultaneously together. However, this criticism can be reversed: those in the free church tradition, especially if they use one large real loaf, find the common catholic practice of using individual wafers equally challenging for the 'one bread' symbolism. Since most commentators on this issue seem to agree that the use of individual wafers need not necessarily invalidate the 'one bread' then by the same logic individual cups do not negate the 'one cup' either. In that case, the same must surely apply to our webinar Zoom eucharists.

It is, of course, undeniable that we all have our own breads and wines before us as we are 'scattered' across the world—yet we are also 'gathered', in the image from the Didache, a very early church document sometimes used over the breaking of the bread:

> As this broken bread was once many grains,
> which have been gathered together to make one bread:
> so may your church be gathered
> from the ends of the earth into your kingdom.[9]

8. Steve R. Holmes, "Can We Celebrate an Online Eucharist? A Baptist Response I", http://steverholmes.org.uk/blog/?p=7716; with part II on possible objections, at http://steverholmes.org.uk/blog/?p=7721

9. This form is taken from the *Prayer Book for Australia*, 141; The Didache, or The Teaching of the Twelve Apostles, states, "And concerning the broken bread: 'We give

Simon Woodman similarly notes "a prayer in the communion section of the Baptist book *Gathering for Worship* which reads, 'As this bread, once scattered over the hills, was brought together and became one loaf, so, Lord, may your Church be united and brought together from the ends of the earth into your Kingdom.' (p. 28)"[10] In Woodman's liturgy, this image is deliberately echoed:

> *We are the people of God,*
> **we are the body of Christ.**
>
> *We are scattered, and the body of Christ is broken,*
> **but as we gather, the body of Christ is re-membered.**
>
> *Each piece of bread that we eat was once scattered across the fields,*
> **and the grain that God gave to grow**
> **has become for us the bread of life.**
>
> *Each sip of wine that we drink was once many vines,*
> **and the grapes that God gave to grow**
> **have become for us the new wine of God's kingdom.**[11]

Thus, Zoom eucharists are a fulfilment of the Didache's vision that its authors could never have imagined. The community that gathers together online through Zoom have in fact previously been physically present with many others in the group; in my case, this is true of nearly everyone. And yet, for various reasons in today's mobile society, we are now 'scattered' across four of the world's continents, like grain scattered across the fields or the vines extending their tendrils in all directions.

But this was equally true for St Paul's missionary journeys across the ancient Mediterranean, so that he could not be with all his churches all of the time. So he writes frequently that "though absent in body, I am present in spirit" (1 Cor 5:3); "for though I am absent in body, yet I am with you in spirit" (Col 2:5). He had to rely on the communications technology of his day to make it clear that "what we say by letter when absent, we will also do when present" (2 Cor 10:11). Even with the network of the Roman roads and shipping lanes, such letters would still take quite some time to reach recipients, and for news to get back to the sender: "whether I come and see

---

you thanks, our Father, for the life and knowledge which you have made known to us through Jesus, your servant; to you be the glory forever. Just as this broken bread was scattered upon the mountains and then was gathered together and made one, so may your church be gathered together from the ends of the earth into your kingdom; for yours is the glory and the power through Jesus Christ forever.'" http://anglicanposse. com/?tag=didache

10. Simon Woodman, 'Scattered Yet Gathered."

11. Simon Woodman, "Scattered Yet Gathered."

you, or am absent and hear about you" (Phil 1:27). However, through the wonders of modern technology, we can now be absent in body—and yet see and hear each other in the same *place* on our screens at the same moment of *time*. So the body of Christ separated by our travels is literally "remembered", to use Woodman's play on words; we "remember Jesus" at the eucharist by bringing together those separated "members" to "re-member" the body of Christ with Jesus as our living head (1 Cor 12). This leads us naturally, but inevitably, into the third possible objection.

3. Is the re(a)lationship between physical/material/offline and digital/electronic/online itself 'real' or 'virtual'?

We have often noted above that terminology and vocabulary do not just determine meaning, but also contain a 'value-judgement' about what is being discussed. Thus, during the writing of this book, I have increasingly avoided contrasting the 'real' (= physical, material, offline) with the 'virtual' (=digital, electronic, online), since it suggests that the latter is somehow *not* real. We have also argued that Christian doctrine requires that the Creator God must be able to be present in all aspects of creation, including those created by human beings as God's pro-/co-creators, such as online communication. If God cannot only *be* there, but *must* be there in the same way that he is present throughout the entire creation, then we cannot say that the online or digital world is any less 'real' than the offline or physical world.

However, in all his emails and articles opposed to 'virtual communions', the Rev'd Dr Paul Roberts, the liturgist from Trinity College, Bristol, has implied this distinction, not least in his use of language. In an interesting and very pertinent article published early in the coronavirus pandemic,[12] Roberts starts with a definition:

> by a 'virtual communion', I mean the practice of *attempting* to celebrate a eucharist, where the president is in a different location from the congregation (who are in different locations from one another), through the medium of an online shared audio-visual linking software, such as Zoom. (My italics for emphasis)

Roberts' negative implication of "*attempting* to celebrate" implies that this 'attempt' is doomed to failure, however well-intentioned. This is confirmed when Roberts states that "What we mean by 'digital' or 'virtual' is really, in scientific terms, *simulation*." 'Simulation' not only suggests that it is

12. Paul Roberts, "'Virtual' Communion Services: Some Doubts"; http://digitaltheology.uk/paulsblog/wp-content/uploads/2020/08/virtual-communion.pdf

not real, but even that there may be pretense or deception involved.[13] Thus the *Cambridge Dictionary* defines "simulate" as "to do or make something that looks real but is not real."[14]

Roberts does not merely consider the 'virtual' as 'simulation', but equates it also with 'digital'. This equation, if extended logically, suggests, bizarrely, that 'digital' TV is somehow a deception, a 'simulation' of the *real* TV, which could only found on old analogue sets, or that 'digital' recordings on CDs or computers are a pretense, simulating 'real' recordings on vinyl LPs—or nineteenth-century wax cylinders, to go further back![15] 'Digital' watches are, according to this argument, a 'simulation' of a 'real' clockwork watch—though perhaps that is itself only a 'simulation' of a sundial! How far back do we need to go to find the 'real'? In fact, they are all just examples of different technologies, and 'digital' innovations are generally viewed in fact as better, rather than a 'simulation', and just as 'real'. Roberts' article continues:

> When a worship service goes out on the internet, sound uttered by a person is transferred into electronic representations of physically uttered speech, and light patterns are, likewise, encoded electronically. Both of these are then transmitted as signals across electronic circuits to numerous destinations (or stored electronically until they are retrieved). At the 'other end', that of the recipient, they are then used to move surfaces on a loudspeaker and to illuminate a matrix of light-emitting-diodes. Through this act of *simulation* [my italics for emphasis], a fair amount of the encoded physical signals at the original end are

13. In his response to the first draft of this chapter, Roberts responded that "On 'simulation', I certainly don't see it as a negative concept at all, but rather as a purely descriptive one"; nonetheless, his email concludes "but pretending simulation is real is, for me, a basic categorical error" (July 16, 2020, used with permission).

14. It even gives these phrases as the first two examples: "in cheap furniture, plastic is often used to simulate wood" and "Ruth simulated pleasure at seeing Sam, but really she wished he hadn't come." See https://dictionary.cambridge.org/dictionary/english/simulate

15. In his response to an earlier draft of this section, even Roberts objected to my drawing this implication from his equation of 'digital' with 'virtual': "The only thing I think you might have misunderstood is that I'm not really making a distinction between digital (TV) and analogue (TV), as—in fact—they both use electronics to display the physical, in the same way that paint does in a painting. I certainly wouldn't make a distinction suggesting that digital is in some sense philosophically inferior to analogue—if the sample rate is high enough, digital is far better than analogue!" (September 1, 2021, used with permission). I am grateful for Paul's response, which further confirms my opinion that 'digital' should *not* be equated with 'virtual', as being somehow less 'real'; in fact, it may be even more real. This is further evidence that we should abandon completely all references to the 'digital' as 'virtual' in future.

reproduced, to a greater or lesser extent, for looking at and listening to. Despite the fact that there are physical (electronic)
'links' between sender and receiver, these links have been set up
and are manipulated by complex human technology—they are
not naturally occurring in the physical universe. It is not *physical transport to render physically present* (as in, "beam me up
Scotty") but merely *simulation*. [His italics][16]

This drives a wedge between the virtual/digital/electronic/online
(which is 'not real' as "merely *simulation*") and the physical or material
(which, for Roberts, alone is real). However, while the "physical (electronic)
'links' between sender and receiver" may result from "complex human technology", they are still "occurring in the physical universe" as part of 'nature'
(the Greek noun *physis* means 'nature' and the adjective *physik-* 'natural').
Roberts claims that "they are not *naturally* occurring" (my italics)—but human speech also does not occur 'naturally': in both, it is I who decide to
communicate, and choose whether to generate sound waves by opening my
mouth, or to do so by sending an electronic signal to vibrate a loudspeaker
in a telephone or a computer, both of which 'vibrate' my eardrum, sending
neuro-electric messages to my brain. Equally, whether another person is
bodily present with me, or someone else in our communion group appears
on screen from the other side of the world, they are both still "in the physical universe", and they both send light waves through my pupil to my retina,
again sending neuro-electric messages to my brain. Both are equally 'real'
before me, and both depend on the 'physics' of the natural world.

Roberts actually had a background in electronics before he studied
theology and, in an email, he restated this view:

> I am far from convinced that a screen constituted of lots of
> light-emitting diodes and a loudspeaker consisting of an elec-
> tro-magnet and a vibrating diaphragm is capable of rendering
> present a real person, made in God's image. Any engagement I
> make with people whom I know and love through this medium
> is *merely simulation* [note that word again, emphasized with
> 'merely'] of their presence, encoded into the passage of electrons
> which shuttle to and fro across wires and other communications
> channels. In the final resort, that is all we have. It's a bit like
> the bereaved widower, each day kissing the photograph of his
> deceased wife. There is intention and love, but there is no longer
> presence.[17]

16. Paul Roberts, "'Virtual' Communion Services: Some Doubts", 1–2; his italics.

17. Paul Roberts, personal email to me of April 25, 2020; my italics for emphasis. I am grateful for his permission to quote from and use these emails between us.

The comparison of a long-distance communication involving "a screen constituted of lots of light-emitting diodes and a loudspeaker consisting of an electro-magnet and a vibrating diaphragm" to "kissing the photograph of [a] deceased wife" is unreasonable. Such communication is indeed electronic and technological, involving diodes and vibrating loudspeakers—but such things were accepted as a real form of communication when the telephone was invented. When somebody real physically speaks into the other end, all we hear at our end are electronic signals and vibrating loudspeakers—but it is still real communication, which can be used in a court of law to bind someone to their word. If we go further back in time, both the invention of the printing press, and before that, the handwritten letter similarly allow someone not bodily present to give binding and real instructions to someone in another time and place. A signed contract is no less legally binding for having gone through the post (or even via carrier pigeon!); lawyers now have software making an electronic signature legally binding (as I had to sign the contract for this book which had been emailed from America); such a signature is emphatically *not* a 'simulation', as the legal warning attached makes abundantly clear.

As noted above, St Paul is explicit that he expects readers to treat his communications—and his judgment—as 'real' and to act upon it just as much if they had heard it physically from his very lips: "for though *absent in body*, I am *present in spirit*; and as if present I have already pronounced judgment" (1 Cor 5:3). He makes the same point about being "present in spirit while absent in body" repeatedly (2 Cor 10:11; 13:2; Phil 1:27; Col 2:5). Roberts' argument suggests that St Paul is only 'real' when "present in body"; the rest is merely ink scratchings on papyrus, and thus a 'simulation'. All that differs is the technology (carrier pigeon, writing, semaphore, printing press, telephone, internet, Zoom); if St Paul could use the technology of his day to communicate with people when physically separated from them, why can we not use the technology of our day?

Our discussion about the Ship and Church of Fools observed how the users began to feel attached even to their clunky, awkward early avatars, and how this is even more true of the newer avatars used in Second Life, as well as my own experience of using the first-person pronoun 'I' naturally and unconsciously to describe what my avatar did in my stead. This is not a 'simulation' but a 'real' expression of a representation or persona, part of

---

However, interestingly another reader of an earlier draft of my manuscript, a bishop who also has a scientific background, suggested that Paul's argument implied "that the use of PA systems in churches reduces the worship to mere assimilation. And that participants that require hearing aids are only pretending to be worshipping." Used by permission—but not attributed!

one's own identity. Similarly, while playing golf, you may ask, "Where am I?" or note that "you are in the water", using the personal pronouns to denote what has happened to the golf ball.

In defence of Paul Roberts, who has been a friend and theological sparring partner over four decades, he admits in his email that "my background in electronics has informed my theology"; his main concern and discomfort is

> arising from theological anthropology and the implications of ever sophisticated simulation technology. There are a lot of implications of steps taken in this area for the historical position that Christianity has taken on key doctrines of humanity, the incarnation, the resurrection of the body, pneumatology and eschatology. . . . It centres around what constitutes 'presence' to one another, and—by implication—what constitutes our humanity.

He is concerned that "big vested commercial interests" want to blur such distinctions: "there is a big financial prize if the distinction between 'real' and 'virtual' is abolished. . . . It is essential that the Church clearly understands what is real and the importance of physical presence, which lies at the heart of creation, justice, who we are, and who God is."[18]

Similarly, in his published article, he states:

> In Christian theology, physical existence matters. God creates a physical universe—it occupies specific space and is earthly. . . . Both beliefs [real presence in bread and wine and bodily resurrection] stubbornly *held on to the physical domain as the domain of salvation*, not merely as a subordinate sign for a more superior spiritual domain of salvation. In each case, salvation is presenced physically. . . . If the Church is the 'Body of Christ' it cannot, by definition, exist in a simulated form. It only gathers as a church physically.
>
> The Church of England's liturgy calls the opening section of the Eucharist, 'the Gathering' for exactly this reason. Without a Gathering (in the fullest, most human sense) there is no eucharist. . . . [W]hat is at stake is our understanding of *what we human beings actually are, . . . what we think salvation is.* What does it mean for me to live a physical existence, which will end with my death, in the hope that through what Jesus, the incarnate Son of God, has done for me and whole creation,

---

18. I am grateful for permission to quote and use Paul Roberts' emails of April 2020.

there is hope for this mortal, physical creature in a New Heaven
and a New Earth?[19]

Paul is often willing to take an unpopular view and argue for what he believes to be true and important, so I admire his courage in tackling this,
which, if he is correct, has implications for many aspects of Christian theology. Along with Roberts, and other theologians like Gregory of Nazianzus
and St Athanasius, we have also rooted our discussion in the doctrine of
God as Creator of the whole universe. Roberts also asserts this, but limits
it: "in Christian theology, *physical* existence matters. God creates a *physical*
universe"—my italics for emphasis.

However, the digital online world is also in the "*physical* universe",
relying on *physics*, or technology, physical atoms and molecules to make the
hardware function; as for "specific space", we have seen that digital space in
Second Life can be bought and sold in a lucrative business (giving rise to
the interesting phrase 'virtual real estate'!). To describe the digital online
world as a 'simulation', and thus 'not real', a space that God cannot 'occupy',
is to fall back into the Greek dualistic view that Roberts wishes to avoid.
God creates the physical universe, but also the intellectual universe, as well
as the moral, the spiritual, the emotional universes—including the digital
universe also—all of which God inhabits and fills with grace and presence.
Otherwise, there is another creator in the cosmos—and that is definitely a
'very bad thing'! With regard to online eucharists using digital technology,
Roberts' email argued:

> The Church needs to realise that the debate between whether
> the 'virtual' is equivalent to the 'real' is a very big theological
> and philosophical one. Changing our eucharistic practice in a
> way that blurs this cannot merely be argued from rubrics and
> precedent. It's too important for that.
>
> We celebrate this biblical and Christian anthropology when
> we celebrate the eucharist, with the interaction of Gathering,
> Attending, Communing, Dispersing—and there are big eccle-
> siological and soteriological implications for being a physical
> 'Body of Christ' which gathers, attends, feeds, and disperses as
> the core of celebrating what it is. If we equate communion with
> a psychological set of responses to twinkling LEDs and vibrat-
> ing speakers, then I think we've essentially changed our whole
> message and purpose.

19. Paul Roberts, "'Virtual' Communion Services: Some Doubts"; his italics in the
original.

Actually, in our weekly Zoom eucharists, we do have all four aspects mentioned above:

- *Gathering* means that people start logging on before the service, and greet one another, share news, just like a real church; I tend to calm it down by playing a Gregorian chant or Taizé chorus while everyone keeps silence, preparing to worship God.

- *Attending*: people have felt so committed to the group, that they will usually email their 'apologies' and explanation if they have to miss a service; equally, the interactive participatory nature of Zoom with everyone's faces visibly filling their camera square makes it immediately obvious if someone is not paying attention or is taking a phone call or disappearing offscreen. Like the so-called 'collegiate style' in university chapels, we face one another, and cannot avoid looking other people in the eye. Thus, the level of 'attending' is actually higher than in a normal physical gathering, and certainly more than watching a livestream or broadcast service.

- *Communing*: see the above description of how we moved from everyone eating and drinking at once to the president communicating each person individually by name—and how that has felt like a deeper 'communing' than queuing up in a physical church to make 'my' individual communion, while other people are nattering about the weather, the inevitable choir member who is off-key, or the vicar's dress sense. Furthermore, as physical people, we do commune in consuming physical bread and wine so that the importance of the physical is not lost in an online eucharist.

- *Dispersing*: again the interactive participatory nature of Zoom means that it is much more difficult simply to slip away anonymously; even though most members are busy in the middle of a working day, everyone waits to say goodbye, or explain what they are 'dispersing' into, and gives a farewell wave.

Far from changing "our whole message and purpose", we have found "big ecclesiological and soteriological implications for being a physical 'body of Christ' which gathers, attends, feeds and disperses as the core of celebrating what it is", even if geographically separated. This is the biggest difference between this *narrow*cast midweek Zoom eucharist and the YouTube *broadcast* or Facebook livestream, like that from my London church on Sunday mornings; in the livestream broadcast, others only know if you have 'gathered' or 'dispersed' if you use the 'live-chat' option to say so, while no one knows if you are attending properly to what is going on, or just have it on in the background like a TV soap opera. In the Zoom eucharist, everything is visible and obvious.

To give Paul Roberts due credit, he does have the grace to conclude, "but I may be wrong".[20] Indeed his own appearance at one of our Zoom celebrations may demonstrate this also. Initially, he was unwilling to join us because of his discomfort, concerned that others would take his presence with us as somehow 'validating' it:

> I do not regard them [these services] as Holy Communion. This is not because I'm being censorious, but because at a conscience level, I do not feel right partaking in something which is being understood by my fellow worshippers as communion, when I do not think it is—for me, it would feel disrespectful on my part.[21]

After we agreed that his presence with us would not be validating or condoning what we were doing, he graciously joined the next Zoom eucharist, and kindly sent me a long email about his reactions:

> It was definitely worth doing: I did have bread and wine with me, because I wanted to experience what everyone else would be doing to the maximum of participation.
>
> My feelings/reactions. Well, first of all, I know how Doubting Thomas felt like at the start of the story. A rather odd way to begin communion. Then, as I said, because the environment was established, but—for me—unfamiliar, I felt (as I said) a bit like someone 'coming to church' for the first time. And that feeling never quite left me. Not sure why . . .
>
> I fully participated ritually and did all the things I would normally do at a communion service (at which I wasn't presiding). The points where I felt I felt most engaged and connected were the prayers and readings, which I'm more used to. The part I found difficult was the communion, for—I guess—a number of reasons: I was not really clear what we were doing (and here, I guess, *lex credendi* was trumping *lex orandi*). I think that were the Church to go down this route, some kind of explanation for people ultimately becomes pastorally essential—which means the Church needs to make its mind up.[22]

---

20. Paul Roberts, personal email to me of Saturday April 25, 2020; I am grateful for his permission to quote from and use these emails between us.

21. Paul Roberts, personal email to me of Saturday April 25, 2020.

22. Paul Roberts, personal email to me of Wednesday April 29, 2020.

He is, of course, quite correct that those responsible for such a service do need to make it quite clear what we think we are doing—but as far as I was concerned, we were '*gathering*' in our usual eucharistic community, where we '*attended*' carefully to a thought-provoking sermon from a professor of biblical studies in a eucharistic celebration beautifully presided over by a priest who combines part-time care of his parish with another ministry in broadcasting; after we had '*communed*' in prayer, praise, and sharing together in the sacrament, which had been taken, blessed, broken, and distributed, despite our geographical separation, we '*dispersed*' back to our separate lives, encouraged by each other, nurtured by what we had learned, and nourished by the very life of Christ present in his body and blood. Thus, it was no different from a communion service in church, or perhaps even better!

Paul also admitted that it "made me acutely aware of how much I was missing the eucharist at church, and kind of skewered that pain", and that afterwards, his wife (also a priest) confirmed that they "both felt uneasy celebrating communion together (which we did over Easter) because it separated us from the wider Body, which is in a long-term 'dismissed' state, under the COVID-19 church situation. We've decided that, as priests, the role we feel most comfortable is to suffer under the same spiritual conditions as the rest of the people." I was sorry to read this, not least because the graphic description of his pain, "skewered", indicated how *real* the online experience was, if it could cause pain that felt as *physical* as skewering! While I respect their noble decision to share in the suffering "under the same spiritual conditions as the rest of the people" in the 'eucharistic fast', it is precisely to find a way to celebrate holy communion in "contagious times" that we have undertaken this long journey through all possible options.

CONCLUSION

Here, in this interactive and participatory webinar software—which allows us to be present to one another and to the Triune God at the same chronological moment in *time* (regardless of what hour our digital watches or sundials consider it to be) and in the same digital and physical *space* mediated through the hardware of our various devices—I recognize true fellowship in the full liturgical context of a communion service that includes reading the scriptures and sharing their meaning together, along with confession, prayer, and praise, culminating as we receive the sacrament of the most precious body and blood of our Lord Jesus Christ together, thanks to the grace of our heavenly Father and the action of the Holy Spirit in coming upon our various breads and wines to make us truly one body, despite our different denominations across the various continents around our world—and for that, I am truly and profoundly grateful. And I am not the only one, as these initial reactions sent from several people after an early experience of this form of communion:

> Once the liturgy began, it felt like we were crossing into a different and holy space, as always happens for me in the communion service . . . the sense of God's grace and giving was the same for me as in a physical-world service.

> Thank you so much for today!!! As a people-person I really appreciated the interaction and it was good to really feel like part of the Body of Christ. Lovely to 'meet' the others.

> Thank you for once again calling us together today to be in Eucharistic community sharing word and sacrament. I think that what we are doing on Wednesdays is discovering ourselves called from our different backgrounds, different locations, and different ecclesial allegiances, into the reality of Eucharistic community, discovering afresh the grace-filled truth that "The Lord is here; God's Spirit is with us." Both my wife and I found ourselves moved to the depths of our hearts with gratitude for the fellowship, love, and blessing we shared with the whole 'congregation', including the dog(!) as we were blessed together in word faithfully opened and sacrament faithfully shared—A truly eucharistic experience—now the challenge is to continue to live eucharistically in the continuing lockdown! Can't wait for next week!

16

Conclusions and Summary of Criteria for Online Holy Communion

WE NOTED THE CENTRALITY for most, if not all, Christian denominations of *regular and corporate worship for a local ecclesial community* gathered in one place, such as a church or chapel, a pattern that also features as its highlight participation in the holy communion, the celebration of the eucharist following Jesus Christ's command to "do this in memory of me" at the Last Supper. Interestingly, while some traditions view it as so important that they need communion at least every week, or even every day (as we saw in the more catholic spiritual discipline of Archbishop Tutu in chapter 4), other churches, especially in the free or independent Protestant tradition, show its importance for them in reserving it for 'special occasions', rather than the everyday. However, the consequences of living in "contagious times", such as the 2020 coronavirus pandemic, unfortunately made such regular and corporate communion services impossible for all traditions of the church.

Therefore, in Part I we explored the *various options* for such times, from abstaining from receiving communion physically, either through a 'eucharistic fast' or 'spiritual communion', to other proposed ways of celebrating holy communion, such as 'solitary communions' by priests alone, 'concelebrating' with other clergy, or extending eucharistic presidency to lay people, as well as examining suggested solutions such as 'drive-in' or 'drive-thru', or 'extended' communions from a local church out into the community. Careful study and examination of these options produced a *list of requirements, or even 'criteria' for a valid and effective communion:*

- The *eucharistic fast* and *spiritual communion* may be temporary so-lutions in very extreme circumstances, but they cannot sustain the physical and spiritual need for holy communion in the long-term and global perspective (chapters 2 and 3).

- *Solo communions* are not acceptable because the *communion*, by defi-nition, requires a *community* or fellowship of at least several people, both lay and ordained (chapter 4).

- *Priestly concelebrations* on their own lack the essential full participa-tion of the laity (chapter 5).

- None the less, in all Christian traditions, since earliest times, *eucharis-tic presidency is confined to an ordained priest or authorized minister*, right across the spectrum from a 'high' doctrine of the 'real presence' (however defined or conceived), through to a 'lower' memorialist un-derstanding (chapter 6).

- Consideration of 'drive-in' communions led to a clear requirement for communion to be celebrated in *the context of a full church service, including the ministry of the word as well as sacrament, with opportuni-ties for praise, prayer, confession, and fellowship*; while this might be possible for some 'drive-in' church services, 'drive-up' and 'drive-thru' collection of previously consecrated elements belongs more to the fast-food world of 'McEucharists' and do not satisfy this requirement (chapter 7).

- We also noted from this discussion that for Catholic, Anglican, and some other traditions, *the bread must be made from wheat and the wine be the fermented juice of the grape*, while for other free church, independent and Baptist traditions, non-alcoholic juice is acceptable (chapter 7).

- Finally, the suggestion of *'extending' communion from a church service to those locked-down and housebound* also does not satisfy the require-ment for the various individuals to be gathered together at the celebra-tion of the eucharist, complete with the ministry of the word and other essential elements. It also raises issues of *health and safety* and the need to *avoid contagion and infection*, while most 'pre-packaged' individual communion elements contain *unfermented grape juice* (chapter 8).

This led to the conclusion in Part I that it was almost impossible dur-ing "contagious times" to satisfy these requirements for holy communion in *the so-called 'real', material, and everyday universe*, and so we turned in Part II to consider the possibilities afforded by *the so-called 'virtual' world of online digital services.* By way of background, we considered the *rise of the internet* in chapter 10; as with all previous communications revolutions—from the discovery of writing inscriptions or manuscripts, the ease and speed of communications in the Roman world, and the invention of the printing press leading to mass publication and the development of printed media—Christian churches have been quick to utilize the internet, beginning with the 'top-down' dissemination of information, through the 'bottom-up' discussions of bulletin boards and bloggers, to the discovery that 'side-by-side' relationships and communities are as possible in cyberspace as in the physical world.

As an illustration of this progression, in chapter 11 we journeyed on the Ship of Fools from its student magazine days to its highly successful website, leading to the voyage of the Ark, which raised the possibility of online worship, resulting in the experiment of the Church of Fools and the development of St Pixels as a truly online or 'digital' church. This raised the inevitable issue of whether the eucharist can be celebrated in digital (cyber) space and holy communion be truly shared online.

This led us in chapter 12 to experience the Anglican Cathedral in the digital world of Second Life, as one example of such online churches or congregations where individuals are represented by their chosen 'avatars'. Here we discovered a true worshipping community of avatars whose users or owners are physically distributed across the globe through all time zones, yet where they study the Bible, discuss the Christian faith, and pray the daily offices and Sunday services regularly together; the quality of their fellowship and mutual concern for each other's situations—after many of them have been together for over a decade—is as palpable as it is moving. In this sense, the Anglicans of Second Life (AoSL) fulfil most, if not all, the requirements or criteria identified in Part I. And yet, following early episcopal advice, they have refrained from celebrating the eucharist, or sharing communion together (or indeed any other sacrament). An examination of the flurry of papers and dissertations written about this over the last decade raised a number of theological issues, including:

- The relationship of the so-called *'virtual' to the 'real' worlds*, first life to second, digital to physical ways of being.

- Whether and how the *one true God can be experienced* in the online world of cyberspace, and in what ways *Jesus Christ* might be able to be *'really present'*.

- Concerns about the *anonymity of avatars* and the possibility for deception, raising *issues of safeguarding* in both the virtual and physical universes.

- Whether and how *consecration by a priest or authorized minister* (and do they need to be ordained in 'real life', or authorized by whom and for what?) can be communicated online—either for avatars to consume *digital bread and wine* in second life, or for their owners/users to consume their own *real bread and wine* wherever they are in the physical world.

To tackle such questions, we needed to step back for more background consideration in an excursus (chapter 13) about *the actual circumstances and methods of priestly consecration in the material, physical world*. A discussion about the practical procedures sometimes followed in large cathedral eucharists or open-air festival communions focussed attention upon several aspects:

- Whether the presiding celebrant needs to be able *physically to touch* the elements of bread and wine in order to effect consecration, and if so how?

- How the *sacramental intention of the celebrating minister* extends to or includes the elements that are intended to be consecrated. (Are they limited to those on a specific area, like a corporal? Or those visible to the celebrant, even if physically distant? And how far can 'intention' extend? Inches, feet, miles, or thousands of miles?) And what role does sacramental intention play in the avoidance of *unintentionally consecrating other elements*, like any bread not required or wafers or wine left over in their boxes or flagons?

- Alongside the sacramental intention of the presiding priest, we noted the importance of a matching *intention on the part of the recipients*, especially the laity, to want to receive 'the body and blood of our Lord Jesus Christ'.

- Ultimately, close attention must also be paid to the *intention of God the Holy Trinity*, to the Father who wishes to bless his children, to Jesus the Son who gives himself to us in his real presence in bread and wine, and to the Holy Spirit who is called down upon both the elements and also the desirous people to enable them to be fed with 'the body and blood' of Jesus.

- Careful consideration needs to be given to what this does to concepts of the '*one bread*' and '*one loaf*' or the '*common cup*' for the '*one body*'.

- And also care needs to be exercised over what happens afterwards for any *left-over consecrated elements* and the traditional requirement for ablutions.

We then turned in chapter 14 to consider the first and most common solution being used in the coronavirus pandemic, that of *a broadcast or livestreamed celebration of the eucharist* (through communications media like Facebook or YouTube) presided over by a priest or authorized minister in their own home (kitchen?) or church, where those watching (audience or congregation?) partake of communion without their community, eating their own individual elements of bread and wine, and whether consecration (however one understands it) has somehow been transmitted through the broadcast or livestream. It is clear that this aspect is much easier for those nearer the 'lower' end of the theological spectrum, where the Lord's Supper is viewed more as a memorial in which nothing actually happens to the bread and wine. For those who hold any 'higher' view of consecration, where the elements are somehow affected spiritually, or even in the catholic tradition, transformed in some mysterious way into the "body and blood of our Lord Jesus Christ" to feed the communicant, this is going to be much more difficult. We noted that this debate goes back to early TV broadcasts of communion services and whether those watching at home could place bread and wine on their television set and expect it to become the "body and blood of our Lord Jesus Christ."

Even this debate from previous decades had raised the difference between watching a pre-recorded event or participating in a 'live' broadcast in the same *time*, if not *space*, and therefore we argued that as far as possible the service, or at least the actual consecration, should happen 'live' in real time, rather than be pre-recorded, or watched later online hours, days, or weeks after everyone else had disappeared. It also opens the question of how the celebrant can 'intend' to consecrate elements of bread and wine that they cannot see, for communicants whom they do not know are there. It was suggested that a better sense of community can be engendered if there is the facility for those watching to type in 'live chat' to be able to indicate their presence to the celebrant and their brothers and sisters in the church, together with asking questions, or requesting needs for prayer.

Finally, we turned in chapter 15 from broad-casting to a narrower, *more participatory 'webinar' technology*, of the sort enabled by packages like Zoom or Microsoft teams. Such technologies rapidly came to the fore during the 2020 coronavirus pandemic simply in order to permit any form of corporate life to continue, from the meetings of governments, through board meetings of businesses and organizations, to classes for schoolchildren and

lectures and seminars for university students. The question was being widely asked about why government decisions affecting millions of people in
different countries could be taken and deemed to be legal and binding—and
yet bishops and church leaders could not agree about something seemingly
easier, like receiving holy communion, which even a child can do. From my
own personal experience of running such a webinar communion service via
Zoom involving a small group of people spanning at least four continents
(USA, Europe, Africa, and Australia) and some five denominations (Roman
Catholic, Baptist, Lutheran, Anglicans of various churchmanships, and even
a non-sacramentalist Quaker!) various things emerged:

- It was a *mid-week service*, in order to allow everyone to attend their
  own churches (even if via a livestream or whatever) on Sundays; it also
  took place at *midday UK time*, in order to allow those in the Far East
  or 'Down Under' to participate in their late evening, while those in
  America were able to have communion at the start of their day.

- We were therefore sharing communion *at the same real time*, regardless of what our clocks or watches said about the time zone, and *in
  the same space*, which may have been *digital* in cyberspace, but was
  physically real in what we could see on the screens before us.

- We saw how quickly the group formed into a *real ecclesial community*
  (a house-church, or cell-group?) and a eucharistic fellowship, sharing
  not just the communion of their own bread and wine, but also the
  joys and sorrows, hopes and fears of everyone else—and learning to
  care for and pray for each other over a period of more than eighteen
  months, which is still continuing.

- This sense of community was further deepened by setting up a Whats-
  App group on our mobile phones where *news, messages, or prayer
  requests* could be posted during the week in between each service.

- The importance was stressed of using a *full liturgical service*, with confession, prayer, and praise, singing hymns or listening to music, watching videos or pictures and illustrations, readings from the scriptures
  with a sermon, homily, or reflections based upon them.

- While different members took it in turn to celebrate or preside over
  the service each week, they were all *ordained and recognized by their
  different churches for this sacramental ministry*; however, many of the
  sermons or homilies were delivered by lay members, most of whom
  were licensed or experienced in preaching and teaching in the ordinary physical world of church life.

- The other *clergy or ordained ministers present and participating could also perform any customary manual acts, elevate the elements, or extend their hands* over their own elements or over all of those visible on the screen if they wished to share in the (con-?)celebration.

- Since each communicant provided their own elements, those whose traditions or even canon law required *particular preparation (wheat or alcohol)* could do so.

- Similarly, those whose traditions required *any particular form of ablutions* could do so after the communion.

- Because we were all locked down in our own homes around the world, there were no *concerns about health and safety, or about contagion or infection,* while the only *virus* that might be transmitted would come from, and affect, only our computers—and of course everyone had their own anti-viral software to prevent that spread!

In this way, we believe that such *participatory, simultaneous, online communion services* using webinar platforms like Zoom or Microsoft Teams met all the *criteria and requirements* that emerged in our real-world considerations in Part I, but without any of their problems, as well as avoiding the problems in chapter 12 about *avatars, anonymity, and digital communion* elements in 'second life', as well as the concerns about *broadcasts and livestreams* in chapter 14, where neither the celebrant nor the communicants can communicate fully with each other at the same chronological time and same geographical space.

Finally, the question emerges of what might happen or is happening already as the world slowly emerges from lockdown into the new, and perhaps frightening, future of learning to live with the coronavirus. Will we be living effectively in what the 1662 Book of Common Prayer calls "contagious times" for the foreseeable future?

The first point to note is the greater realization through the pandemic that we all live in one physical world, which is increasingly linked by the digital online world. This is demonstrated by the many people returning to St Luke's Holloway or joining its services for the first time even from the opposite side of the planet. Similarly, our little Zoom communion group also spanned many continents in an enlarged example of the worldwide body of Christ. A return to our own private services in our respective little churches would necessitate a limiting of that vision of a wider community and a global communion. Thus, St Luke's Holloway is experimenting with a 'blended' approach of not only broadcasting the physical gathering on Sunday mornings in the local church, but enabling others who had joined us from around the world to continue to participate, including contributing to or leading certain parts of the service.

Secondly, this global background brings the sober realization that not all people nor all countries are as fortunate as some of the wealthier and more privileged parts of Britain or the United States. American friends are concerned for their poorer and less cared for communities still suffering without widespread vaccination, while my South African colleague who first inspired the idea of the Zoom communion is back under her umpteenth lockdown as the virus threatens to rage unchecked not just in South Africa but across the whole continent. And that is before one thinks about places like India or South America. The pandemic is certainly not over yet—and may never be, given the apparent ability of the virus to mutate, so the considerations raised in our discussions remain hugely important for perhaps the majority of the world. As some countries who were perhaps the most effective at immediately locking-down and keeping the virus away from their shores are now discovering, such isolation cannot continue for ever, and sooner or later they too will have to learn to live with the virus if they are to share once more in the global community. The coronavirus pandemic seems to be bringing the same message to the human race as the increasingly obvious problem of climate change: the simple fact is that we are all in this together, and no one country or people will be safe unless we care for each other and ensure that all are safe.

Thirdly, it is true that our Zoom eucharistic community has become a little smaller as some members, especially those ordained, have found themselves called back to presiding at communions in various local churches and simply do not have the need, space, or time for the group any more. On the other hand, even they are the first to admit that the sense of being an ecclesial gathering and eucharistic community was so strong, even online, that they miss this weekly experience, and still wish to attend when they can. Meanwhile, others of us—especially those under renewed lockdowns or without opportunities in their local churches—still need, as well as value, these services to maintain our sacramental and spiritual lives.

On the other hand, an interesting recent development that I have noticed as we have been emerging from lockdown under the pandemic has been the development of a 'blended' approach in both church services as well as academic seminars and conferences, where some people are able and willing to meet again physically in buildings or classrooms, but where the online provision continues for those who do not (yet?) feel comfortable or safe about that. However, significantly, this also gives the opportunity for those online from a physical distance away who joined in (or in many cases, rejoined, having moved away years previously) the church community, or services, or seminars, or lectures and paper discussions during lockdown, to be able to continue to do so, rather than being disenfranchised by a return to meeting solely in the material world of churches and university buildings.

In recent weeks, as well as my weekly online Zoom communion, I have taken part in regular online morning prayers daily at 9.30am London time, attended not only by local parishioners, but also by former church members scattered across the UK, and even as far away as Australia (even if that means doing 'Morning' Prayer in the early evening!); I have found the same mixture in church on a Sunday morning with the large TV screens on the pillars beaming people in from many places; I physically presented a paper at a conference on the Gospels to a full seminar room in Durham, but which was attended by biblical colleagues online from Japan and the USA; finally, the weekly Erhardt biblical studies seminar at Manchester University includes as many staff and postgraduate students attending online as are physically present in the theology departmental seminar room. I suspect that such 'blended' approaches may well become the 'new normal', rather than a return to the old ways of pre-pandemic times.[1]

Therefore, the issues raised by all the options for holy communion in "contagious times" throughout most of these chapters on our journey of exploration have not gone away—and the possible solutions discussed and offered by broad- and narrowcasting in the last two chapters still require further thought and theological reflection—especially if a 'blended' approach combining meeting in both the physical world with the opportunity for others to join in online does become part of 'the new normal'. While I welcome the latest practical advice issued by the Church of England bishops about the return to communion services in local churches, the need remains for that "further theological reflection" promised in the Appendix section 11 of all versions of the "Guidance on the Celebration of Holy Communion."[2]

As we have noted during the course of this book, it was a privilege for me to share in the English bishops' study day on October 26, 2020, and for a paper about my work to have been considered by the American Episcopal bishops at their Table in the Wilderness. But as far as I know, the Anglican church on neither side of the Atlantic has produced anything further by way of publications or announcements at the time of writing these conclusions, nor have I seen anything from any other denomination. I would love

1. The advantages and need for continuing with such 'blended' approaches with livestream taking place online alongside physical gatherings became even more clear as the latest variant of coronavirus, Omicron, caused a worryingly rapid rise in infections, hospitalizations and potential deaths just as this book went to press.

2. See all the documents available at https://www.churchofengland.org/resources/coronavirus-covid-19-guidance

to be proved wrong about this, and to be able to enter into such further theological debate. It is therefore in that spirit of truly eucharistic sharing and communion that this book is offered—and I cannot wait to see what emerges from it all!